Elihu

Burritt:

Crusader

for Brotherhood

Elihu
Burritt:
Crusader
for Brotherhood

PETER TOLIS

ARCHON BOOKS

Hamden, Connecticut 1968

341.1
TS7e
67153
Sept. 1969

First Printing, 1968

Library of Congress Catalog Card Number: 68–31609
Printed in the United States of America

*To my mother Alexandra
and my wife Dorothy Ann*

Foreword

This study was originally begun at Columbia University under the guidance of Dr. Robert D. Cross and Dr. R. K. Webb. I am deeply indebted to both of them for their countless suggestions, criticisms, and corrections. Thanks especially to Dr. Cross, the life of Elihu Burritt was rescued from the numerous meanderings and digressions to which I had committed it. Needless to say, whatever infelicities or errors have crept into this work are my responsibility.

I am grateful to Merle Curti both for allowing me the use of his Burritt manuscripts and for his encouragement. Professor Curti was not only the first scholar to recognize the significance of Elihu Burritt, but also the first to write extensively on Burritt's contributions to 19th century international pacifism.

The staffs of many libraries and state historical societies were very helpful in my search for materials. I express my appreciation particularly to the following: American Antiquarian Society, Boston Public Library, Central Connecticut State College Library, Chicago Historical Society, Connecticut Historical Society, Connecticut State Library, Dartmouth College Library, Duke University Library, Friends House Library (London), Harvard University Library,

Haverford College Library, Henry E. Huntington Library, Historical Society of Pennsylvania, Indiana University Library, Illinois Historical Society, Library of Congress, Massachusetts Historical Society, New Britain Public Institute, Newark Public Library, New York Historical Society, New York Public Library, Pierpont Morgan Library (New York), Rochester University Library, Swarthmore College Library, Syracuse University Library, Yale University Library.

To my wife Dorothy Ann, and to Spencer, Darrell, and Peter, I can only say thanks.

Peter Tolis

Contents

Introduction 1

1. From Village to Learned Blacksmith,
   1810–1840 3

2. A Frustrated Literary Career 28

3. On the Lyceum Circuit 42

4. A Serious Young Man 65

5. Into the Antislavery Orbit 84

6. Apostle of Peace 115

7. The League of Universal Brotherhood 145

8. International Peace Crusader 173

9. Ocean Penny Postage 203

10. Slavery and Civil War 235

11. The Faith Remains Firm 269

    Bibliography 293

    Index 303

Introduction

Elihu Burritt is now one of the least known of the host of Yankee reformers who participated in the ferment of reform that engulfed most of the United States in the generation preceding the Civil War. Yet his enterprises for the promotion of peace and brotherhood, spanning two continents, made him a widely popular international figure in his own day. In America and Europe he was intimately associated with distinguished philanthropists and reformers, most of whom accepted him as a singularly earnest coworker. To many American and European pacifists he was the symbol of the international peace movement of the mid-nineteenth century.

The story of Elihu Burritt is an interesting commentary on some of the social values and religious attitudes of the times in which he lived. The emphasis on "self-culture" caused him to elevate himself from a poor, untutored blacksmith to a successful lyceum lecturer with the reputation of being a linguist *par excellence*. The moralistic preoccupations of the period, as well as Burritt's extremely sensitive religious conscience, drew him into the arena of reform and benevolence. Once in, he found a real meaning and purpose in his life as he strove to make Christian morality serve as the basis for world peace and brotherhood.

Burritt was a militant moralist who had most of the virtues and faults of that generation of American reformers which confidently set out to eradicate social wrongs. He offered simple solutions to enormously complicated problems, he was impatient, and at times he was too self-satisfied. But he was also uncompromising in his denunciation

1

of iniquities, unstinting in his labors, and completely dedicated to his beliefs. His entire career as a reformer reveals a remarkable consistency with the plain Christian principles he preached. There was much he said and did that might today appear to have been silly and unrealistic. At the time, however, his words and deeds had a meaning that was fully understood and accepted by thousands who like himself believed peace was practicable.

1

From Village to Learned
Blacksmith, 1810-1840

Elihu Burritt was born on December 10, 1810, in the Yankee village of New Britain, Connecticut, the third youngest of a family that by 1816 included ten children—five boys and five girls. His birthplace was a plain, wooden house, one and a half stories high, situated on a lot of about one and a half acres. Elihu, Sr., was a struggling laborer who farmed a few stony acres during the summer and repaired shoes during the winter. In 1810 New Britain, located in central Connecticut, was a comparatively poor parish of the town of Berlin with a population of slightly over one thousand. Most of the male inhabitants farmed during the summer and pursued some craft in the winter.[1]

The elder Elihu, "a man of nervous temperament, quick apprehension, and vivid sympathies," had unsuccessfully engaged in several small commercial enterprises.[2] He managed a bare living for his family. To make ends meet, Mrs.

1. Elihu Burritt, *Ten-Minute Talks on All Sorts of Topics* (Boston, 1873), pp. 9–10; Lewis L. Burritt, *The Burritt Family in America* (published by the author, n.d.), p. 12; David N. Camp, *History of New Britain* (New Britain, 1889), p. 83.

2. Mary Howitt, "Memoir of Elihu Burritt", in E. Burritt, *Thoughts and Things at Home and Abroad* (Boston, 1854), p. vii. (This article first appeared in the *People's Journal* (London), Oct. 31, 1846.)

Burritt practiced a rigid economy, and the children performed numerous chores. There was no future on the Burritt farm, and four of the sons, including Elihu, eventually traveled far in search of better things. Before their time came to leave home, however, they learned a few important facts of life from their mother.

Elizabeth Hinsdale Burritt was the dominant influence in raising the children. A strong-willed and intensely pious woman, she made religion the staple of the household. The Burritts were dutiful Congregationalists who attended the First Church and listened to the sermons of the Reverend John Smalley, an orthodox Calvinist known throughout New England. The character of young Elihu bore unmistakably the stamp of his mother's deep-rooted religious convictions. Her ideals and ethics were decidedly Puritan, of the old-time variety, and they rubbed off, more or less, on all of the children.

Elihu remembered his mother as one who "watched and prayed over my infancy . . . a kind of guardian angel set apart to lead me in the path of duty." To him, "as to all her children—both in heaven and on earth," he later recalled, "she was the most precious friend this side of Jesus Christ."[3] He extravagantly acknowledged his debt to her: "I would not exchange the efficacy and influence of her treasured precepts, her early and affectionate counsels, her timely and tender reproofs, her morning and midnight wrestlings with her God on my behalf—for all that glittered in a monarch's crown, or was ever hidden in the earth or sea." Even when he was past thirty, she was still dinning religion into his ears and praying mightily for his salvation.[4]

Mrs. Burritt was a fearless defender of the timeworn Cal-

3. Burritt, MS Journals, Oct. 7, 1844 (hereafter cited as Journals).
4. Burritt to Mrs. Chrystie, Worcester, March 8, 1841, Klingberg Collection. Elizabeth Burritt to Elihu Burritt, New Britain, Feb. 22, [1841] Central Connecticut State College Library.

vinist doctrine of predestination, a doctrine, Elihu wrote, "she would sooner lose her right arm than give . . . up." Well before 1800 that doctrine retained adherents only among the staunchest Calvinists. When friends gathered in the Burritt house for conversation, they discussed predestination "by the hour." Young Elihu was horrified by the concept. At the age of seven he trembled at the thought that "the chance of my election in such a large family seemed so small, and my risk so terrible"; such "sad thoughts worked in my mind night and day," but he "dared not" tell his mother.[5] Elizabeth Burritt's dislike of the increasing liberalization of Protestant dogma, however, could do little to prevent her son from finding satisfaction and relief in it.

Mrs. Burritt supervised Elihu's pre-school education. After grappling with the family spelling and grammar books, he did his first reading in the Bible. His enthusiasm for the Bible as narrative his mother often misinterpreted as unusual religious fervor. As a young boy, Elihu's appetite for reading could scarcely be satisfied by the few books at his disposal. A small Library Association existed in the village, but only once in every two months could a subscriber procure books. There were about 200 volumes in the library, mostly histories, sermons, and homilies. His mother allowed him to select one-half of the prescribed allotment of books. He chose the histories while she selected the sermons and homilies. The library contained a few of Scott's historical romances and some of the works of Shakespeare and Milton. Sometimes Elihu persuaded his mother to select only one volume of sermons, so that he could choose another book for himself.[6]

His formal education was limited to the Southeast District School "for three months every winter until he was

5. Burritt. *A Voice from the Back Pews to the Pulpit and Front Seats* (London, 1872), pp. 6–11.
6. Mary Howitt, pp. x-xii.

sixteen years old."[7] The district school, one of five in the village, was a crude structure, in which the 3 R's were monotonously hammered into the children after the usual Testament readings began the day's exercises. Each of the district schools operated on an annual appropriation $125.00.[8] A few private schools were available for those children whose parents could afford the tuition. The curriculum and instruction in New Britain's district schools did not vary from the mediocre standards and practices of other New England towns and villages.

Elihu's district-school teacher recalled that he was "the best scholar in his class," although Elihu believed his parents considered him "the dullest child in the family."[9] Apparently as a young boy he looked a bit dull and acted somewhat strangely, for the children in his neighborhood teased him constantly and had all sorts of uncomplimentary nicknames for him. He later confided to a friend that he

was full of romance from my earliest childhood. When I could scarcely mount above the door-stone of my father's house, I used to muse by the hour on the still, pure golden sky that zoned the North West, and as I gazed upon it in harvest time through green maple trees, I thought the people that lived under that sapphire drapery never died, and wore that robe of golden sky to meeting, and did nothing but sing psalms and eat apricots all the week.[10]

If he disclosed such speculations to his school friends, it is little wonder that they thought him odd.

7. Rufus W. Bailey, "Elihu Burritt", in *Southern Literary Messenger*, IX (April, 1843), p. 234; Burritt to Frederick T. Stanley, New Britain, April 1, 1875, Connecticut Historical Society.

8. Camp, pp. 216–225.

9. Burritt, *Lectures and Speeches* (London, 1869), p. 180; Burritt, *A Voice from the Back Pews;* p. 10; Journals, Aug. 5, 1842.

10. Burritt to [Anna Mary Southall], Hamburg, Germany, September 5, 1853, Friends House Library, London.

The Burritt house was a kind of temporary refuge for the weak and poor. Though unsuccessful in business, Elihu's father got along well with people. He had a real concern for those whose fortunes were less than his, and some of the meager means at his disposal he used to help the needy. Often when returning from the market, he would walk "two or three miles out of his way to leave a few oysters or oranges, or some such acceptable present, to some sick person or poor sufferer." Young Elihu inherited his religious convictions from his mother, but he learned his first lessons in philanthropy from his father.

After the latter's death in 1827, Elihu apprenticed himself to Samuel Booth, a New Britain blacksmith, and began learning the trade with which his name would always in the future be associated. He worked diligently, but he could not forget his books. "I carried," he wrote in 1838, "an indomitable taste for reading" into the blacksmith shop.[11] Too poor to give up work for more schooling, and probably too old—he was now about twenty—to consider it seriously, he decided, when his apprenticeship was a little more than half over, to study Latin on his own. This decision at an age when more practical boys would have been considering marriage was due to the incentive provided him by his oldest brother, Elijah.

Elijah Hinsdale Burritt, sixteen years Elihu's senior, was a man of considerable ability and wide-ranging interests. While apprenticed to a blacksmith as a young boy, Elijah had an accident which disabled him for several months. During his convalescence he continued private studies in mathematics, for which he had a strong bent. Some charitable friends were so impressed by his intellectual promise that they sent him off to Williams College, paying part of his expenses; he earned the rest through part-time teaching.

11. Burritt to William Lincoln, Worcester, 1838, in *Common Sense in Education* (New York), May, 1882.

Insufficient funds caused him to leave Williams. He moved to Georgia, where he edited a newspaper in Milledgeville (then the capital) and began to acquire property. Unfortunately, Elijah was "much given to ostentation and display, imperious in his manner, and too fond of change and adventure to make the success in life which his great talents would otherwise have accomplished."[12] In 1830 he fled from Georgia, as Elihu liked to believe, "in consequence of persecution for antislavery sentiments"[13] and returned to New Britain, where he established a school that specialized in science and astronomy. In 1833 Elijah wrote *The Geography of the Heavens*, a popular astronomy textbook which went through several editions and which had sold over 300,000 copies by 1856.[14] In 1834 he had an article published in Benjamin Silliman's *American Journal of Science*.[15]

When Elihu finished his apprenticeship in 1831, he enrolled in Elijah's school for a quarter's study, concentrating on mathematics and giving a "few half hours and corner moments to Latin and French." At the end of his enrollment he returned to the forge happy with what he had accomplished but worried over the time and money lost while away from work. He decided to undertake the work of two men to make up the money he would have earned had he not attended school. For the next six months he worked fourteen hours a day. Despite the long hours, he carried on his studies independently, devoting most of his study time to

12. W. H. Lee, "Reminiscences of the Early Life of Elihu Burritt" in New York Genealogical Society *Proceedings* XXXVI (New York, 1881), p. 5.

13. Journals, May 29, 1854.

14. Elijah Burritt, *The Geography of the Heavens*, Greatly Enlarged, Revised and Illustrated by H. Mattison (New York, 1856), p. iv. For Elijah's estimation of his book see his letter to President Fisk of Wesleyan University, New Britain, August 14, 1833, Wesleyan University Library.

15. *American Journal of Science*, XXVI (July, 1834), pp. 129–131; Elijah Burritt to Edward C. Herrick, New Britain, Jan. 16, 1834, Yale University Library.

languages rather than to mathematics.[16] Confident he could study languages and work at the same time, he purchased a Greek grammar and conjugated verbs as he cast brass cow-bells. (Years later, he enjoyed relating this improbable scene.) At night he studied Latin, French, and Spanish. "This circumstance," he wrote, "gave a new impulse to the desire of acquainting myself with the philosophy, derivation and affinity of the different European tongues."[17]

It was not peculiar that Elihu, a bright young man eager to learn, should have charted out for himself such an ambitious if desultory educational course. Not until 1850 did New Britain have a free high school, and even at that late date it was one of the first Connecticut towns to provide free secondary education.[18] His passion for self-improvement was a fairly common emotion during the period. The generation in which he reached young manhood was given over to what Professor Merle Curti has called the "cult of self-improvement,"[19] convinced that any mind could be elevated, morally and intellectually, through persistent application. This idea had its roots in America's colonial past, and was part of the larger meaning to America of the eighteenth-century European Enlightenment, with its emphasis on the essential goodness of man and the perfectibility of mankind. The Scotch scientist-philosopher, Dr. Thomas Dick, a good friend of Elijah Burritt, helped popularize the concept in America through his widely read book *On the Improvement of Society by the Diffusion of Knowledge.*[20]

16. Burritt, *Ten-Minute Talks*, p. 11.
17. Burritt to William Lincoln, Worcester, 1838, in *Common Sense*.
18. Camp, pp. 229–230.
19. Merle Curti, *The Growth of American Thought* (New York, 1943), p. 355.
20. *Ibid.* Dr. Dick had corresponded with Elijah Burritt over the latter's *Geography of the Heavens;* Elihu Burritt from Worcester "to Thomas Dick, L.L.D. Scotland, on the death of his brother Elijah," MS Family Album and Letter Book, 1822–1838, American Antiquarian Society.

The fetish for self-improvement received its most sophisticated literary synthesis in William E. Channing's essay on *Self-Culture*, published in 1838. Throughout the first half of the nineteenth century "improving" literature stimulated the enthusiasm for self-help and expressed sentimental hopes for the upward progress of the poor, self-motivated working man.[21]

Burritt seemed determined to make himself an obedient practitioner of self-culture. He revered Elijah, whom he considered "the noblest man that ever bore the name of Burritt,"[22] and with friendly envy he sought to emulate Elijah's scholarship. Perhaps because he realized that in the fields of science and mathematics he could never match Elijah, he turned to languages. But the untoward conditions under which he studied made him realize that, if he was to learn languages, he would have to find more time. Accordingly, in the winter of 1832, he went to New Haven in the naive belief that mere presence in the rarefied academic atmosphere of that college town would facilitate his study of languages. He had no intention of enrolling at Yale, as he had just enough money for room and board to last a few months. Neither did he think seriously of asking some of the Yale professors for free instruction. That idea he dismissed because he was "then naturally timid, and also half ashamed to ask instruction in the rudiments of Greek and Hebrew at twenty-two years of age."[23] Elihu's New Haven plan, viewed from any angle, was strange. Since he did not plan to seek free help from Yale Professors, there was little purpose in going to New Haven, unless, of course, he would have felt guilty to have remained at home and have done nothing but study languages. New Britain folks had sus-

21. Carl Bode, *The Anatomy of American Popular Culture*, 1840–1867 (Berkeley, California, 1959), pp. 119–132.

22. Burritt to A. Southall, Washington, D. C., April 10, 1854, Friends House Library.

23. Burritt, *Ten-Minute Talks*, p. 12.

pected that there was something queer about him, and he probably did not want to confirm their suspicions.

Almost immediately upon taking a room in a New Haven inn, he commenced his studies:

> As soon as the man who attended to the fires had made one in the common sitting room, which was at about half-past four in the morning, I arose, and studied German till breakfast, which was served at half-past seven. When the boarders were gone to their places of business, I sat down to Homer's Iliad, without a note or comment to assist me, and with a Greek and Latin lexicon. A few minutes before the people came in to their dinners I put away all my Greek and Latin, and began reading Italian, which was less calculated to attract the notice of the noisy men who at that hour thronged the room. After dinner I took a short walk, and then sat down to Homer's Iliad, with a determination to master it without a master. The proudest moment of my life was when I had first possessed myself to the full meaning of the first fifteen lines of that noble work. . . . In the evening I read in the Spanish language until bedtime. I followed this course for two or three months, at the end of which time I had read about the whole of the Iliad in Greek, and made considerable progress in French, Italian and Spanish.[24]

After he had memorized the first fifteen lines of the *Iliad*, he strolled "among the classic trees of the Elm City and looked up at the college . . . with a kind of defiant feeling."[25] It was quite like him to have done just that.

In the spring of 1832, after he had returned to New Britain, Elihu was offered a teaching position at a small academy in nearby Glastonbury. Wanting to put his studies "to practical account," he accepted, teaching languages and other subjects. Toward the close of the school year he became ill, the result, he thought, of the lengthy suspension

24. Quoted in Mary Howitt, pp. xiii-xiv.
25. Burritt, *Ten-Minute Talks*, p. 12.

of manual labors. He believed that health required hard exercise, and that without it neither body nor mind could function properly. He gave up his job and went back to New Britain, never again giving much thought to teaching.[26]

This was Burritt's first opportunity to make use of his mind professionally, and his decision to quit teaching appears arbitrary. His health was not so impaired as to prevent him from resuming his duties after a sufficient rest. But the low pay and inferior social rank of rural New England teachers were poor inducements even to a self-taught blacksmith. Burritt tossed teaching aside because he sought a higher station in life.

Instead of returning to blacksmithing for the physical labor he thought so necessary for his health, Burritt became a travelling salesman for a small New Britain manufacturer. The job kept him away from home for long periods, but he enjoyed travelling through New England and New York. He also began studying Hebrew and by the time he resigned from his job around 1835 was able to read a Hebrew Bible.[27] His most notable achievement as a "commercial traveller" was the story he wrote entitled *My Brother's Grave*, the first of a plethora of stories and essays from his ever-active pen.

My Brother's Grave was so bathed in mawkish sentimentalism and banal moralism that it makes much of the profuse moralistic literature of the period seem like high drama. It was based on an incident which involved Burritt as he travelled through Vermont on business, though it is hard to imagine that the event could actually have happened the way he described it. Journeying through the countryside, Burritt came upon a young girl swinging an axe, "which she could scarcely lift," against "a hacked billet of hickory."

26. *Ibid.*, p. 13; Mary Howitt, p. xiv.
27. Mary Howitt, p. xiv.

While doing for the frail girl what she herself could not, Burritt told her that, if he were her brother, he would never permit her to do a man's work. With tears watering "her soft blue eyes" she pointed to "a coarse chip of granite standing in a corner of a little garden spot" and said, "so would he, and did when he was pale and sick, until cold drops of sweat would run down his hollow cheeks." Burritt was downhearted as he walked her to the door of her little dwelling and turned around "to bid adieu to a spot of earth more precious than the ashes of the Pantheon." The story continues with Burritt reading to the girl (who, naturally, lived with an aged grandmother) from a much-used Bible. Just as he was ready to leave—and while she stared long-ingly at the heavens—he substituted a bank note for the broom-splinter the girl had used as a bookmark in her Bible. The stealthy act of philanthropy consummated, Burritt de-parted.[28]

The reader is puzzled whether the story is about a poor, pious girl, or about what a beneficent fellow Burritt was. Though the scene and action are trite even by the criterion of sentimental fiction of the time, for the reader of popular literature during this period the "greatest enticement into romantic melancholy was probably the graveyard."[29] Bur-ritt was an incurable sentimentalist and moralist whose childhood had been filled with paternal injunctions and ex-amples to "think holy" and to do good. Undoubtedly he had read much "graveyard" literature—he could hardly have es-caped it. It is therefore not surprising that "his first essay in original authorship"[30] should have been patterned after the style of Lydia H. Sigourney, the master writer of maud-lin melancholy.

28. Burritt, *Sparks from the Anvil* (Worcester, 1846), pp. 17–22.
29. E. Douglas Branch, *The Sentimental Years, 1836–1860* (New York, 1934), p. 154.
30. Mary Howitt, p. xiv.

Burritt did not long remain a Yankee peddler. His family and relatives complained of his frequent absences from home and prevailed upon him to set up a business in New Britain. In 1836 he used what few dollars he had saved, along with brother Elijah's good credit rating, to open a grocery store. The "memorable period of artificial prosperity," as Elihu called it, under which most of the nation, including New Britain, was basking convinced him that the grocery business, if mundane, would at least be profitable. He was not at the time unwilling to make money. But no sooner had he started his business than he was forced to close. The panic of 1837 swept it aside with thousands of others.

"I accordingly came to the ground," he wrote in his autobiography, "and lost all the avails of years of industry." The business failure came as a shocking blow to him, but he was determined to pay his debts in full from the "fruit" of his manual labors.[31] He began to understand that, though he had a good head for figures, it was not for business figures. He had no way of knowing then that this was to be for him just the first of a series of financial setbacks which would keep him poor throughout his life.

A failure in business at twenty-seven, Burritt was now more inclined than ever to resume his language studies, which he had never entirely neglected. The study of Hebrew had sparked an interest in Oriental languages, and he began to formulate in his mind a grand project to master as many Oriental languages as he could. He thought that nowhere in New Britain, or in all Connecticut, could he find the requisite books to begin such a program. He "concluded to seek a place as a sailor, on board some ship bound to Europe, thinking in this way to have opportunity for

31. Journals, Nov. 30, Dec. 3, 1841; Burritt, Ten-Minute Talks, p. 13.

collecting, at different ports, such works, in the modern and Oriental languages, as I found necessary for my object."[32]

His earlier New Haven plan was somewhat impractical, but this one was wild. Obviously he was uncertain about what he wanted to do, or be. In any event, to propose a trip around the world to study languages illustrated the extent to which he would go to satisfy his instincts and that his instincts were not of a common order. The Burritts were not people who suffered from indecision or shrank from adventure. Elijah was about to lead several members of the family to Texas "to plant a colony from New Britain."[33] If Elijah was to be the Moses of an expedition to Texas, Elihu was prepared to lead himself around the world.

He chose Boston as the most likely port from which to secure passage as a hired hand aboard any ship sailing for Europe. With all his worldly possessions in his pockets, which included three dollars, an old silver watch needing repair, and "a change of linen tied in a handkerchief," he started off on his pilgrimage in May, 1837. He told neither his mother nor his friends the reason for going to Boston because he was afraid of what they might think. To save money, he decided to walk the 120 miles to Boston. When he arrived, he learned that no ship would be sailing to Europe for some time. He was about ready to scrap his plans when by accident he heard that the American Antiquarian Society library in Worcester had a large collection of rare language books.[34] He set off, on foot again, to Worcester, forty miles from Boston.

32. Burritt To William Lincoln, Worcester, 1838, in *Common Sense*.
33. Burritt to Southall, Washington, D.C., Feb. 27, 1854, Friends House Library. Elihu declared that members of his family went to Texas "to establish a mechanical enterprise." See Extract of an address by Elihu Burritt at a conference-meeting, Worcester, April 1, 1838, MS Family Album.
34. Mary Howitt, pp. xv-xvi; Journals, Nov. 29, 1843.

"I visited the hall of the Antiquarian Society and found there, to my infinite gratification, such a collection of ancient, modern, and Oriental languages, as I never before conceived to be collected in one place."[35] Most of his first day in Worcester he spent inspecting the library. His frequent visits there, and his transparent eagerness, elicited an invitation from the Society to use all its facilities.

To support himself, Burritt took a job as a journeyman blacksmith, receiving twelve dollars a month and board. He had less time for study than he had hoped, but was able to spend about three hours a day in the library and to study all evening. His recording in 1838 of a typical week of manual and academic travails points out how hard (and aimlessly) he worked:

> *Monday,* June 18, Headache; 40 Pages Cuvier's Theory of the Earth, 64 Pages French, 11 Hours Forging. *Tuesday,* 65 Lines of Hebrew, 30 Pages French, 10 Pages Cuvier's Theory, 8 Lines Syriac, 10 ditto Danish, 10 ditto Bohemian, 9 ditto Polish, 15 Names of Stars, 10 Hours Forging. *Wednesday,* 25 Lines Hebrew, 50 Pages Astron., 11 Hours Forging. *Friday,* Unwell; 12 Hours Forging. *Saturday,* Unwell; 50 Pages Natural Philos., 10 Hours Forging. *Sunday,* Lesson for Bible class.[36]

Within a year's time he reported having made substantial progress in languages. He was "able to add so much to my previous acquaintance with the Ancient, Modern, and Oriental languages, as to be able to read upwards of fifty of them with more or less facility."[37] Though the number of languages he could read (he spoke none of them) was closer to thirty than fifty, and though his fluency in reading

35. Burritt to William Lincoln, Worcester, 1838, in *Common Sense.*
36. MS "Journal of Elihu Burritt, A Connecticut Blacksmith", 1838, Central Connecticut State College Library. This Journal is an outline of Burritt's work and study routine June 4-Aug. 2, 1838.
37. Burritt to William Lincoln, Worcester, 1838, in *Common Sense.*

varied markedly with the language, this was no mean accomplishment. In spite of the rather breathtaking scope of
his endeavors, he insisted that nothing came easily to him.
"All that I have accomplished, or expect, or hope to accomplish, has been and will be by the plodding, patient, perse-
vering process of accretion which builds the ant-heap—particle by particle, thought by thought, fact by fact."[38]

Whatever satisfaction he derived from his first year's exertions in Worcester was mixed with grief over the fate of
Elijah and other members of his family in Texas. In less
than two months "the fatal disease of the climate swept
. . . away" his two brothers, Elijah and William, and his
brother-in-law, Jabez Cornwall.[39] Emily Burritt, the second
oldest sister who had also gone to Texas, wrote to her sister
Eunice (Cornwall's wife, who had remained in New Britain) about how she had "wiped the sweat of death from
his forehead." Emily asked, "Will you let the religion which
you have long professed be your support in this hour of
trial?" She also wrote to Clarissa Burritt, William's wife,
that "God has promised to be a father of the fatherless and
the widow's God and judge."[40] In a few days Emily would
painfully write to Ann, Elijah's wife. A short time later,
Emily died in Galveston. Only Hezekiah Seymour, a brother-in-law, lived to return to New Britain "to tell the tale of
their suffering and death."[41]

Elihu was thunderstruck over the death of the "amiable

38. Burritt to Thomas Nelson, Worcester, Dec. 16, 1839, in *Sparks
From the Anvil*, pp. x–xiv.

39. Burritt to [A. Southall], Washington, D.C., Feb. 27, 1854.

40. Copy of a letter from Emily Burritt "on the death of two of her
brothers at Houston, Texas, Nov. 30, 1837," MS Family Album. . .

41. Burritt to [A. Southall], Washington, D.C., Feb. 27, 1854,
Friends House Library. Elijah's last words were: "The battle is not
to the strong—a short race." Copy of a Letter from Emily Burritt
"communicating intelligence of the death of her eldest brother," MS
Family Album.

Cornwall," the "lamblike William," and the pious Emily, but he was more deeply hurt by Elijah's death. "My Dear girl," he wrote to a friend about Elijah's death, "you and I will never look upon that noble man again. Those golden locks are hidden in a grave which neither of us will ever visit . . . The hand of death touched that majestic forehead —has passed over that heavenly countenance and it is changed and hidden in the unnoted sands of a foreign desert."[42] Not only was Elijah "the eldest of our brothers," he wrote at another time; "he was the pride and pillar of our family: our souls were bound up in him."[43] The second oldest brother, the "meek George," had died in Georgia, where he had accompanied Elijah in 1822.[44] Of the brothers there remained only Elihu and Isaac, a Southington farmer. Elihu never for a moment questioned God's right or fairness. He would have unhesitatingly replied in the affirmative to the inquiry his sister Emily had made of Eunice: "Will you say the Lord gave and has a perfect right to take away?"[45]

42. Elihu Burritt to Miss Laura Cook "informing her of the death of his Brothers in Texas," 1837, MS Family Album.

43. Extract of an address by Elihu Burritt . . . April 1, 1838, *ibid.*

44. George Burritt ran a school in Columbia County, Georgia. E. H. Burritt, Columbia Co., Georgia, to his parents "communicating to them the intelligence of the death of George Burritt," *ibid.*

45. Emily Burritt to Eunice Burritt, Houston, Nov. 30, 1837, *ibid.* Elihu wrote Eunice: "Alas, I have nothing alleviating to mingle in this bitter chalice which is forced upon your lips—nothing to mitigate the wormwood of this afflicting draft, save those melting sentiments of commiseration, which flow freely and freshly, both night and day, from the bruised heart of an affectionate Brother . . . Let not the cankerworm of consuming grief feed upon your widowed heart . . . Think also you have a God to go to;—that there is a 'tree of life' planted for you. Go and try the virtue of its healing leaves, for they will cure those wounds which no human anodyne can reach;—they will cure those wounds which no earthly lenitive can modify." (Elihu Burritt, to Eunice, "in answer to hers communicating the intelligence of the death of her husband, Jabez Cornwall," *ibid.*)

The Texas tragedy weighed heavily on Burritt's mind as he maintained a steady pace at forging garden hoes and at studying abstruse languages. Because blacksmithing brought him very little money, he wondered whether his linguistic talents could be turned to profit. He wrote to William Lincoln, a prominent literary-minded Worcester resident, giving a none-too-bashful account of his background and ability in languages, asking if he knew of any publishers who would pay for German translations.[46] Burritt was aware of the national interest in German literature and philosophy. Such journals as the *North American Review*, the *New York Review*, the *Knickerbocker*, to mention only a few, regularly published translations from the works of Goethe, Heine, Schiller, and Herder.[47] For Burritt a few such translations would both establish a reputation as a language scholar and enhance his income. Judging from the letter he wrote Lincoln, however, it is doubtful that he cared much about the money. He was trying to let the people in Worcester know of the uncommon blacksmith in their midst.

Not long after he had written Lincoln, Burritt was "dumbfounded and almost overwhelmed with confusion," so he wrote in his self-effacing autobiography, when he saw his letter to Lincoln published in a newspaper.[48] Lincoln had sent the letter to Governor Edward Everett, a brilliant classical scholar and patron of education, who in addressing an educational convention in Taunton, Massachusetts, on October 10, 1838, referred to the linguistic feats of a poor young blacksmith recently arrived in Worcester. By the late thirties educational conventions were familiar occurrences throughout New England as the free public school movement created a demand for more and better common

46. Burritt to William Lincoln, Worcester, 1838, in *Common Sense.*
47. Frank L. Mott, *A History of American Magazines, 1741–1850* (New York, 1930), I, 401.
48. Burritt, *Ten-Minute Talks*, p. 15.

schools. Education for responsible citizenship and for moral enlightenment were dominant educational themes at this time.[49]

At the Taunton Convention Everett enumerated the various civil obligations of citizens living in a republic and stressed the importance of education in helping them perform those duties wisely. Education assisted men in making "an independent and rational judgment of their own, and . . . diminished as much as possible the numbers of the opposite class, who, being blinded by ignorance, are at the mercy of anyone who has an interest and the skill to delude them." As proof of the scholastic heights within the reach of ordinary workingmen, Everett read aloud Burritt's letter. "It discloses," the Governor said, "a resolute purpose of improvement under obstacles and difficulties of no ordinary kind, which excites my admiration, I may say my veneration." It was "enough to make one who has good opportunities for education hang his head in shame."[50] Thus did the village blacksmith become the "learned blacksmith."

Burritt feebly maintained that the Everett incident had brought him unwanted "sudden notoriety." His first thought, he declared, "was to change my name and abscond to some back town in the country, and hide myself from the kind of fame I apprehended."[51] But he did not change his name, nor did he run away. He was able to cope with the publicity, enjoy it, and in due time capitalize on it.

Soon after the Taunton episode, Governor Everett invited the learned blacksmith to dinner. Less than two years before, Burritt had walked to Boston with a vision that failed

49. Lawrence A. Cremin, *The American Common School* (New York, 1951), pp. 44–62.

50. Taunton *Whig*, Oct. 24, 1838; excerpts from Governor Everett's Taunton address can be found in Cremin, pp. 32–33.

51. Journals, August 17, 1841, Burritt, *Ten-Minute Talks*, p. 15.

to materialize supposedly for want of a ship. Now he made his way there by coach, to dine with the governor, who, apparently, had been formulating plans for him. Everett, according to Burritt, had secured the pledges of several wealthy men to finance his education at Harvard. Burritt graciously demurred, saying weakly that he deemed it imperative for his health to couple his academic endeavors with manual labor.[52]

It is not puzzling that Burritt should have refused such a splendid offer. He was probably wary of the competition he would face at Harvard and afraid that he might not do well. He did well with languages because he was ambitious, methodical, and willing to study without stint. But his mind was neither creative nor reflective. His compulsive and erratic study of languages was not an end in itself but a means of social escalation, a kind of intellectual stunt he used to emancipate himself from the blacksmith shop. Now that he was "the learned blacksmith," Harvard might have been, at best, an anticlimax or, at worst, a source of personal embarrassment.

Burritt's "notoriety" caused him to plunge precipitously into a literary project. In 1839 he began publishing a small monthly magazine called the *Literary Geminae*, whose design was to "add to the facilities of the young ladies and gentlemen of New England, for their acquisition of the French language."[53] American readers were not suffering from a lack of journals and periodicals when Burritt decided to enter the literary field. On the contrary, the market for magazines was glutted and the chances for success were slim.

Half of Burritt's monthly contained selections from various French authors (probably because at the time most "magazines paid far less attention to the French writers

52. Burritt, *Ten-Minute Talks*, p. 15.
53. *Literary Geminae*, August, 1839, p. 72.

than to the German"[54]), and the other half mostly his own articles and translations. The periodical was moral and didactic in the extreme: "My Brother's Grave", "My Own New England Home", and "An Apprentice's Way of Acquiring a Library" were typical short stories full of the asphyxiating moralism that characterized most of his early writing. The translations were usually from the works of German romantic poets (Herder and Klopstock) and German moralists (Zollikofer and Gessner); selections in French included the writings of Buffon, Massillon, Raynal, and Voltaire. Now and then the magazine published an original poem by Mrs. Sigourney or a brief essay by Longfellow, whose acquaintance Burritt had recently made.[55]

Burritt sent a copy of the first number to Mrs. Sigourney, seeking, he wrote, "the approbation of *one* whose very name is identified with all the trends to the salutary cultivation of the minds and hearts of the youth of our country."[56] He mailed free copies to people who he thought might spread the word about his magazine. To the editor of the *New Yorker* he not only sent a copy of the *Literary Geminae,* but also a garden hoe—no doubt for the express purpose of reminding the editor that he was merely a simple blacksmith.[57] Mrs. Sigourney wrote Burritt "a very flattering expression of her approbation of the character and design of the magazine." But the *Literary Geminae* never received the public's approval. The magazine had fewer than one hundred subscribers, though they included Longfellow and

54. Mott, p. 404.
55. *Literary Geminae,* June-Oct., 1839.
56. Burritt to Mrs. L. H. Sigourney, Worcester, June 15, 1839, New Britain Public Institute.
57. The volume of the *Literary Geminae* at the Yale University Library belonged to the editor of the *New Yorker,* who wrote about the garden hoe on p. 11 of the Nov., 1839 number.

Governor Everett.[58] It was too literary, pedantic, and didactic, and its editor too little known to gain the circulation needed for survival. By January, 1840, Burritt withdrew his magazine "from the already too crowded list of periodical publications."[59]

This abortive literary venture cost him over five hundred dollars of his "hard-earned wages," and almost all of his savings.[60] It is difficult to visualize even a hardworking blacksmith having saved so much money, but as Burritt told Longfellow, he was no "amateur workingman. With my own hands I earned last year [1839–40] nearly $1,000, besides some little time devoted to my magazine."[61] Evidently his abstemious habits made it possible to save a large portion of his wages. He had also rented the use of a small blacksmith shop to hammer out garden tools to sell on his own.

In 1840 the affairs of Elihu Burritt, learned blacksmith, reached well-nigh national consideration when the *Southern Literary Messenger*, a reputable magazine published in Richmond, Virginia, paid high tribute to him. Knowledge of Burritt had been brought by a Richmond doctor, Thomas Nelson, who was travelling in Massachusetts about the time Governor Everett was introducing Burritt to the public. Dr. Nelson had met Burritt in Worcester and was impressed by him. The two began to correspond, and one of Burritt's immodest autobiographical letters to Nelson was sent by the latter to the *Southern Literary Messenger*, which published it.

58. *Literary Geminae*, August, 1839, p. 72; MS Cashbook, American Antiquarian Society.
59. *Literary Geminae*, May, 1840, p. 287.
60. Journals, Nov. 30, 1841.
61. Burritt to Longfellow, Worcester, Dec. 1, 1840, in Merle Curti, *The Learned Blacksmith, The Letters and Journals of Elihu Burritt* (New York, 1937), p. 11.

The editor of the magazine royally saluted Burritt as a paragon of self-culture and implied that he was one of the foremost linguists of his time. He conceded the brilliant philologist, Mezzafonti, a professor of Oriental languages at the University of Bologna, to be the world's most learned linguist. However, "Mezzafonti has not been obliged to labor one-third of his time at the anvil for subsistence."[62]

What the *Southern Literary Messenger* did for Burritt's reputation as a linguist was surpassed by what the *American Phrenological Journal* did for his reputation as a universal genius. In 1840 Burritt had permitted a phrenologist to make a plastic cast of his head, a picture of which was inserted in the October number of that journal. The characteristics of the size and shape of Burritt's head were meticulously explained in phrenological language. Burritt eventually regretted that he allowed such a cast to be made; but for the moment he was happy to read that the "anterior lobes" of his brain, which were "the seat of the intellectual faculties," were "decidedly large, compared with the middle and posterior lobes." He was also comforted by the fact that his head showed "a very large organ of Firmness, and rather deficient Self-esteem, which explains his extreme diffidence and modesty."[63] Six years later, his head again graced the pages of that periodical, this time nobly flanked by the heads of the poet Moore and the statesman Pitt; Burritt's head, readers were told, compared most favorably with Moore's and Pitt's.[64]

In Massachusetts the deeds of Burritt very much inter-

62. *Southern Literary Messenger*, VI (March, 1840), pp. 202–203. Dr. Nelson's letter to the editor is also included in this number, as is Burritt's letter to Nelson.

63. See John Davies, *Phrenology: Fad and Science* (New Haven, 1957), Chapters 1–2; *American Phrenological Journal*, III (Oct., 1840), pp. 27–28.

64. *Ibid.*, VII (Nov., 1846), pp. 327–328.

ested Longfellow, who, in addition to his growing fame as a poet, was a Harvard professor of modern languages. Longfellow wrote Burritt and suggested that he move to Cambridge and devote full time to literary matters. He offered Burritt some financial assistance. Burritt replied that he might consider taking up residence in Cambridge if he could gain access to the college library. He whimsically asked: "[M]ay I bring my hammer with me? [M]ust I *sink* that altogether?" He assured Longellow that his "hammer is as much predisposed to *swim* on top of all my ideas, as was the axe to float on the surface of the water at the touch of the prophet," and that he had "long ago resolved to make them [his studies] subservient to the more necessary and important avocations of life, and not to indulge them at the expense of valuable time or the price of labor." He always confined his "literary leisure" to those parts of the day *"when no man can work."* He hoped that Longfellow would not think him eccentric because he wanted "to stand in the ranks of the workingmen of New England and beg and beckon them onward and upward . . . into the full stature of intellectual men." There was "no higher human reward" coveted by Burritt "than the satisfaction of having stood in the lot of the laboring man."[65] Burritt's letter included practically everything but a definite answer to Longfellow's request that he move to Cambridge.

Longfellow had not asked Burritt to state his ambition in life, but Burritt was only too glad to volunteer the information. Earlier Professor Edwards A. Park, of the Andover Theological Seminary, had solicited from Burritt an account of himself. Burritt replied that he could not "conceive that there is anything in my past history or present pursuits, that could be of use or interest to any individual." Yet he

---

65. Burritt to Longfellow, Worcester, Dec. 1, 1840, in Curti, *The Learned Blacksmith*, pp. 9–11.

enumerated enough of his "trifling attainments" to fill three closely written pages.[66]

Burritt was an extraordinary young man, but he was also a genuine product and expression of the utilitarian Yankee milieu in which he grew up. He had been, as he told Park, "brought up in the most rigid habits of industry," and he actually did think "it a criminal prodigality of time, to devote the best hour of the day . . . in prosecuting such studies as I have been accustomed to choose as the diversion of a brief pastime." His belief in the felicitous results of combining intellectual exercise with manual labor was not unconventional. It was a commonplace notion subscribed to by leading educational reformers. Manual labor schools, such as the famous Oneida Institute which the Reverend George W. Gale had established in Whitesboro, New York, and Oberlin College in Ohio, gave students an opportunity to use their brawn along with their brains.[67] But Burritt was not a student. He needed to remind himself (and others too) that "a certain amount of manual labor is as necessary for me as daily food." After all, he was a blacksmith whose mental gymnastics would not have excited much notice had he been formally trained in languages.

Burritt's whole course of development by 1840 followed closely the advice W. E. Channing gave workingmen regarding self-elevation. He had told them that self-improvement "is not an outward change of condition. It is not political power. I understand something deeper. I know but one elevation of a human being, and that is elevation of soul. . . . There is but one elevation for a laborer and for all other

66. Burritt to E. A. Park, Worcester, Nov. 27, 1839, Boston Public Library.
67. Cremin, p. 36; Benjamin Thomas, *Theodore Weld, Crusader for Freedom* (New Brunswick, New Jersey, 1950), pp. 16–20; Journals, Oct. 3, 1842.

men. There are not different kinds of dignity for different orders of men, but one and the same to all."[68]

In less elegant words Burritt had been told the same thing by his mother. He had responded with enthusiasm to the strident call of his generation for self-improvement. Considering the point from which he had begun life to that at which he had arrived by 1840, he had already made significant advancement. But for the bold, ambitious, and adventuresome the young nation offered boundless opportunities. Progress was the keynote of the period. It was only natural that Burritt was affected by the nervous, rash energy that propelled countless Americans, like his impulsive brother Elijah, to lofty goals. Elijah had studied the stars and had run a newspaper in Georgia and a school in New Britain before he died in Texas. At the age of thirty Elihu, although he had already been involved in diverse enterprises, was still searching. Now, as the learned blacksmith with a vaunted ability to devour languages, he looked ahead to a bright future while he continued to profess "ineffable surprise" at his burgeoning fame. He had indeed come a long way, but he was in a hurry to go further.

68. W. E. Channing, "On the Elevation of the Laboring Classes", in *Works*, II, 411.

2

A Frustrated Literary Career

Burritt's failure to make the *Literary Geminae* a success did not discourage him from continuing his literary activity. A minor celebrity whose name was now known beyond the boundaries of Massachusetts, he embarked upon a literary career somewhat bold and comprehensive in light of his self-professed timidity. As befitted a young man of growing reputation and promise, in 1841, he resolved "to commence and continue a kind of journal, which . . . shall embrace the important occurrences of each day, whether they interest *me* personally, or relate to the interests of the civil, religious, political, or intellectual world."[1] Thus he began a journal which for eighteen years he maintained with characteristic steadiness.

Soon after the demise of his periodical, he started contributing German and French translations to the New York *Evangelist*, an influential Protestant religious journal. He submitted lengthy translations from the sermons and moralistic writings of eighteenth- and nineteenth-century European scholars and clergymen such as G. J. Zollikofer, a Lutheran minister from Leipzig, Friedrich Jacobs, a German classical scholar, and Alexandre R. Vinet, a Swiss Protestant theologian and critic.[2] About the same time the

1. Journals, August 27, 1841.
2. New York *Evangelist*, June 6, 1840-Dec. 8, 1842, *passim*.

28

New York *Observer,* a Protestant journal edited by two brothers of Samuel F. B. Morse, also included Burritt's translations in its columns, though not so regularly as the *Evangelist.*[3] Burritt assumed he would be paid for his articles, but he made no arrangement with the editor of either journal. For a while he was content to let it go at that. Later he would be sorry.

His admiration for the rich and at times soaring Christion moralism of Zollikofer spurred him to prepare for pamphlet publication a translation of the German's discourse on *Moral Education, or the Culture of the Heart of the Young.*[4] It was a heavily didactic piece, but perfectly suited to the reading tastes of a New England public.

Burritt's translations in the *Evangelist* and the *Observer* attracted the attention of the *American Eclectic,* a scholarly bi-monthly magazine begun in New York City in 1841. The editor, the Reverend Absalom Peters, a Presbyterian minister and secretary of the Home Missionary Society, requested translations from Burritt. The magazine contained selections from the periodical literature of foreign countries and translations from rare foreign works. In the prospectus of the first number Peters cited those prominent literary and scholarly persons who had manifested "a lively interest" in the periodical, and Burritt's name was included in a list of distinguished men: George Bancroft, Longfellow, the Reverend Dr. Theodore D. Woolsey, George P. Marsh, and many others.[5]

The Royal Society of Northern Antiquaries of Copenhagen had issued publications of early Scandinavian history and folklore, in Danish, Swedish, Latin, and sometimes

3. New York *Observer,* Jan. 16, 23, 1841.
4. G. Zollikofer, *The Moral Education, or the Culture of the Heart of the Young,* trans., E. Burritt (Providence, 1840), Burritt's name did not appear on this pamphlet, but only the words, "translated by a distinguished linguist."
5. *American Eclectic,* I (Jan., 1841), p. ii.

in Icelandic, under the title *Antiquitates Americanae*. Fewer than 150 persons in Great Britain and America subscribed.[6] Burritt did not—the price was high and the American Antiquarian Society had whatever copies he needed. Peters wanted his magazine to include this material, and for that reason secured George Marsh, the Vermont philologist, and Burritt, still fresh from the praise of the *Southern Literary Messenger*.

The *American Eclectic's* first number contained translations from Scandinavian sources by both Burritt and Marsh, prefaced with historical introductory notes. Marsh translated from the Swedish a selection from Olof Rudbeck's *Atlantica*. Burritt's translation was from *Njals* saga, "considered the greatest of the sagas of Icelanders,"[7] and from *Grunlaug Ormstungs* saga. He used Professor Peter E. Muller's *Sagabibliothek*, in Danish, as his source. He also contributed a translation from *Egils* saga.[8]

His dexterity and precision in translating difficult languages is noticeable in his translation from the Samaritan of *The First Letter Addressed By the Samaritans of Sichem, to Their Brethren in England, 1672*, as well as other letters to and from the Samaritans, originally in Hebrew, Samaritan, and Arabic. He accompanied the first translation with a lucid historical sketch of the Samaritans derived from the Old Testament and various other sources.[9] At the time there was considerable learned debate over the historicity of the Ten Lost Tribes of Israel. Burritt refuted the notion that the Ten Lost Tribes were "wandering about upon the

6. *New York Review*, II (April, 1838), pp. 6–7.

7. Stefan Einarsson, *A History of Icelandic Literature* (New York, 1957), p. 146.

8. *American Eclectic*, I (Jan., 1841), pp. 99–109—in the same issue Burritt also translated from Icelandic "The Narrative of Thorstein Ericsson"; I (May, 1841), pp. 488–494.

9. *Ibid.*, II (Sept., 1841), pp. 250–263; II (Nov., 1841), pp. 481–490.

earth . . . It may occasion some remark [it did not]," he thought, "but I shall stand ready to maintain it."[10]

If the *Eclectic* afforded Burritt the opportunity to pursue his scholarly interests, the *Patriarch* gave him a chance to gratify his moral instinct. The *Patriarch*, edited by the Reverend Rufus W. Bailey and W. H. Cutter, was a family magazine whose purpose was "to show what a family ought to be." In format and scope it was much like several other magazines already in print. It laid great stress on the importance of religion, morality, social duty, and self-improvement. Bailey believed that "the mind is *its own society*, and must finally depend on itself for its improvement." Nathaniel Bowditch and Benjamin Franklin were adduced as examples of the limitless powers of self-discipline. Bailey also referred to Burritt: "The learned blacksmith of Massachusetts, who pounds his anvil eight hours in the day, and reads his fifty different languages at night has had no master."[11]

For his contributions to the *Patriarch* Burritt relied on his old favorite, Zollikofer, in addition to a few of his own moralisms from the *Literary Geminae*, whose articles were now exhumed one by one. "Bury Me in the Garden", which had appeared in the *Literary Geminae*, was Burritt's first literary offering to the *Patriarch*. Though a less complicated affair than "My Brother's Grave", it was equally sentimental. It concerns a dying young girl who whispers to her mother from "ashy lips . . . Mother! Mother! don't let them carry me away down to the dark, cold graveyard, but bury me in the garden—in the garden, mother." Unfortunately the reader never learns whether the girl, who again uttered the plea before "all was still," had her wish granted.[12]

10. See the New York *Observer*, Nov. 27, 1841, for an interesting account of this debate; Journals, Sept. 2, 1841.
11. *Patriarch*, I (Jan., 1841), pp. 3, 15.
12. *Ibid.*, I (Oct., 1841), pp. 168–169.

"An Apprentice's Way of Acquiring a Library" was another contribution to the *Patriarch* which had originally appeared in the *Literary Geminae*. A bluff young man visiting a fellow apprentice is surprised to see that his companion's library embraced "a long list of outlandish names" such as "Milton, Shakespeare, Young, Pope, Dryden, Cowper, Bacon, Locke, Goldsmith, and all the other Smiths in creation, as well as those in America." Lighting an expensive Havana cigar, he asks his friend "to explain how you, an apprentice, with only forty dollars a year, contrive to scrape together a library half as large as Parson Dayton's." The interrogator is told that what he spends weekly on cigars, "nuts, raisins, oranges and figs" would in a year's time more than pay for "the several neatly bound volumes of the *North American Review*, and a handful of those of the *Knickerbocker*" also included in the library. The book-minded apprentice declared that his employer, impressed by his reading habits, allowed him to work during his lunch time in order to earn more money for books. The cigar-smoking, nut-eating young man was admonished that employers prefer "to see them with a book in their hands, when they have done their work, rather than to be lounging about at the taverns or in vicious company." The story ends with the visitor throwing his half-dozen cigars, "a week's stock of comfort," out the window and saying: "I'll try it."[13]

The Reverend R. W. Bailey had made a special trip to Worcester to get Burritt to write for his magazine. He offered Burritt one dollar per page and appointed him the Worcester agent for the *Patriarch*. Bailey desired an account of "the leading incidents" of Burritt's life to accompany an engraving that was to appear in the magazine. ("He had better," wrote Burritt with implausible modesty, "introduce an engraving of a jackboot!") It was Bailey who proposed that he contribute some of his *Literary Geminae*

13. *Ibid.*, I (Nov., 1841), pp. 224–227.

articles, a suggestion to which Burritt happily acceded, "as they are entirely original except to about 100 individuals in this state." Bailey's financial offer made Burritt hopeful that his "literary labors may yet contribute something to my support instead of being that consuming moth which they have hitherto been to my pecuniary ability."[14]

Burritt thought much about leaving Worcester and moving to Cambridge. Four strong inducements prompted him: first, he would have access to Harvard's library of 41,000 volumes; second, he felt he would be "more in intercourse with the literary world, and be better able to acquire a literary reputation"; third, he might meet people in Cambridge and Boston "who may introduce me to some situation less laborious than my present one"; and fourth, the change in residence "would favor a secret design which I have long cherished to commence a polyglot of 40 languages."

The polyglot enterprise involved the translation of select passages from the Scriptures into many languages. Burritt had this plan in mind since 1838, when he prepared a chart on which a short Biblical quotation was translated into forty languages.[15] Though he was sincere about his polyglot scheme, the main reason he wanted to move to Cambridge was to gain a literary reputation. Having drifted to Yale nine years earlier to be among the "classic elms," he now wished to be closer to the literati of Harvard—apparently he thought some of their literary lustre would rub off on him. In 1840 he may have viewed his literary and academic efforts "as matters of mere recreation" and expected nothing from them "but a species of transient gratification."[16] By 1841, however, his impatience for a life as a writer was too

14. Journals, Sept. 4, 1841.
15. *Ibid.*, August 17, 1841.
16. Burritt to Longfellow, Worcester, Dec. 1, 1840, in Curti, *The Learned Blacksmith*, p. 9.

disquieting for him to practice literally what he had written.

To pay for his room and board in Cambridge, Burritt thought he "might hire or build a little blacksmith shop about as large as a hogs-head tub, and procure work from Boston." He estimated he must earn at least $1.25 a day at his trade, since he could not depend upon his writings "for a single *sixpence*." For several weeks he debated the Cambridge move. He was feeling low—persistent headaches, no orders for his garden tools, and no remuneration for his writings. He felt like "burning my books, and giving up forever my literary pursuits." The idea of living in Cambridge became less and less feasible as money became increasingly scarce. "I presume," he wrote, "that if I should apply to some of the wealthy citizens of this place [Worcester] they would cheerfully extend to me all that counsel & aid which I could expect from any gentlemen in Boston and Cambridge." But he could not force himself into making such an application.

Burritt now began taking more positive steps to gain an income from his writings. He asked Peters to inquire of the editors of the *Evangelist* and the *Observer* if in the future they would pay him one cent a line for his contributions. He wanted them to be aware of "how my many gratuitous communications to their columns have trenched upon the necesarries [*sic*] & comforts of my life." In a letter to Harper and Brothers he offered to translate a series of Icelandic sagas, enough to fill a four-hundred-page volume, at fifty cents a page. He realized it was "a poor straw to catch at."

As he waited for replies, he brooded: "I have been feeding myself with the chaff of ambitious hopes too long." He was so despondent that he half-seriously considered "applying for some district school; get married to some poor worthy girl whose situation would not be likely to be rendered worse by the union—and try if it would not afford me a humble home."

Harpers was interested in Burritt's proposal and requested him to send some samples of his translations for their perusal. This was the first of many similar offers to publishers which received attention. It gave him an increased "incentive to industry" to think that he could "get anything but by the sweat of my brow, and the most arduous manual labor." He translated seventy-five pages from the *Antiquitates Americanae* and sent the manuscript to Harpers.

Notwithstanding his deep desire for a literary career, Burritt continued to pass himself off as a contented blacksmith who had no ambitions beyond the forge and anvil. Walking home from church one Sunday, he was given a roll of paper, which had been left off at the railway depot by a passerby. Opening the roll, he discovered it was

a little piece of sheepskin written over with Latin, and sent me by the President and faculty of Amherst College, telling me in particular and the world in general, that they have nicknamed me *Magister in Artibus*—I suspect some of them have seen some of my *garden hoes*. I hope God will preserve me from any appeals to my vanity.

He wrote a letter of appreciation to Heman Humphrey, president of Amherst, thanking him and the college faculty for the tribute. The letter is worth quoting in large part because of Burritt's studious efforts at maintaining a reputation for modesty:

You may easily conceive, Sir, that I could not but be deeply affected at the reception of such an honorable and unsolicited mark of distinction. Nor need I say that I prize it richly, *not* as an evidence of merit, but of debt to a generous public, which will inspire me to more assiduous exertions in the future. I accept it with inexpressible sentiments of pleasure, not as a personal honor, but as a pledge of encouragement, on your part, Gent, given to the young work-ingmen of New England, for whom I am living and for whom I shall die. It is with them that I desire to share this honor, and all others that may attend my future career; and my earthly ambition will have attained its goal, when I shall have left some feeble wayworks to the temple of knowledge and virtue. . .

Yet there were occasions when Burritt refused to help people interested in their self-improvement. A stranger in Zanesville, Ohio, for instance, wrote, asking how Burritt had acquired his "tact" for learning languages. This was the sixth letter making the same inquiry he had received "from a distance." He answered none of them because he knew of "no royal road to learning."

Harpers' reply concerning his manuscript was encouraging, if not precisely what he wanted. They proposed a translation of the sagas bearing upon the question of the ante-Columbian discovery of America, a topic, wrote Burritt, "much agitated of late." Before hearing from Harpers he had made plans to visit Providence and Newport. He had sixteen sorely-needed dollars owing him there in unpaid subscription money for the *Literary Geminae*. Money problems now became acute. His work at the forge was slow, and prospects for steady work dim. (One wonders how he had been able, as he claimed, to have earned a thousand dollars the previous year.) The Reverend Absalom Peters' letter regarding remuneration by the *Evangelist* and the *Observer* was only half-satisfying. "The *Observer* man," Burritt noted, "seems disposed to fill his pockets by making his contributors work merely on the Roman Catholic principle, viz—'for the love of God.' " But the *Evangelist* appeared "more liberally disposed" to pay him.

Burritt's Journal, for September 24, 1841, testifies to his growing despair over finances: "My money is all gone, and if I should get sick I should be in an unpleasant predicament. I have relinquished the hope of obtaining anything by my pen; such a hope is a delusive phantom, as thousands have realized whose claims upon it were stronger than mine." He was determined to write Peters to ascertain what he intended to pay for the *Eclectic* articles. Burritt had begun "to suspect the propriety of thinking that others 'will do what's right,' without any specific obligation."[17]

If he was having trouble receiving pay for his articles, he was, after all, no exception. Although payments to magazine writers had improved somewhat after 1842, as late as 1848 one writer ascribed the "inferiority of American periodical literature" to the painful fact "that its contributors are mostly unpaid"; and the elder Richard Henry Dana, admitted that had he been "tolerably successful in a pecuniary way, I should have been a voluminous writer" by 1848.[18] The *North American Review* maintained its customary payment of a dollar a page from 1825 to 1850—the same amount Bailey had promised Burritt—and comparable periodicals paid even more. But Burritt did not write for well-established journals. It is inconceivable that the *North American Review*, or its kind, would have published "An Apprentice's Way of Acquiring a Library", "Bury Me in the Garden", or "The Drunkard's Wife". The *Children's Magazine* and the *Mother's Magazine*, among many other family journals, catered to that sort of bathos, but they were well supplied with articles. For the lachrymose prose Burritt wrote at this time he certainly could not have competed with Peter Parley. As for the third-rate poetry he toyed with, Mrs. Sigourney was the undisputed lioness.

The *Patriarch* published Burritt's writings because it could not be fussy, and though Bailey had assured him a

17. Journals, Aug. 17-Sept. 25, 1841, *passim*. A copy of Burritt's letter to Humphrey is in Journal entry for Sept. 22.

18. Quoted in F. Mott, *A History of American Magazines*, I, pp. 511–512.

dollar a page, he was unable to pay anything. The *Eclectic* used Burritt because of his translating ability and because Peters, like "the *Observer* man," also acted on the so-called Roman Catholic principle, "for the love of God." In anticipating remuneration so soon after he had begun writing for periodicals, Burritt was unrealistic; in receiving none, he was in good company.

In the fall of 1841, on his way to Providence, Burritt stopped off in Boston for a day. He spent most of the evening drinking tea and chatting with Samuel C. Drake, proprietor of an antiquarian bookstore and celebrated for numerous writings on the Indians. Burritt told him about a new literary venture he had in mind, which he proposed to call "Tales of the Pensioners". The project would entail interviewing Revolutionary War veterans and gleaning from them accounts of their war experiences. Drake thought the idea good. But this intended work never went beyond one interview with an old veteran "so deaf that I could get nothing out of him except that he was in service only 6 months, and was in the battle of White Plains."[19]

Burritt's literary ambition was temporarily curbed by the numerous invitations to lecture he began receiving from various lyceums. By 1842 both the *Patriarch* and the *Evangelist* sought to capitalize on his expanding reputation as a lecturer, without of course any cost to them. Bailey offered to make him the third editor of the *Patriarch* and suggested that he purchase a share of the magazine. The money-conscious minister planned to arrange a series of lectures for Burritt "*a la Lardner*,"[20] that is, he would rent a lecture hall, sell tickets, take care of all other matters, and allow Burritt to pocket the profits after expenses. With his profits Burritt could buy into Bailey's magazine. Burritt refused because he thought the proposition mercenary and "re-

19. Journals, Sept. 28, Oct. 19, 1841.
20. A reference to Dr. Dionysius Lardner, an English mathematician and very successful popular lecturer.

pugnant." Bailey, anxious to retain Burritt's services, thereafter promised him $100.00 a year for his editorial and literary efforts.

Meanwhile the *Evangelist* offered him $2.00 a page for the forthcoming year. Heartened by the offer, Burritt wrote the editors: "I now hasten to say that I shall hereafter be on the *qui-vive* for all the interesting scraps in literature, and religion, which I may *weld* together, and forge an article worthy of being filed for reception into the columns of the *Evangelist*. I flatter myself that there are neglected *mines*, which I may smelt out a *chain* of interesting facts, if not a string of orient pearls."[21] During the first few months of 1842 he contributed several translations to the *Evangelist* and some original articles to the *Patriarch*. For the *Patriarch* he wrote two articles on "The Dignity of the Parent's Office", in the form of "Letters to a Young Father".[22] They counseled male parents to be extremely vigilant over the moral and religious education of their children.

In the summer of 1842 Bailey sold the *Patriarch*, and the Reverend Absalom Peters was on the verge of disposing the *Eclectic*. Peters told Burritt that he was unable to pay anything because "he was worth nothing when he commenced that publication and had been worth less since."[23] One of the last numbers of the *Eclectic* contained a reference to a work just completed by an Englishman on the ante-Columbian discoveries of America. Thus what little work Burritt had done on this project for Harpers was rendered superfluous.[24] Having received no money for his literary labors, he now vowed to give up writing for "ephemeral publications."

21. New York *Evangelist,* June 6, 1842.
22. *Patriarch*, II (Jan., Feb., 1842).
23. Journals, Dec. 3, 1842.
24. *American Eclectic*, III (March, 1842), pp. 242–243. North Ludlow Beamish had written *The Discovery of America by the Northmen, in the Tenth Century, with Notice of the Early Settlements by the Irish in the Western Hemisphere* (London, 1841).

He was not yet willing to abandon all expectations of writing for profit. He wrote Little, Brown and Company in Boston, offering to translate Garcilaso de la Vega's *History of the Conquest of Florida* for fifty cents a page, with part of the payment in books.[25] The firm turned down the proposal. Burritt's hopes of establishing residence in Cambridge had practically vanished. "Do you not see as plain as the sun," he mournfully asked himself, "that your great polyglot scheme is the most chimerical, impractible [sic] useless enterprise that ever entered into a visionary's brain?" But failure to derive any money from his writings had at least made him wary of seemingly sound literary offers. Theodore Foster, the veteran New York journalist, invited him to become editor of his magazine, the *Indicator*, a bimonthly devoted to self-cultivation. Foster had issued three numbers of the journal before he realized that it would not succeed. By unloading it on Burritt, he saw a way out of an expensive predicament. Burritt demanded a salary of $400 a year, for which he promised to take complete charge of the periodical and furnish it with all the articles. Foster discontinued negotiations.[26]

The editors of the New York *Observer*, who had paid Burritt nothing for the approximately 130 manuscript pages of translations he had contributed, sent him a bill for the copies of the *Observer* he had received during the past three years. Indignantly Burritt replied: "Poor as I am, or as I may be, my mind spurns the inspiration of the 'almighty dollar' . . . If you prefer that I should pay you for the privilege of reading my own thoughts and composition in your columns, then I am ready to demonstrate your appreciation of them, by footing your bill." The editors were not humbled by this tart letter. Sidney Morse, the senior

25. Burritt to Little, Brown and Company, Worcester, May 17, 1843. New Britain Public Institute.
26. Journals, Feb. 9, Jan. 11, 1841.

editor, informed Burritt that he had no right to expect payment since practically all of his contributions were translations rather than original articles. "We could not, therefore, have continued the insertion of your translations, even gratuitously, without some self-sacrifice . . . It would have been more pleasant to have suffered you to remain under the impression that you had conferred upon us a great favor."[27] Burritt stopped supplying translations to the *Observer.*

By 1843 Burritt's literary status left everything to be desired. He had in fact written little except translations. The rest was very ordinary. It was not that he lacked energy or range of interests. His difficulty was that he believed a literary reputation could be established simply by writing a few moral tales and contributing translations to several periodicals. He had a remarkable self-discipline for translating, but he had not yet developed a flair for serious expository writing. His literary style was overwrought, his vocabulary trite and ornate, his themes puerile. Burritt's later writings, for the most part, were never entirely free of these blemishes, yet they do reveal the considerable intellectual growth that came from a life of constant writing and almost continuous labors in reform enterprises.

27. *Ibid.*, March 1, 26, 1843.

3

On The Lyceum Circuit

While Burritt's primary goal during the years 1841 to 1843 was to achieve a "sprinkling of literary fame," his major accomplishment in that period was the substantial reputation he earned as one of America's more popular and successful lecturers. Whatever failures he experienced with the printed word he more than made up for with the spoken word. Whereas he had been paid nothing for his writing, the lyceum, in the beginning at least, paid him well in gold and silver.

The lyceum has been called the "town meeting of the mind." Established in England in the early 19th century, it had sunk its American roots in Massachusetts soil under the guiding hand of Josiah Holbrook, who organized the first lyceum in Millbury in 1826. By 1830 close to one hundred lyceums had sprung up in New England. To a generation of Americans bitten by the bug of self-culture and showered with numberless handbooks extolling self-improvement, the lyceum was an extraordinary agency serving the three-fold purpose of education, enlightenment and entertainment. With "a dollar or two a year" all that was required for membership, even thrifty Yankee farmers and mechanics could not complain.[1] In most cases, regard-

1. Carl Bode, *The American Lyceum: Town Meeting of the Mind* (New York, 1956), pp. 3–19.

less of the reputation or ability of the lecturer, lyceum halls were well-filled; it was a night out, and a cheap one.

At the time of Burritt's entree into the lyceum limelight, the institution had undergone some significant transformations. The most important change was that "the lyceum in the sense of a local, public education movement was finished by about 1840." As the tie-in with adult education loosened, it became more formalized. Lectures were now "more cultural and less informational," and the lecturer more polished and professional.[2]

Burritt's first invitation to lecture came from the Lowell Lyceum in the winter of 1841. He prepared a speech on "Natural Philosophy Prior to the Construction of the Newtonian System." It surveyed the history of astronomy up to the time of Isaac Newton, "containing a view of what had been written or done upon the subject of gravitation before his day."[3] His knowledge of astronomy came from the work his brother Elijah had done in that area, and it was a topic with which he was completely at ease. When he gave this lecture in New York City several months after the Lowell engagement, the New York *Tribune* described it as "a rapid and lucid history."[4]

In anticipation of more lecture engagements Burritt prepared a talk on "The Influence of Mythological Figures and Metaphors on Education." Of the various lectures he gave during his lyceum phase, this one contained his most controversial principle and the one for which he was best known; it also provided the theme for several slightly different lectures. His aim was to prove that "*Nascitur, non fit* was false: that there was no native genius, but that all attainments were the result of persistent will and application."[5] In this particular lecture he illustrated the harmful

2. *Ibid.*, pp. 133, 250.
3. Journals, Oct. 24, 1842.
4. New York *Tribune*, Nov. 24, 1841.
5. Burritt, *Ten-Minute Talks*, p. 16.

effects the doctrine of native genius had upon school-children led to believe that unless they were born geniuses they would always remain ignorant.

In order to learn the techniques of delivering a lecture, Burritt bought a copy of *The Columbia Orator, Containing a Variety of Original and Selected Pieces: Together with Rules, Calculated to Improve Youth and Others in the Ornamental and Useful Arts of Eloquence.*[6] The odds were heavily in his favor that he would receive invitations to speak throughout the country, for there were more good lyceums than good lecturers, or even poor ones. Many lyceums, as advertisements in the *American Journal of Education* show, solicited lecturers who had "a faculty of speaking to an audience with plainness and perspicuity; salaries are offered such gentlemen."[7] Burritt fulfilled these meager qualifications and had, besides, a decided advantage: he was considered an intellectual phenomenon or, as he in time regretfully understood, an "oddity" or "prodigy."

By the fall of 1841 he had received several lecture invitations, including three from New York City. Since he had only two prepared speeches, he wrote a third on "Roman Patriotism," asking the question "Is Roman patriotism or Christian philanthropy most congenial to the Republican principles?" Burritt hoped "to intimate pretty distinctly that there is such a thing as a republic being a republic of democrats among themselves, but a republic of Nebuchadnezzars to the rest of the world." He had "apprehensions of my success in New York, where they have the ablest lecturers in America." But a neat rationalization gave him some solace: "I know they only invited me to gratify their Yankee curiosity, and therefore I shall feel less concern at their

6. The New Britain Public Institute has over 200 books, including *The Columbian Orator*, that comprised part of Burritt's personal library; most of the books are foreign grammars and dictionaries.

7. Bode, p. 189.

disappointment."[8] Of course he was being artlessly humble again; but there was an element of truth in what he said: curiosity was involved in his New York invitations—people wanted to see "the learned blacksmith." As for his lack of "concern" in the event he failed, this was untrue. What people thought of him, in any of his capacities, was always a matter of importance to him.

Before travelling to New York, Burritt lectured in Newburyport, Massachusetts, on "The Influence of Mythological Figures and Metaphors on Education" before "a very full audience of intelligent looking ladies and gentlemen." He was disappointed with his performance because he had forgotten parts of the lecture, not having reviewed it carefully enough beforehand. But the audience was satisfied, and the Newburyport *Herald* gave it special attention, something seldom done for other lectures, by reproducing much of it.[9]

The lecture was an impassioned plea for the abandonment of the principle of native genius and the substitution of the more congenial one of self-culture. Burritt declared that "The knowledge of the men who lived before the flood would hardly in these days furnish an aliment for the tenant of the cradle. The single truth, known to every schoolboy, of the revolution of the earth around the sun, cost the concentrated labor of centuries." Mankind's progressive accumulation of knowledge, in other words, was the consequence of painstaking individual efforts of men whose only genius was a capacity for hard work. Schoolteachers must stop emphasizing the role of genius, for that "pagan title [was] deceptive and injurious to infant minds." It was wrong to stuff young students with ideas that denied the democracy of knowledge and thus snuffed out aspirations for learning. "Better believe in Jupiter and all the gods and

8. Journals, Sept. 9-Nov. 13, 1841, *passim.*
9. Newburyport *Herald,* Nov. 23, 1841.

goddesses of the pagan heaven," Burritt announced, "than in that popular little hobgoblin 'native genius.' "[10]

The lecture was surfeited with exasperating analogies, metaphors, and similes intended to debunk the concept of native genius. It contained one sentimental illustration which became a kind of personal trademark and which caused tears to well in the eyes of tender-hearted listeners. It was the story of the Natural Bridge in Virginia and of the heroics of a young boy determined to make his mark on "that vast arch of unhewn rocks, which the Almighty bridged over those everlasting butments 'when the morning stars sang together.' " The adventurous youth and his friends had climbed the rocky structure, etching their names where hundreds had done so before. A foot above all the others was the name "Washington", carved by George, according to the imaginative lecturer, just before he joined the ill-fated Braddock expedition against the French. Not to be outdistanced even by so formidable a predecessor, the boy carved his name alongside Washington's: 'What man has done, man can do.' But the lad continued to climb higher and higher; and when he dropped the knife he had been using to cut fissures for his hands and feet, he had no way of getting down. A large crowd watched breathlessly as this exemplar of courage and persistence was assisted down by means of a rope.[11]

Though the connection between climbing and book-learning is obscure, Burritt was sure that he had got the point across that native ability was no substitute for determination. Just in case there were those in the audience who needed more concrete examples, Burritt's peroration was autobiographical:

10. *Ibid.*

11. It is probable that Burritt lifted this anecdote from a similar account related by Harriet Martineau in *Retrospect of Western Travels* (New York, 1838), II, 65–68.

Don't sit down in despair. Too late! It is never too late. If you have worn the fetters twenty or thirty years break them now. Do not believe in this native genius—inborn talent. I come to give you my experience. For twenty-one years, the yoke rested on my neck. 'Nascitur non fit'—is a lie. The same invitation is extended to drink at the wells of knowledge—as to drink at the fountains of grace.[12]

Burritt received twenty dollars for the Newburyport lecture and assurance of a future invitation. The fee was a little above what the average lyceum paid at this time, and it represented twenty times more money for speaking less than two hours than he had earned for over a year's writings. With confidence he went to fulfill his New York engagements. Recalling that several years earlier he had visited that city as a neck-stock salesman, he felt honored to be "invited to the great metropolis to assume the position of a *teacher* or *lecturer* to its citizens."[13] He was scheduled to lecture before three societies on successive evenings.

He first spoke on "Roman Patriotism" before members and guests of the New York Mercantile Library Association, trying "to show that the true republican principle belonged to the human race and not to a single sect of mankind."[14] He traced the history of great nations and empires from the Assyrian to the Roman and found them all wanting in human dignity, individual rights, and liberty. The history of Rome he equated with "the insatiable cupidity of empire," which marked the downfall of all nations past and present. Ancient Greece, the cradle of democracy and teacher of Rome, was no exception. Her supposedly democratic city-states had espoused "the democracy of a band of pirates, conceding equality to each other that they may

12. Newburyport *Herald*, Nov. 23, 1843.
13. Journals, Nov. 20, 1841.
14. *Ibid.*, Nov. 21, 1841.

the more effectually war upon the rights of all mankind." Thus fell Greece, "self-destroyed, a victim of unhallowed ambitions." Republicanism was the natural political condition of man, he declared. But it had been America's destiny to give that system of government root: "There is no pure republicanism anterior to the period of our own history. Its advent was upon the rock-bound shores of our country; and here is its home."[15]

This was one of Burritt's best lectures. It was sharp, emphatic, and reasonably well-grounded in historical knowledge. Its theme had been explored before in lyceum hall and would be again. But it was no panegyric on the glories of American democracy. Rather it was a survey of history as the story of liberty. The New York *Tribune* praised Burritt's "rapid and vigorous" analysis and thought his "elegant and forcible" conclusion was "calculated to keep alive in the hearts of his hearers the flame of *true* Democracy, as distinguished from the delusive and pernicious counterfeit— a lust of power and impatience of just restraint—which has too long and too widely usurped its name."[16] Several gentlemen of the Mercantile Library Association "who seemed desirous of making my acquaintance" accompanied him back to his hotel.[17]

Burritt passed the next day accepting the compliments of the many gentlemen who called on him. That evening he delivered his astronomy lecture before the General Society of Mechanics and Tradesmen. The *Tribune* correspondent was unable to report on more than a fragment of the lecture because, "being of necessity a few moments too late,"[18] he could not find even standing room. Again Burritt was

15. New York *Tribune*, Nov. 23, 1841. For a very thorough report of this lecture, see *Pennsylvania Inquirer and National Gazette* (Phila.), Jan. 11, 1842.

16. New York *Tribune*, Nov. 23, 1841.

17. Journals, Nov. 21–22, 1841.

18. New York *Tribune*, Nov. 24, 1841.

swarmed by a crowd of congratulators. Not until one in the morning did he retire, but he was so excited over his apparent success that he lay awake two or three hours.[19]

His voice was extremely hoarse the next morning, and he had still to lecture for the New York Lyceum in the spacious Broadway Tabernacle. The Lyceum had engaged him first, and he began to question the propriety of having lectured twice elsewhere before discharging his initial obligation. The president and secretary of the Lyceum, Dr. John Griscom and Isaac Smith, tested the strength of his voice by standing in the remotest corner of the vast Tabernacle. They were unable to hear him even faintly. Burritt, embarrassed and distracted, drank lemon water and bought "a paper of Pease's candy" to soothe his throat. At lecture time the hall was thronged with a very respectable audience. Three times he attempted to announce his subject; each time his voiced cracked. He turned to Dr. Griscom in despair and for help. Griscom motioned to the audience to fill the seats behind Burritt. With "tolerable distinctness" he waded through his lecture, having won the sympathy and "deathlike stillness" of the compassionate listeners. He "was interrupted several times with expressions of approbation; especially at the close, when I wound up with a bold appeal to the young men, uttered with unusual vehemence & force."[20]

He had spoken on "Self-Cultivation", which was in essence the old address urging men "to a self-cultivation without any reference to native genius." The central illustration remained that of the Natural Bridge. He would like, he said, to be shown the artistic productions of Praxiteles, Phidias, da Vinci, and Raphael when each was a boy so "that he might compare them with the rude etchings or sculpture of the Sandwich Islanders or aborigines of Amer-

19. Journals, Nov. 23, 1841.
20. Ibid., Nov. 24, 1841.

ica." Burritt "referred to Demosthenes as an instance of self-culture, [and] commented on his midnight studies, his practice before a mirror to detect and correct disagreeable grimaces and gestures." In refuting the "heathen lie" of native genius, he "alluded to his own course" and beckoned young men to follow his example and "offer no more incense to Native Genius."[21]

The *Tribune* called the lecture "an original and powerful incitement to universal effort in the great cause of intellectual culture and elevation." In "size and appearance," it continued, he "resembles Hon. Benjamin F. Butler, and dresses and speaks among us rather like a country clergyman." Burritt's hands, however, showed "the dents of the hammer upon them." The *Tribune* thought his elocution "distinct and clear, but not impressive; and his pronunciation is often faulty, evincing an acquaintance with classical names from reading merely."[22] Sidney Morse of the New York *Observer*, perhaps since he had given Burritt nothing for translations, paid him an extended compliment. Burritt's "strength of language . . . was wonderful. His sentences came forth as if they had been forged on his anvil." As minor criticisms of style and delivery (since "improvement is his aim"), Morse suggested that Burritt "prune his style of . . . its present redundancies."[23]

Burritt was conscious of his oratorical deficiencies. His voice was weak and "lacked the flexibility and compass to command attention in ordinary assemblies."[24] But he compensated for this shortcoming by the enthusiasm and sincerity he displayed in delivering a lecture. "He has extraordinary energy," wrote a later assistant, "great power of concentration of thought and feeling, and when he is thor-

21. *Pennsylvania Inquirer and National Gazette*, Jan. 11, 1842.
22. New York *Tribune*, Nov. 27, 1841.
23. New York *Observer*, Nov. 27, 1841.
24. Lee, "Reminiscences of the Early Life of Elihu Burritt", p. 108.

oughly aroused, he makes up for the lack of natural graces of oratory in burning, impressive, intense eloquence."[25] A Cincinnati resident who had heard Burritt lecture gave a more accurate description: "that strong sledge-hammer style . . . you would expect from a self-educated blacksmith, is not at all his characteristic. His style is ornate, almost to orientalism."[26]

Burritt was startled by the large fees he received for his New York lectures. The Lyceum gave him fifty dollars, as did the Society of Mechanics and Tradesmen, and the Mercantile Library Association paid forty, making a total of one hundred and forty dollars for three nights' work.[27] The fees represented as much a reward for his own personal attainments as for the actual worth of the lectures, which, though good, were hardly in a class with those of Emerson, Holmes, or E. P. Whipple, whose addresses were not only well received but highly literary.[28] Burritt's speeches were neither erudite nor scholarly, and it was evident to most observers that he was not "a truly philosophic thinker." Like his literary productions, his lectures were too moralistic. Yet this is one reason why they appealed to moralistic listeners of average intelligence. Though the contents of his lectures and his method of delivery never rose much above respectable mediocrity, his popularity was assured. He was a romantic symbol of initiative, steadfastness, and swift success, and these were key qualities of Young America. Audiences derived vicarious pleasure from seeing and hearing a Yankee blacksmith who had made self-culture a special calling.

25. David W. Bartlett, *Modern Agitators: or Pen Portraits of Living American Reformers* (New York, 1855), p. 108.

26. Account from the Cincinnati *Gazette* reprinted in the Worcester *Aegis*, March 2, 1842.

27. Journals, Nov. 25, 1841.

28. Bode, pp. 204–205, 209–211, 216–217.

On the day of the second New York lecture, the *Journal of Commerce* commented that

> the great usefulness of these lectures cannot be doubted. They are objected to by no one, but approved by all, while the theatres are now almost universally considered the most efficient schools for all sorts of vices. The lectures have opened up a source of income to literary men. A man who has rendered his country great service by his scientific labors yet hardly acquiring for himself a daily competence, may turn his fame to solid account by becoming a lecturer and in a few weeks fill his pockets as they were never filled before.[29]

Fees for lecturers were better than they had ever been and continually rose throughout the forties and fifties. The ease with which the pockets of lecturers became crammed with money, however, was overstated by the *Journal of Commerce*, as Burritt would eventually discover.

After a successful lecture tour through Massachusetts, Connecticut, and New York, Burritt returned to Worcester in December, 1841, more self-confident than ever. He criticized the "elegant apathy" of a lecturer he heard at the Worcester Lyceum and regretted having to write six letters "to correspondents, who are drawing upon my leisure rather seriously." Honorary membership in the Mercantile Library Association of New York and the Whig Society at Princeton College produced no emotions.[30] An invitation to lecture again for the New York Lyceum elicited from Burritt a pretentious reply:

> Under the persuasion that I had finished my campaign in the city of New York for this season, I have made no provision to appear there again at present. I shot away all my

29. New York *Journal of Commerce*, Nov. 23, 1841.
30. Journals, Dec. 14–16, 1841.

cartidges [*sic*] during my last visit, and I have not time to *load* again. . . Your citizens are unlike the Bostonians '*as cheese & chalk.*' *These Bay State democrats* cannot be reached by an impulse unless it is given by a galvanic battery of a hundred *hoss-power,* and then they will freeze up in warm weather. By the way, however, there is now a 'sign of change,' and their phlegmatic character bids fair to receive a little enthusiasm by inoculations with your state, *via* the *Western Railroad.* Boston is getting quite gallant, *a la Melbourne—,* in her old age and she is carrying on quite successfully a kind of *intrigue d'amour,* or an *amorous dalliance* with your fair little sister of Albany. I would not play the eavesdropper to provoke your jealousy; but they *do say* that she receives the addresses of the Old Bay [Bey] State with *open arms,* and that the *suit* is this moment going on at Albany in the same fashion as Jacob courted Rachel at the well, with this *exception* I fear, *that your* coquetish [*sic*] *sister is proffering her suitor something stronger 'in the gourd' than the Syrian maiden ever carried in her* pitcher.[31]

Such a cumbersome letter bears ample testimony to Burritt's lack of social sophistication. He could not decline a simple lecture request without writing a letter of outlandish proportions and bizarre humor. He disliked "affectation" in others, yet there was a streak of it in himself. He had not lectured in Boston and had "scarcely ever been invited into a private residence" in that city. New York, on the other hand, had treated him with deference. So, for a while at least, his loyalty was to New York, though he would much rather have impressed Boston. The letter also reflected his joy at having recently paid off some of the debts he had

31. Burritt to Isaac Smith, Worcester, Dec. 30, 1841, Dartmouth College Library. For other examples of Burritt's graceless wit, see Burritt to Mrs. Elwell, Worcester, Jan. 1, 1842, American Antiquarian Society, and Burritt to Mrs. Cutter, May 16, 1843, Klingberg Collection.

incurred while running a grocery store and editing a literary periodical. Thanks to the fees he had so far received, he "cherish[ed] a faint hope that I may finally discharge these debts which have so long kept my head under water, and made me feel like an exiled Cain upon the earth."[32]

The first resistance to his theory of native genius he detected while lecturing at the Salem Lyceum. The audience was stolidly unsympathetic. Burritt attributed his poor reception to the fact that the majority of hearers wanted to be thought "the favorites of genius . . . born with greater faculties than common men."[33] When he lectured to audiences that comprised the substantial citizens of the community, he noticed their transparent unwillingness to accept his thesis. The editor of the Worcester *Aegis* wrote an article on "Talents and Genius" to prove that "the distinctive qualities of men are innate. There have been millions of shepherds, but it requires no great arithmetical power to count the Burnses."[34]

In Philadelphia, after having lectured on "Self-Cultivation" before a huge audience in the Music Fund Hall, Burritt was challenged by a Protestant minister who objected to his criticisms of native genius. A Protestant clergyman in Bridgeport, Connecticut, believed Burritt's doctrine "was dangerous because it made intellectual and moral eminence *too democratic*, diminishing the dignity of the scholar and Christian, by intimating that either of those characters may be attained by the *general herd*." One of Lyman Beecher's sons told Burritt that his views of native genius were contrary "to the gospel, to philosophy and experience." Burritt recorded: "I told him that his position was alike contrary to all these, and was the doctrine of Jupiter Amon rather than that of Jesus Christ."[35] In Baltimore, where he

32. Journals, Nov. 30, 1841, Feb. 4, 1842.
33. *Ibid.*, Dec. 23, 1841.
34. Worcester *Aegis*, Mar. 10, 1841.
35. Journals, Jan. 8, 9, Mar. 8, 23, 1842.

gave three lectures, the *Patriot* refused to accept his "new
doctrine," stating that many who attended the "Self-Cultivation" lecture were similarly unconvinced. The *Patriot* declared that Burritt himself was "living evidence—a worthy
and distinguished one—against his own doctrines—that no
man is an extraordinary genius."[36] The New Haven *Herald*
wrote that the next time Burritt lectured on native genius
he "should leave his own head and history behind."[37]

In Geneva, New York, after "a conceited phrenologist"
had taken him to task over the question of native genius,
Burritt lashed out in his Journal at the "mongrel, illegitimate
science, which perpetuates a kind of heathenist fatality."[38]
Phrenologists expressed views of native genius antithetical
to his. While he informed audiences that all minds were
capable of infinite intellectual refinement, phrenologists advertised in newspapers that parents "anxious to know the
propensities and faculties of their children" need only submit the child's head for scientific scrutiny.[39] Burritt believed
they managed to "stifle whatever good seed" he had sown.
He was annoyed that he had "not found a single believer,
or made a single proselyte to this doctrine. Every one seems
to prefer to ascribe their intellectual attainment to an inherited genius rather than to his own efforts."[40]

Though Burritt consistently denied the existence of "a
royal road to learning," he acted as though the road to languages was but a short path. When his sister Eunice came
to Worcester for a short stay, he instructed her in Hebrew,
French, Arabic, Latin, German, and Flemish. She already
knew a little French, but was totally unfamiliar with the
other languages. Because she was a Burritt, apparently, he
started her off reading Virgil, and vouched for her "pretty

36. Baltimore *Patriot*, Jan. 13, 14, 1842.
37. New Haven *Herald*, Jan. 20, 21, 1842.
38. Journals, Mar. 12, 1842.
39. Newburyport *Herald*, Mar. 20, 1841.
40. Journals, Jan. 9, 1842.

good progress" after the first day. He gave her an Arabic grammar and expected that the next day she would be able to read from the Old Testament in Arabic the same verses she had earlier covered in Hebrew. After six weeks he declared she "gets along faster than I ever did." By then she was supposedly reading each day a chapter from a Hebrew Bible, "German till noon; afterwards she reads Virgil and Flemish."[41] Burritt was trying to prove through Eunice that his much-rebuffed position on native genius was valid.

Newspapers generally reported Burritt's lectures in glowing terms, overrating his intellectual acquirements and capacity. The Albany *Evening Journal* paid a supreme tribute by appraising his "attainments, considering age and opportunity," as "probably greater than those of any man living." Thurlow Weed, editor of the *Evening Journal*, later wrote: "As a popular and interesting lecturer Mr. B. has few equals and no superiors."[42] The Baltimore *Sun* invited "those who wish to see a prodigy" to attend Burritt's lecture; it told how Burritt had "supported himself by his daily labors at the forge, and yet has found time to make himself master of *fifty* languages, with nearly the whole circle of useful learning."[43] The Providence *Journal* stated casually that Burritt "reads fluently" fifty languages.[44] The *National Intelligencer* referred to his "extraordinary mental powers."[45]

When attending lectures while on his swing around lyceum circles, Burritt seldom passed up the chance to be critical of his competitors. A discourse on literature by the poet Richard Dana, Sr., was adjudged by Burritt to be "rather transcendental and metaphysical." At the Worcester Lyceum he listened as the Reverend Henry Giles, of Liver-

41. *Ibid.*, June 2–3, 13–14, July 20, 1842.
42. Albany *Evening Journal*, Jan. 29, April 18, 1842.
43. Baltimore *Sun*, Jan. 10, 1842.
44. Providence *Journal*, Feb. 11, 1842.
45. *National Intelligencer*, Jan. 17, 1842.

pool, England, "poured out such a torrent of eloquence as I never heard from the mouth of man" on British efforts "to enforce Protestantism [in Ireland] at the point of the sword." Burritt applauded the lecture but ridiculed the lecturer's physical stature: his "bodily presence is contemptible as he is scarcely 4 feet high." After listening to George Bancroft lecture, he felt that his own ideas were "puerile conceptions" and "*baby talk*" by comparison. But, said Burritt, on second thought, "there was an incoherence in his thoughts that rendered at times the drift of his subject imperceptible. His ideas were all splendid and lofty, but too much resembled detached meteors meeting, glittering and disappearing without any preconceived coincidence in the heavens."[46]

Burritt was equally captious in assessing important people whom he met on his travels. Before leaving Albany, he talked with Horace Greeley of the New York *Tribune*. Burritt raked him over pretty thoroughly in his Journal: "He looks as if the winter of old age had suddenly set in upon him in youth, and preserved all his puerile features in icy rigidity; or perhaps it would be a better figure to compare him to a *petrified bog*." After a New Haven lecture Burritt had been introduced to Professor Benjamin Silliman, the Reverends Eleazar Fitch and Leonard Bacon, and the taciturn Josiah Gibbs, a brilliant philologist and professor of sacred literature at Yale. Towards Gibbs he felt not a little jealousy, describing him as "the very personification of a man of *learning* but not of knowledge. He is a walking lump of ice without radical heat enough to thaw out a place within him large enough for a heart. He is the most awkward ungainly man that I ever saw come into a social circle."[47]

46. Journals, Nov. 11, 18, 1841, Dec. 16, 1842.
47. *Ibid.*, Jan. 19, 30, 1842. See Burritt's laudatory article on Greeley in *Ten-Minute Talks*, pp. 289–297.

In Providence, Burritt had the opportunity to pass judgment on Emerson. At the time Emerson, according to the
historian of the American lyceum, was "perhaps the only
lecturer in the [lyceum] movement who could unhesitatingly
be called great," and "he was also enormously popular."[48]
Burritt heard Emerson lecture "On the Times" and seemed
to find peculiar satisfaction in noting that the audience
"amounted to about 80." This lecture, like Emerson's "Man
the Reformer," advocated a bold revision of all institutions.
It was typically Emersonian, simple, abstruse, powerful,
something for every mind.[49] Burritt thought it too radical:

> The reformists and conservatists were the principal actors
> on the stage. He decided in favor of the reformists, not be-
> cause that the innovations which they might introduce
> would be improvements in the social system, but because
> that the inner soul, the abstract principal [sic] of innova-
> tion or reform is true & just, although it broke up society
> with the wildest anarchy. He touched slightly upon the
> Brownsonian theory of property. . . He complained that the
> present laws hampered our young man, and that, with all
> the brave impulses of his nature, they were able to wring
> out of him a certain respect for the rights of others. Or,
> in other words, he hinted that it was an unjust restriction
> when an individual tells our brave young man that he shall
> not take away the *ewelamb* of industry and toil, to save him
> from the trouble of honest labor.[50]

The analysis was unfair. Emerson's ideas on property
were not similar to those held by the radical Orestes Brown-

48. Bode, p. 205.
49. Ralph W. Emerson, *Nature, Addresses, and Lectures* (Boston,
1883), pp. 246–267.
50. Journals, Feb. 10, 1842.

son.[51] Yet Burritt was convinced that if Emerson "were capable of exerting any influence, he would be a dangerous youth *corrupter*."[52]

In small New York and Massachusetts towns Burritt was not always received with a splash of newspaper print, large and well-behaved audiences, and good fees. In Danvers, Massachusetts, he was introduced to the audience by an individual who referred to him as the learned blacksmith "with just such a kind of chuckle as he would exhibit a kangaroo." Well before Burritt finished speaking, many listeners had begun putting on their wraps and started moving about the hall. In Canandaigua, New York, the treasurer of the organization he addressed "seemed desirous of apprising the whole audience that the society was not going to suffer merit to go unrewarded; for he commenced a surprising evolution with four or five one dollar bills, which he fluttered around with so much adroit ostentation." Burritt was unceremoniously informed by a Utica group that they would be honored to have him lecture, "especially if it would not subject them to any greater expense than my bill overnight."[53]

Burritt noticed a difference in the interest with which various cities received him the second time around. When he lectured again in the Broadway Tabernacle, he "could easily perceive that the interest of novelty which they felt in my first lecture, had worn away, and I scarcely secured that attention which I usually receive." No one shook his hand after the lecture, and he was left to find his way back

51. Brownson advocated the abolition of hereditary property. What disturbed Burritt, apparently, were Emerson's words: "Grimly the same spirit looks into the law of Property, and accuses men of driving a trade in the great boundless providence which had given the air, the water, and the land to use and not to fence in and monopolize." Emerson, p. 261.
52. Journals, Feb. 10, 1842.
53. *Ibid.*, Feb. 14, Mar. 2, 10, 1842.

to his hotel "alone and on foot." Only fifty persons were present at his Brooklyn Lyceum lecture, which was proof to him that the large audiences he had become accustomed to "were no evidence of any great merit of mine, but an indication of a transient curiosity to *see* a kind of literary *oddity*, and that *one* such a sight, as in the case of all shows, was sufficient for the majority." He read his astronomy lecture as he "would read a newspaper aloud to a dozen boys and girls."[54] The *Tribune* was more sparing with its plaudits and more concerned with his "faulty" pronunciation, weak voice, and "lack of ease and grace." It would later comment that Burritt's style was "graceless and often turgid to a very displeasing degree,"[55] a harsh but not unfair statement.

He was worried about lecturing in his "own country." After he spoke at the Worcester Lyceum, he complained that it was "the most restless and inattentive audience that I ever appeared before"; he determined never to "lecture to them again." None of the Worcester newspapers reported the lecture. The wealthy people of the town ignored him. His successes elsewhere made him all the more scornful of "the shabby aristocracy which reigns in Worcester."[56] In a letter to his brother Isaac he explained why he thought Worcester was neglecting him: "Worcester is a noble place, but tinged with an air of aristocracy. I do not receive the deference & respect here I should in any other place, because I came here in obscurity and arose from obscurity here, which subjects me to suspicion or jealousy."[57]

54. *Ibid.*, Mar. 28, 31, 1842.
55. New York *Tribune*, Mar. 29, Dec. 14, 1842.
56. Journals, Dec. 30, 1841, Mar. 23, 1842.
57. Burritt to Isaac Burritt, Worcester, April 20, 1842, Central Connecticut State College Library. Burritt had thought of moving to Bridgeport, Connecticut, "a place of refined society"; but, as he wrote Isaac, "it is a little out of the way, and it is in *Connecticut* (. . . I would like to live in Old Massachusetts, for I feel it to be an honor and a priviledge [sic].)"

The smaller crowds in cities in which he had previously lectured were in part due to the widespread newspaper coverage of his lectures. If people had not heard him speak, they at least had the opportunity to read what he had said. But the aspect of "novelty" was also an important factor. The New Haven *Herald* commented after a Burritt lecture: "It is curious to witness with what avidity the public crowd to see anything *learned*."[58] Sidney Morse of the New York *Observer* shrewdly attributed Burritt's early success as a lecturer to a popular desire "to *see* an individual who by his own unaided exertions had overcome untold obstacles, and mastered more than fifty of the various languages of the earth."[59] The decade of the forties, in its social setting, was "engrossed in natural wonders . . . eager for prodigies of all kinds . . . and consumed with credulous curiosity."[60] Some of those who attended Burritt's lectures undoubtedly were interested in gazing at what they thought was an intellectual freak. "It is wonderful," remarked Burritt, "how much *fustian* and *fudge* has come into requisition in this wonder loving age."[61] Ironically, it was precisely this trait in American popular culture which accounted for much of his lyceum success.

In Richmond, Virginia, in December, 1842, Burritt was showered with the adoration that had marked his first appearances in New York, Philadelphia, and Baltimore. The Mechanics Association had reserved "a suite of splendid rooms" for him in a fashionable hotel. His hosts were so "embarrasingly [*sic*] respectful" that he wondered if "the very *Dickens was* in me."[62] Burritt met his friend Dr. Thomas Nelson and was introduced to Thomas Ritchie of

58. New Haven *Herald*, Jan. 21, 1842.
59. New York *Observer*, Nov. 27, 1841.
60. Meade Minnigerode, *The Fabulous Forties* (New York, 1924), p. 222.
61. Journals, Oct. 22, 1842.
62. *Ibid.*, Dec. 19, 1842.

the Richmond *Inquirer*. "Mr. B.," Ritchie wrote after Burritt had lectured on "Roman Patriotism," "is a man of great merit, blended with much modesty—and has succeeded in making himself, by untiring perserverance and a wise distribution of his time, the most distinguished master of the Languages (Ancient as well as Modern, Asiatic as well as European) in America." Ritchie described Burritt's "Self-Cultivation" lecture as "impressive, occasionally eloquent, and . . . liberal in its sentiments and correct in its counsels."[63] Burritt received seventy dollars for the two lectures, which marked his last major triumph as a popular lecturer.

He wrote three new lectures on "Elements of Genius", "The Rubicon of St. Peter", and "The Want of Individuality of Character." The former amplified his two earlier lectures on native genius, but was less hortatory, less filled with awkward personal and historical anecdotes, and much more sophisticated. It was a fairly successful attempt to analyze the claims of genius in a philosophical way, and it was the best popular lecture he ever wrote. "The Rubicon of St. Peter" was the first of a series of short lectures he intended to write contrasting "the political and moral principles of the gospel with those of the world."[64] "The Want of Individuality of Character" was a blistering assault upon the increased "massification" of society in which "the *individual* had been compressed out of his proportions. Individuality of character, opinion, sentiment, and responsibility had been going for the last ten years into a kind of liquefaction."[65]

By October, 1842, Burritt had delivered sixty-four lectures and had travelled 3,500 miles. Lecture invitations in 1843, however, were sporadic, mostly from small towns in

63. Richmond *Inquirer*, Dec. 22, 24, 1842.

64. Both lectures were later published in the *Christian Citizen*, Mar. 9, 16, May 4, 11, 25, June 18, 1844; Journals, Nov. 30 1843.

65. The actual title of this lecture was "The Social Principle"; the manuscript is in the Connecticut Historical Society; New York *Tribune*, Dec. 14, 1842.

Massachusetts and Connecticut—the fee offered was usually not more than ten dollars and frequently it was less. If Burritt now had a greater variety of lectures, he had fewer opportunities to give them. Moreover, he was not fond of New England audiences, finding them churlish and difficult to please: "A New England audience is an emotionless, icy body, full of light but cold as a stone." He began questioning the wisdom "of peddling my *genius*, as one would peddle wooden nutmegs." He was growing tired of being an "itinerant lecturer" and was "undetermined as to what I ought to turn my attention." He did "not fancy the profession of the travelling lecturer on the same plan that is pursued by Phrenological and Animal Magnetical adepts."[66]

Burritt thought the duty of a lecturer was to edify people, not to beguile or entertain them. Finding it increasingly difficult to sustain popularity, he was no longer sure that his lectures were enlightening the public. He began to suspect that audiences were interested in seeing rather than hearing him. "Most of the cities and towns about have had me once before them, which will probably suffice their curiosity." Having exploited the theme of self-culture, he had little else to offer audiences save a bloated reputation for scholarship. And though lyceum-lecturing had proved financially profitable, it was not a full-time vocation. He still had to forge garden hoes and pruning hooks to make ends meet. He could have continued on the lyceum circuit if he had wanted to, addressing thinner gatherings and receiving smaller fees. But by the beginning of 1843 he had become affected by the twin viruses of evangelism and reformism. He wished to fill a "useful place in society" and be of "benefit to mankind."[67] He never abandoned the lecture rostrum, but he was nearing the time when he would use it principally to endorse humanitarian causes.

For Burritt the lyceum was the springboard for partially

66. Journals, Sept. 15, Dec. 6–7, 12, 1842, Feb. 4, 1843.
67. *Ibid.*, Oct. 3, 1842, Jan. 1, 1843.

validating and thoroughly enhancing that reputation which
Everett had cavalierly bestowed on him in 1838. Three
years of lyceum-lecturing was an education for him more
rigorous and intellectually rewarding than the study of forty
pages of Cuvier's Theory, fifteen names of stars, and eight
lines of Syriac or Arabic. Addressing audiences ranging in
size from 2,000 to fewer than twenty-five persons—and varying appallingly in attention and behavior—bolstered his
self-confidence. It seems reasonable to suppose that his lyceum stint was of general benefit to the population. But it
is no conjecture that he himself gained much from it. As
his lectures brought him within drawing-room distance of
lawyers, doctors, merchants, and bankers, he was quick
to appreciate the social style of the upper classes. Their
"beauty and brilliance" fascinated him; in their presence he
was "perfectly at home, which I feel to be a proof of the
effect of the company of refined ladies and gentlemen."
Fraternization with the genteel taught him much about tact
and bearing. "I have acquired a great deal of tact & facility
from these daily discussions with intelligent men, and I
feel my mind much enlarged by this instructive intercourse."[69] It is interesting to follow in his Journals the way
in which he moved in select social circles, acting as if he
belonged there, if not by birth, then by destiny. When he
left the lyceum for what he was certain was a far nobler
adventure, he left as a more confident and capable man.
Everett's 1838 remarks had catapulted him to local fame;
the lyceum had given him a wider audience and, more important, a chance to develop a necessary social maturity.

69. *Ibid.*, Dec. 1, 8, 10, 1841, Jan. 25, 1842.

4

A Serious Young Man

The Christianity to which Burritt subscribed was infinitely more liberal than that which his mother had professed. Hers was a grim Puritan faith stressing original sin, total depravity, and making salvation absolutely dependent upon the inscrutable will of an awful God. Her unyielding protestations in defense of predestination had frightened Elihu. Like the large majority of American Protestants of his time, he was repelled by the dour Calvinism that stressed the inability of man to work for his salvation and focused on a monarch-God who had arbitrarily selected a limited number of Christians to receive His irresistible grace.

New England Calvinism had become a cultural anomaly by the 18th century. Calvinistic determinism, with its emphasis on human inability, came into conflict with an aggressive American society that had made rapid political and economic strides through the application of considerable human freedom and ability. The genius of Jonathan Edwards, however, had infused it with new light and meaning and made it a formidable theology which had still to be contended with. He resurrected the piety of Calvinism, explored the infinite glory and greatness of God, spoke of "holy affections" and of a mystical "virtue", and ingeniously modified the concept of free will without substantially changing it. Thanks to Edwards, Calvinism made no basic compromises with the modern spirit of the times: God's sovereignty remained unchanged and man's ability was "sophistical."[1]

Edward's profound spirituality had forestalled the decline of Calvinism, but he could not prevent its ultimate disintegration. Even in the hands of dedicated and first-rate disciples Edwardseanism reverted to the dry and formal legalism that had paralyzed Calvinism. Joseph Bellamy and Samuel Hopkins thought they were amplifying the theology of the great master; but by making concessions to the expanding republicanism, humanitarianism, and rationalism of the late 18th century, they unconsciously sacrificed the piety on which the Edwardsean system had been based for the moralism of their day. Forced to contend with deism and Unitarianism, they had surrendered much of Edwards' determinism for the sake of reasonableness. Hopkins himself marked "the transition from Calvinism to moralism."[2] Edwards had taught that true holiness "consists in a disposition to love Being in general," or God. Hopkins had understood holiness to be not only a love for "Being in general" (God), but "a love of our neighbour, as it regards the highest good of the whole as its chief object." Such "disinterested benevolence," he had asserted, "is not really a distinct thing from seeking the glory and kingdom of God, as they perfectly coincide."[3] By equating the love of God with the love of man Hopkins had fatally undermined the piety of Calvinism and had opened the door for even more drastic revisions by those who had no use for that theology.

1. Frank H. Foster, *A Genetic History of the New England Theology* (Chicago, 1907), p. 78.

2. Joseph Haroutunian, *Piety vs. Moralism: The Passing of the New England Theology* (New York, 1932), p. 92.

3. Quoted in *ibid.*, p. 86.

With the glory of God fast becoming synonymous with "the highest good of the whole," the New England Theology became less Calvinistic.

By 1830 orthodox, moderate, and liberal Calvinists had gone their separate ways. Moderate Calvinism, exemplified by the New Haven Theology of Nathaniel Taylor, conceded a real freedom of will. Man had a propensity to sin, to place his own interests ahead of his love for God. But through the workings of the Holy Spirit man was capable of realizing that his selfishness had vitiated his love for God. The Holy Spirit could act as "the means of regeneration" for sinful man.[4] Taylor's effort to synthesize Calvinism and common sense coincided with the rise of the common man. The same acquisitive Americans who demanded the freedom to sink or swim in any enterprise they chose to engage in also required of God a fighting chance to save their souls.

Burritt believed in the Christianity of the Gospels which proclaimed the fatherhood of God, the divinity and humanity of Christ, and the brotherhood of man. Christianity was to him not an institution finalized for all time, but a movement of dynamic faith in the kingdom of God and in the reign of Christ. He felt that, while Christians should look to the past for historical bearing and insight, they must understand that the gospel of Christ provided a knowledge of God for "every age . . . every condition . . . every grade of human advancement." The "revelations of nature and of the Bible have been, are, and will be made for *man* in a *progressive* state."[5]

The example and teachings of Christ together with the epistles of St. Paul convinced Burritt that there was "a unity in true Christianity as perfect as the unity of God's attributes." All Christians were "children of the same Heavenly Father—all made of one blood, and members of one family

4. Foster, pp. 369–400.
5. Burritt, *Thoughts and Things*, pp. 94–96.

circle."[6] Denominational Christianity—that is, institution-alized divisiveness among professing Christians—he labeled "mistaken, earth-wedded religion." Burritt could never be more than a nominal Congregationalist because he could never substitute a pragmatic gospel for the essential gospel.

Burritt distrusted the excessive rationalism that was creep-ing into Protestantism and derogating from the primacy of the Bible. Intuitive reason, or the so-called "revelation or illumination within us," on the other hand, was powerless "without the light of the gospel" and by itself too feeble "to wade into eternity in search of human destiny beyond this terrestial [sic] existence." If the intuition relied on by transcendentalists "was worthy of more reliance than the written word of God . . . then France under Robespierre and his infamous associates would furnish an example of the religion which human reason, with all its inborn illumi-nation is able to offer to the world." The predestinarian principle of orthodox Calvinists, he believed, "had more of mythology in it than the Bible." He was sure Jesus Christ never "preached any such doctrine."[7]

He insisted that "religion must begin in the heart and be a thing of *soul* as well as *form*."[8] This essentially evangelical definition of religion he would always adhere to, and his concession to religious form was no more than a token one. The practice of subordinating the head to the heart charac-terized all Evangelicals. In Burritt's case, the result was frequently a mild form of religious enthusiasm or a hazy sentimentality.

One of the first things Burritt did after he had arrived in Worcester in 1837 was to join the First Congregational Church, or the Old South as it was commonly called. Then

6. MS Lecture on the Constitutional Unity of Christians and the Natural Bonds of Brotherhood, Connecticut Historical Society.

7. Journals, Feb. 10, June 9, 1842.

8. *Ibid.*, Oct. 19, 1842.

twenty seven, he may have been a "poor, bashful, humbled wight," but he did not act like one in the religious affairs of the Church. He was in his element when attending an Old South prayer or conference meeting. Neither his shyness nor the fact that he was a new parishioner deterred him from addressing these gatherings, as he was never timid in professing his love for God. Less than a year after his arrival he delivered an address at a church meeting in which he unblushingly rambled on about the blessings God bestowed upon the poor and the afflicted:

> What though the humble professor of the Christian's hope be some maimed, houseless object of charity—though he be clad in the unsightly rags of a beggar, and sit down upon the door-stone of the rich and mighty and there solicit in vain for the crumbs that fall from the rich man's table, yet he can then raise his eyes to Heaven and say: I, also, have a house—I have a building in the heavens! A building founded and fastened up on the immutable promises of an unchanging God! I have a mansion there that never can be exposed to incendiary conflagration or ever subject to decay! A building that shall remain as long as the heavens endure.[9]

Burritt's Journals reveal his religiosity. His intense faith repeatedly forced him to take stock of his obligations to God and to man. On the first day of every new year he invariably recorded in his Journal some deep-felt homage to God:

> Another year! [1842] May God who has thus far led me on prepare me for all the events which are laid up for me the coming year. Unto [H]im I commit all the interests of my soul and body. . . I will trust in God and try to render him more perfect obedience.[10]

9. Extract of an address by Elihu Burritt at a conference meeting, Worcester, April 1, 1838, MS Family Album . . .
10. Journals, Jan. 1, 1842.

Burritt usually attended the three Sunday services at the Old South, and he admired the evangelical sermons of the Reverend Rodney Miller. When in 1841 lecturing began to keep him away from Worcester for long periods, he complained about "the loss of inestimable priviledges [*sic*] both social and religious." If he "could only carry the Old South with me, and the circle which worships there, I should be at home anywhere."

Evangelicals, from the time of the Great Awakening of the 1740's, had been skeptical about the value of learned ministers whose approach to religion was too rational and intellectual and who seemed more interested in doctrines and liturgical forms than in genuine religious experience. In the 19th century this evangelical inheritance had been enlarged upon to the point where "The Puritan ideal of the minister as an intellectual and educational leader" was largely displaced by the conception "of the minister as a popular crusader and exhorter."[11]

Burritt typified this evangelical scorn for intellectually oriented ministers. In his Journals he treated kindly only those ministers with strong evangelical proclivities. He noticed that the Reverend Gardiner Spring, an influential New York Presbyterian, spoke with "a kind of affectation in manner and pronunciation which is getting rather common to city clergymen." Methodist ministers he thought inclined towards "ostentation, magniloquence and pomposity." He derided the sermons of Horace Bushnell, of Hartford, because "he never aims lower *or* deeper than the intellect." Bushnell's "manner . . . was disagreeable. To give a nasal, snivelling twang, he exercises the nerves of that region of his face with the kind of effort which is visible in a German's throat, while *egorging* his most unspeakable words." Burritt enjoyed the sermons of Joel Hawes, also of Hartford,

11. Richard Hofstadter, *Anti-intellectualism in American Life* (New York, 1964), p. 86.

because their "ideas are all reduced to the comprehension of children, without any dilution or diminution of their force." Hawes's homilies "pressed home to the heart," and to Burritt this was a minister's primary obligation. The "everlasting and universal defect in ministers," he said, was "a lack of personal interest & feeling in their discourses" and the absence of "a heartfelt zeal." Logical and placid sermons "come like hail upon the heart," leaving an "impression" much "like the chill of ice." Episcopal services, in his judgment, were drearily sedate and dispassionate; thus Episcopal churches "have more spare seats than anywhere else."[12]

Once in a while Burritt attended Roman Catholic services. Anti-Catholic feeling in the United States was rampant during the first half of the forties, and the notorious Philadelphia riots of 1844 were the culmination of a long and carefully nurtured Protestant antipathy to Romanism.[13] Burritt rebuked such violence;[14] but, like most contemporary Protestants, he viewed Catholicism as a spurious religion. His description of a Catholic service in Baltimore, therefore, was unkind but not unusual:

> The excercises [sic] were an imposing mummery, a pompous dumb show, a heartless routine of forms which resembled idolatry if it was not in fact sheer profanity. I can no longer wonder at the success of the Catholic religion in throwing a spell of enchantment over the minds of the ignorant; for indeed there is about it the jugglery of a species of religious *mesmerism*.[15]

His observation of the celebration of Mass in a Roman Catholic Church in Boston was equally denunciatory:

12. Journals, Nov. 21, 1842-Jan. 15, 1843, *passim*.
13. Ray Allen Billington, *The Protestant Crusade, 1800–1860* (New York, 1938), pp. 220–234.
14. *Christian Citizen*, July 27, 1844.
15. Journals, Jan. 16, 1842.

It was a ceremony of imposing mummery well suited to the character of a physical religion. The bishop was a real Falstaff, weighing, I should think, 400 overdupois [*sic*]. Dressed in all the trappings of the pontificate and surrounded by priestly assistants, he went through with the rites, with a species of lazy gravity that struck me ludicrously.[16]

He abhorred the cold, formal, intellectual offerings of the Unitarians and mocked the silent services of the Quakers. He attended his first Quaker meeting in Philadelphia in 1842 and wrote a flippant account of "the dumb show" he witnessed:

As I expected, I found it difficult to retain my gravity during the dumb show which was a prelude to the 'working of the spirit.' There was a sort of board fence running through the centre of the house, which might well be said to divide the *sheep* from the [ewe] or *what is the same thing*, the men from the women . . . On one side of the fence, sat about 500 male quakers in a kind of snoozy meditation . . . On the other side appeared the sisters, with their gravity pleasantly tempered with sweetness & simplicity . . . In the front rank were the regular *continentals*, consisting of a hundred of the really confirmed sisters with the 'bonnets so brown.' The rest were a class who seemed to be lingering wistfully on the confines of the *world*. They were mostly coy young maidens with bright laughing eyes, which they could not fix so steadily & devoutly on vacancy as their mothers . . . After sitting in immoveable [*sic*] silence for half an hour, a young quaker arose and commenced a very edifying exortation [*sic*] enjoining a greater simplicity and pureness of life, and a nearer conformity to the divine teachings of our own nature, or the law within our hearts independent of written revelation. Another silence ensued upon his taking his seat, and I was wishing that some of the sisters might be moved, when one of them arose, and made a short exhortation in

16. *Ibid.*, April 13, 1843.

one of the sweetest voices that I ever heard . . . The exercises were brought to rather an abrupt termination by two elders shaking hands upon the forum, when the spell was broken and the assembly dissolved.[17]

On September 5, 1841, the Reverend Rodney Miller urged Old South parishioners "to feel and act as if it was high time for a revival of God's work in our midst." Miller had previously directed four "seasons of special religious interest"[18] at the Old South, and he believed a fifth "season of refreshment" was imminent. Burritt agreed that the time for a religious revival was long overdue: "How faint, cold, and vascillating [sic] is our love! Christians seem to act as if they must have a five years' sleep for watching with the Savior *one hour*."[19] Throughout New England at this time, and in New York's "Burned-over District," revivals were revitalized after the deadening effect of the panic of 1837.[20] Lecturing in upstate New York in March, 1842, Burritt saw "indications of a general revival"; in Rochester, which was peculiarly susceptible to revivals, he had trouble finding an empty hall or church basement in which to lecture, as prayer meetings were being held everywhere.[21]

The evangelistic labors of Charles G. Finney, during the 1820's and 1830's, had succeeded in making revivals not only a respectable function of the clergy but an indispensable one as well. By 1840 saving souls by converting sinners had been accepted as a legitimate role for pastors. Revivals had become institutionalized. They had been a key factor in the transformation of American Protestantism into

17. *Ibid.*, Jan. 9, 1842.
18. Edward Smalley, *The Worcester Pulpit: with Notices Historical and Biographical* (Boston, 1851), p. 221.
19. Journals, Sept. 5, 1841.
20. Whitney R. Cross, *The Burned-Over District* (Ithaca, 1950), pp. 269–270.
21. Journals, Mar. 1–5, 7–8, 1842.

an evangelical faith, but they were more than just a wholesale way of reaching the unconverted. Their overriding importance was in creating a kind of national evangelical con-
sciousness which optimistically looked ahead to the day
when all Americans would be united in a genuine Christian
commonwealth. From this happy religious condition Evangelicals expected to proceed to the next logical and necessary step—the evangelization of the world. This was no
frivolous idea, but a deeply felt conviction shared by all
Evangelicals, and they were not at all shy about expressing
it in the clearest and strongest terms. Burritt had great confidence that "Protestant Christendom can evangelize *the
whole world* in a very few years."[22]

Burritt's mother had something to do with his concern
over the need for a religious revival. She had written him
about the revivals going on in central Connecticut and
wished the contagion of piety would "reach even to you."
She hoped Elihu would "invite the Lord to come and pour
out such a Blessing that their [sic] will be not room to contain it." Mrs. Burritt asked him to "mix some religious sentiments" in his public lectures and to give at least some
thought to becoming a minister. It was important to her
that he get involved in "the blessed work of converting
souls to Christ."[23]

When Burritt returned to Worcester in April, 1842, after
a brief lyceum stint, he found the Old South in the initial
stages of a revival. "The Lord is indeed here," he wrote,
"and it seems we could hear and feel the breath of [H]is
spirit in our midst." It inspired him to watch both the young

22. William G. McLoughlin, Jr., *Modern Revivalism: Charles
Grandison Finney to Billy Graham* (New York, 1959), pp. 35–67;
Perry Miller, *The Life of The Mind in America, from the Revolution
to the Civil War* (New York, 1965), Ch. 1. *Christian Citizen*, May
18, 1844.

23. Elizabeth Burritt to Elihu Burritt, New Britain, Feb. 22, April
16 [1841], Central Connecticut State College Library.

and the old come forward hesitantly to the "inquiry seats" and then, ecstatically, to the "anxious seats," after which conversion normally followed. "The work goes on gloriously and many are flocking into the fold of Christ," he rejoiced.[24] At first Burritt participated in the evening prayer meetings "with a sense of unworthiness which I tried to express." While alone in his boardinghouse room he "knelt in prayer often" and sensed "an unusual nearness to the Saviour." Before long he began assuming a primary role at the prayer gatherings and with those unconverted persons who "came forward to be conversed with upon the subject of religion." With the shy and self-conscious people who attended the Old South "inquiry meetings" he worked diligently to instill the proper mood and attitude necessary for conversion. He beseeched, assured, supplicated, and coaxed, firmly and quietly, never arrogantly. His spiritual labors with a Miss Elizabeth Eaton illustrate his gentle method of persuasion and the profound seriousness with which he took his work as evangelist:

> I . . . found her in the most interesting state of feelings. She had in a measure lost her insupportable burden, and had begun to catch a glimpse of a dawning twilight, but was in a state of trembling hesitation whether to admit it into her soul. Never did I see one in such a crisis: It seemed as if I was assisting at a *new-birth*. Her heart was broken and voice too, and she spoke like a child who had scarcely recovered from a spell of sobbing. Dear girl; I never shall forget that interview. I said everything that I could conceive proper for one in such a situation; and we all knelt down and prayed.

When he met Miss Eaton on the following day, "there was a serenity resting on her countenance, and her eyes were swimming with a joy that the world cannot give nor take

24. Journals, April 4, 6, 1842.

away. I stood and looked her in the face and told [her] to say not a word, for I knew it all. Oh who shall be the next soul to bow to the mild sceptre of Jesus!"[25]

Burritt was so wrapped up in the revival that he thought of little else: "I begin to feel less inclined to my studies, and desire that I may become a *fool* that I may learn the mystery of godliness in Christ Jesus." He prayed that Jesus would keep him "under the shadow of [H]is wings, that I may stray no more from [H]is side!" As the revival became more intense, so did his religious thoughts. After he and a male companion had walked two sisters home following an evening prayer meeting, Burritt decided not "to do it again for there is a tendency adverse to entire devotion in it." Reflecting on all of his varied experiences since he had arrived in Worcester in 1837, he felt that none would "be so more precious or memorable than this heavenly season of the presence of God." At a prayer meeting he declared "that all the heaven I wished was the love of Jesus, and to be permitted to be a servant of [H]is hired servants, and eat of the crumbs that fall from their table."

By the end of May the revival had virtually subsided. Prayer meetings were still held, however, and Burritt kept searching for "more unconverted souls." Some thirty individuals had been converted and added to the Old South. He conceded that "every susceptible person was brought into the Kingdom." But there was God's work to be done in the villages surrounding Worcester. So, assisted by several brethren of the Old South, he organized religious meetings in Quinsigamond, Northville, and New Worcester, and took the "lead" at the Old South prayer meetings. Burritt had become a very active lay exhorter. He "spoke with some ease" at the prayer meetings he organized and could "present a few considerations from any passage of Scripture."

25. *Ibid.*, April 6, May 2, 3, 8, 1842.

Having addressed a spate of prayer meetings, he found it difficult to unwind after such a galvanic religious experience. He wanted more souls to conquer. That he had been helpful in "saving" a few persons affected him far more deeply than had his linguistic or lyceum successes. He explained to the Reverend Rodney Miller his plan for "extending our operations about the towns, taking in the different districts into a kind of circuit, so as to set all the brethren to work in the vinyard [sic] two by two, as the disciples of old." He suspected he "might do more good in the conference than the lecture room." "It would certainly seem more genial to the natural heart to speak to a vast and applauding audience in the Tabernacle in New York than to address a handful of simple people in a retired dim lighted schoolhouse, but it might make a heaven's difference to some soul."[26] His ripening evangelism may have been related to his declining stature as a public lecturer, but it is clear that he was already a complete Evangelical.

It took Burritt a while to realize that religious revivals were commonly followed by long spells of religious lethargy. He trudged five miles in the snow to Quinsigamond to conduct a prayer meeting attended by "only 2 men & 2 boys & 6 women." God's vineyard appeared to be withering, and his efforts to prolong the revival were of no avail. He was, however, becoming a familiar "religious" figure in Worcester. People who saw him for the first time—dressed "in a plain suit of black—set him down as a clergyman."[27] A friend's remark that he "should be licensed to preach!" did not strike him as "preposterous." Burritt felt "that God has given me talents sufficient for such a station, if he would superadd grace enough to get my heart aright."[28]

26. *Ibid.*, May 9-Dec. 11, 1842, *passim.*
27. Worcester *Aegis*, Mar. 2, 1842.
28. *Journals*, Feb. 1, 10, 1843.

The revival had vividly re-enforced in him the conviction that in matters of religion and morality he was indeed his brother's keeper. Samuel Hopkins' doctrine of "disinterested benevolence" had undergone modification early in the 19th century. By then it had been widely interpreted as meaning that man served God best by leading a sound moral life and by keeping a careful eye on the morality of his fellow man. With the triumph of moralism over piety came the advent of humanitarianism and social reform. The proliferation of benevolent societies by 1820 offered palpable proof of the power of disinterested benevolence.

Burritt was acquainted with the new twist given Hopkins's concept. He had carried out its injunction during the Old South revival: saving a soul, after all, was the most benevolent act a Christian could possibly perform. When in the heat of the Old South revival he received an "abrupt" letter from a cousin, he did not become angry because he could "never hereafter feel but love and friendship for every human." It was natural that he should have sought ways to channel his moralism into benevolent works. "I thank God for his mercy in sparing my life to see this glorious epoch of humanity, and to take a part in the great deeds of philanthropy which are enacting for the race."

Corollary to the doctrine of disinterested benevolence was the widespread belief of American Protestants in the nearness of the millennium. "Among the Christians of America, at least," writes H. Richard Niebuhr, "the optimism of the nineteenth century was intimately connected with the experience of the anticipated Christian revolution." Evangelicals agreed that the kingdom of God would be established in America once they had thoroughly propagated the gospel and attended to the moral and social evils that kept so much of the country under the devil's dominion. Burritt was a millenarian. But, unlike the famous William Miller, the New York Baptist who had picked a date in

1843 for the Second Coming, Burritt was certain that God's kingdom on earth "will not come by observation."[29]

A visit to the Worcester County Jail, in July, 1842, to see Sampson Wilder, "a recent *millionaire*, who is confined for one of his protested drafts," culminated in Burritt's assuming the role of self-appointed chaplain to the prisoners. Wilder, "a noble looking man, a gentleman and a Christian," the kind of man "few jails . . . were ever honored" to have as an inmate, had taken it upon himself to conduct religious meetings among the prisoners. After Wilder's release, Burritt carried on the work. The jail had a room set aside for religious worship, as well as an official chaplain.[30] But this did not dissuade Burritt from becoming an unofficial spiritual overseer of the prisoners. Several members of the Worcester Union Congregational Church who had pre-empted the task of redeeming the prisoners' souls looked upon him as an interloper. He was aware of their disapproval of his "forwardness," but he continued his labors. He often addressed his captive audience from the parable of the Prodigal Son. Burritt candidly "asked them if Satan had done any better by them for all their years of faithful service, and whether they thought God would have turned them off with such fare, and suffered them to be thus incarcerated, if they had served [H]im as faithfully."

After three and a half months of listening to Burritt's lay sermons some of the prisoners grew a little weary of being told that they had followed in the footsteps of Satan and began to manifest their displeasure in ways that embarrassed him. One prisoner, for instance, laughed so loudly during a prayer meeting that "the floor shook." Burritt thought it "quite evident that many of them feigned an

29. H. Richard Niebuhr, *The Kingdom of God in America* (New York, 1959), pp. 150–151. Journals, May 13, 18, 1842, April 23, 1843, Jan. 1, 1844.

30. E. Smalley, p. 529.

interest" in the meetings because they thought "it would facilitate their escape from confinement." Their increasing unruliness was enough to make him vow, on November 6, 1842, to "preach as the Methodists say, my *farewell sermon* next Sabbath." There was no "next Sabbath," however, for he never preached to the prisoners again. He had no intention of making the word of God the means for a jail-break.[31]

Once the Old South revival had quickened his latent evangelism, Burritt was ready to tell men how they should prepare themselves for spiritual regeneration. A convenient platform from which to reach sinners who seemed unconcerned over their salvation was temperance. The nexus between revivalism and reformism was strong. There was a very close kinship between soul-saving and temperance, as revivalists regularly inveighed against the Demon Rum for keeping men in a chronic state of sinfulness. With the bane of intoxicating beverages removed, revivalists reasoned, conversion would be easy.

Burritt gravitated to the temperance cause because he believed that "if there is any tangible devil in this world it is rum." Whenever he was invited to social affairs at which liquor flowed freely, he always rejected offers to drink: "I never mean to concede anything to this fashionable custom at all events, nor ever compromise between my temperance principles and the pernicious practices of high life dissipation." In Albany he had watched with keen interest as Eliphalet Nott, president of Union College and a temperance zealot, illustrated through diagrams "the situation of the stomache [sic] during the different stages of drunkeness [sic]." Burritt was relieved that he had early in life taken the total abstinence pledge as he "shudder[ed] to behold such a planispheric exhibition of the drunkard's fate." It galled him when on an occasional Sunday he was forced to take lodging at a tavern, where he felt contaminated by

31. Journals, July 23, Sept. 1-Nov. 6, 1842, *passim*.

the sickening fumes of tobacco smoke and rum, and the loathsome effluvia of the rum-drinker's breath, which even as bad as it is, is the breath of flowers compared with the breath of his coarse profanity. What a place to spend the Sabbath! What sights, sounds, and odors mingle to pollute the air, and revolt the senses! O how much better to spend one day in the house of God than ten thousand in such a tabernacle of wickedness.[32]

Like most of the social and moral reforms of the time, the temperance movement suffered from conflicting opinions among leaders over method, rationale, and scope. Total abstinence, as opposed to the older principle of moderate drinking, did not gain a significant following until after the inception in 1840 of the Washingtonian movement, begun by six Baltimore imbibers who had decided, while in a state of partial inebriation, to organize a society pledged to total abstinence from all intoxicating beverages.[33] Scarcely a town or village in America did not shortly thereafter establish a Washington Temperance Society. One was created in Worcester in May, 1841; it numbered nearly 4,000 members by 1845,[34] one of whom was Burritt.

In Worcester the most popular temperance orator in America, the English-born John B. Gough, got his start. Abandoned there by a theatrical company because of his bottle-bouts and crushed by the death of his wife, Gough was persuaded to take the pledge in October, 1842.[35] Burritt attended what was probably Gough's first temperance address in November of that year. Gough spoke only ten minutes, but made a profound impression on his listeners,

32. *Ibid.*, Jan. 8, 28, Oct. 23, 1842.
33. John Allen Krout, *Origins of Prohibition* (New York, 1925), pp. 181–183.
34. *Worcester Almanac, Directory, and Business Advertiser, for 1846* (Worcester, 1846), p. 42.
35. Krout, pp. 192–194.

especially Burritt, who "almost unconsciously" left his seat and walked to where the reformed drunkard was movingly recounting "his own thrilling experience in the degradation and misery of drunkeness [sic]."[36]

In June, 1842, Burritt delivered his first temperance lecture in New York City, which, now that he had been subjected to the moralizing energies of the revival, he likened to a "great brick Babel." He told his audience that there was no place for alcohol in the new evangelical "era of man, the epoch of humanity that was dawning." He prophesied that the day of the rumseller would cease when moderate drinkers pledged themselves to total abstinence. Moderate drinkers, he charged, posed a greater threat to temperance than rumsellers or habitual drunkards. The seller "dug the drunkard's grave, but he never placed the syren there to entice him in. Moderate, fashionable drinkers, thou art the man!" Drunkards exerted "an influence all on the side of total abstinence." They plead the cause "with all the eloquence of . . . [their] misery."[37]

Burritt had hoped to present temperance in a novel light, but despite his great pains his lecture was a stereotype which did not fail to mention "little, shoeless, shivering children" severely fixing on their tipsy fathers "large, hungry, glassy eyes for bread." It was boring. When he delivered the same lecture in New Haven, the audience was inattentive and noisy. He abruptly stopped and labelled the gathering "the most stupid" he had ever addressed. After he repeated the lecture in Worcester, "a tall, haggard looking Irishman came up before the desk and called me to order for endeavoring to preach a sermon." From then on, Burritt gave only scattered temperance lectures, though he

36. Journals, Nov. 7, 1842.
37. Burritt, "The Influence of the Drunkard", in *Thoughts and Things*, pp. 118–120; New Haven *Herald*, Aug. 20, 1842.

continued to believe that total abstinence was "the greatest reformation since Luther's day."[38]

Early in 1843 he began to "feel that I had almost come to an end in Worcester, and that there is nothing that I can do of any use here." He was becoming highly sensitive to the pressing social problems of the day. He thought about writing a lecture on "the political duties of Christians," asking "whether the institution of slavery shall receive such a powerful auxiliary as the accession of Texas to the Union." He also started composing a peace lecture to deliver in Boston. In addition he decided to confine his public speaking "to peace, temperance, and righteousness." But having already tried without success to be of service to the temperance movement, he believed it wiser to leave temperance exhortations to men like Gough, whose personal experiences with the iniquities of drink would be more meaningful to audiences than his own conventional assessments. Burritt now turned to abolition and peace because both causes seemed more promising and urgent, as well as more in need of evangelical assistance.[39]

38. Journals, Mar. 20, Aug. 19, 26, 1842; *Christian Citizen*, Sept. 7, 1844.
39. Journals, Feb. 1, April 23, May 5, 1843.

5

Into the Antislavery Orbit

Burritt's interest in the plight of the slave dated to the troubles his brother Elijah had experienced in Milledgeville, Georgia, in February, 1830, for possessing several copies of *Walker's Appeal*. Written in 1829 by David Walker, a free Negro, *Walker's Appeal* was an incendiary antislavery pamphlet which boldly exhorted slaves to insurrection and violence to gain freedom.[1] The Georgia legislature had recently passed a law proscribing the publication or circulation of antislavery literature.[2] Elijah was arrested. When released, fearing mob violence, he fled Georgia, leaving behind his possessions and his family, who, after a delay of

1. For the Southern reaction to *Walker's Appeal*, see Clement Eaton, "A Dangerous Pamphlet in the Old South," *Journal of Southern History*, II (1938), pp. 323–334.

2. Ulrich B. Phillips, "The Public Archives of Georgia", in *The Annual Report of the American Historical Association for the Year 1903* (2 vols. Washington, 1904), I, 469. The executive board of Milledgeville decreed that, "Whereas the board has received information that Elijah H. Burritt has violated the statute of the last Georgia legislature by the introduction of certain insurrectionary pamphlets, resolved that the town marshal be directed to enter his name as prosecutor in the case and this board will pay all expenses necessary to bring the offender to punishment."

several months, finally managed to rejoin him in New Britain.

Elijah later gave his version of the affair. He had written to several Northern friends for copies of *Walker's Appeal* because he, his newspaper partner Mr. Polhill, and several "distinguished Georgia friends" were "exceedingly anxious to see the work." Elijah received not only the pamphlets, but a letter from Walker himself. Polhill showed the pamphlets to some of his friends, loaned copies for inspection and spoke freely of owning such inflammatory literature. "On seeing some extracts from this same pamphlet in a Boston paper," Elijah explained, "we even republished them in our paper [*The Statesman and Patriot*] with nearly half a column of Editorial remarks," which treated the pamphlet with great circumspection and censured its sanguinary sentiments. When Elijah went away on a short business trip, Polhill took "the residue of these pamphlets to the Governor [George M. Troup] with an unmeaning letter from the author [Walker], and raise[d] in his mind, and the minds of the public, the most perfidious unfounded and damnable prejudices against *me* individually."[3]

Besides blaming Polhill, Elijah vigorously maintained that the "conspirators" plotted against him for reasons having nothing to do with the pamphlet. Intent upon "dethroning the *Statesman and Patriot* of its Editor," he wrote, they seized upon "the firebrand of slavery, *chiefly* because it is ever the easiest kindled against a Northern man." Ever since the passage of the Tariff of 1828 and the efforts of the Supreme Court to prevent the Georgia legislature from rescinding Cherokee land titles, Southerners had "manifested the most virulent and indecorous purposes of revenge against us all." It was his spirited stand in "the cause of humanity and justice towards this hunted and abused [In-

3. Copy of a Letter from Elijah Burritt to D. Whittlesey, Klingberg Collection.

dian] race" that led the people of Milledgeville "to visit
upon *my* head their accumulated wrath." On other political
matters he also "had opposed with equal fidelity their mad
Governor Troup, and his disorganizing coworkers for which
my life had more than once been sought and threatened in
good earnest."[4]

Safe in Connecticut, Elijah became a hero to his friends
and attracted the attention of a few abolitionists. The Reverend Simeon S. Jocelyn, a home missionary agent who had
established a Negro church in New Haven, interviewed
Elijah, and wrote to William Lloyd Garrison, suggesting
that he enlist Elijah in the abolition movement:

> He is the gentleman who suffered so much on acct of
> Walkers' pamphlet. I had an interview with him yesterday
> —he is a noble soul—lived 20 years in Geo.—has facts on
> the subject of slavery most horrible and would make one of
> the most commanding and interesting agents for our society
> that can be found—he is pious and warmly devoted to the
> cause of the oppressed. He will I think write something for
> you bye & bye.[5]

Elijah neither joined Garrison's New England Anti-Slavery Society nor wrote for the *Liberator*. It is unlikely that
he was an abolitionist, or that he intended to circulate
Walker's Appeal to stir up sympathy for the slave. Never-

4. *Ibid.* Elijah wrote Mark A. Cooper, Solicitor General of Georgia,
requesting an investigation of the "famous pamphlet affair". He
assured Cooper that such an inquiry would "unmask the Iago who
stabbed me in the dark." Should Georgia justice deprive him of his
property, as he suspected it might, "I can but take my wife under
one arm, and my children in the other & seek some corner of God's
domain, where integrity of purpose and honest industry may regain
what it lost me in Milledgeville." (Burritt to Cooper, New Britain,
August 14, 1830, Klingberg Collection. See also Elijah Burritt to
Ann Burritt, New Britain, May 22, 1830.)

5. S. S. Jocelyn to W. L. Garrison, New Haven, July 12, 1832,
Boston Public Library.

theless it took courage to send away for the pamphlet and no doubt at heart he abominated slavery. Elijah's contention that it was his outspoken criticism against "the Georgia policy of exterminating their red brethren" that engendered the obloquy against him is probably the truth of the whole episode.[6] He was a brave defender of human rights.

Elihu never forgot his brother's Georgia ordeal. By the time he had reached his twentieth birthday, he had been vicariously confronted with the irrationality and militancy with which the South defended the institution of slavery. While passing through Milledgeville many years after the incident, Elihu visited "the site and scene of my dear brother Elijah's life and labors for many years, and from which he fled" because of his "antislavery sentiments."[7] He knew that Elijah had attributed his harassment to the Indian removal issue, and Elihu had even written some poor prose on "The Cherokee", in which he mourned "the last vestige of the Indian race . . . trampled under foot of these pale-faced favorites of the Skies."[8] But he chose to remember Elijah as a martyr to the slave rather than to the Indian.

In 1841 and 1842 Burritt's Journals contain only random references to abolitionism. But they point to his unequivocal faith in the reform and his approval of the political direction it had taken. At an antislavery convention in Worcester in October, 1841, he listened to Joshua Leavitt unleash a torrent of invective against slavery, urging those in attendance

6. An incomplete appraisal of Elijah's misfortune is found in Herbert Aptheker, *To Be Free* (New York, 1948), p. 47. Aptheker accepts the view of Merle Curti that Elijah was forced to flee Georgia because of his abolitionist sentiments. Elijah, writes Curti, "made great sacrifices for his abolitionist principles during his residence in Georgia." Curti, *The Learned Blacksmith*, p. 118, n.1. Neither Curti nor Aptheker had access to Elijah's letters.

7. Journals, May 29, 1854.

8. MS Family Album.

to acknowledge the wisdom of political abolitionism by supporting the Liberty Party. Burritt agreed that Liberty Party men

> have seized upon the right plan to meet the emergency. The institution of slavery has given a direction to almost every political question; it has overshadowed all our institutions; its militates against every republican principle; it renders our government an anomaly to the world. The people of New England have been enjoined by every moral consideration to keep it from mingling with politics, as if it was a cause too holy to be involved in political action. Never was a more delusive humbug foisted upon the credulity of our northern freemen than this.[9]

In 1842, Burritt received an invitation to lecture in Richmond, to which he graciously responded: "It would give me peculiar pleasure to appear before the young men of your city as a representative from their brethren at the North." But previous lecture commitments made it necessary to decline the offer. When several months later the request was repeated, he hesitated to accept because he did not wish "to breathe the air that *slaves* breathe."[10] (He had lectured in Baltimore on several occasions, and the slave air in that city had not affected his oversensitive nostrils.) Finally accepting the invitation, he journeyed to Richmond full of suspicion.

As he approached the capital of Virginia, he noted the geographical and cultural differences that, in his own mind, set the South far apart from New England. Neither villages nor "cheerful bright painted houses" nor "church spires" nor "elegant farm houses" broke "the monotony of a half cultivated waste." Only "once in two miles" did a "slovenly

9. Journals, Oct. 7, 1841.
10. Burritt to C. J. Richards, Baltimore, Jan. 16, 1842, Historical Society of Pennsylvania; Journals, Dec. 11, 1842.

residence of a planter" emerge from the wastelands, or the
squalid huts of slaves, "constructed like . . . an Irishman's
cabin on the railroad." The Southern planter, he wrote with
some insight, "seems wedded to the idea of territory, and
he sows and reaps over vast tracts of land, as if occupying
space rather than filling his barns." A planter with whom
Burritt conversed on slavery "tried to divest the system of
slavery of those features which are so obnoxious to the
North, and whittled it down to the mere abstract, which he
granted was wrong."[11] That the planter did not advance
the "positive good" theory in defense of slavery, but instead
admitted its moral wrong, failed to impress him. Burritt
had already reached the conclusion that slavery was not
just a moral abstraction, but an evil the exorcising of which
demanded immediate action.

Burritt's impatience corresponded with that of the abolition movement during the 1840's. Abolitionists of all shades
cried for action, but could not agree upon a common course.
The Liberty Party's political efforts alienated those abolitionists who wanted to keep the cause purely moral. Garrison and his confederates savagely condemned political
abolitionism; but by denigrating the churches and the national government, they irreversibly reduced their own control, if not influence, over the reform. In 1843 there was
no national leadership as "abolitionists became . . . mere
sects."[12] Though abolitionism grew progressively more political, its moral tone remained none the less shrill.

The secretary of the Liberty Party of Massachusetts peti-
tioned Burritt to address antislavery gatherings. Earlier
John Greenleaf Whittier had asked him for a letter expressing his opinions of the abolition movement.[13] Whittier,

11. Journals, Dec. 18–22, 1842.
12. Louis Filler, *The Crusade Against Slavery* (New York, 1960),
p. 157.
13. Journals, Feb. 8, 1842, Sept. 23, 1843.

then in his Liberty Party phase, had learned that Burritt was sympathetic with political abolitionism, and hoped that he would contribute his oratorical talents. It is probable that, like many others, Whittier had heard the exaggerated accounts of Elijah's difficulties in Georgia and thus presumed that Elihu would be equally warm toward abolition.

In Boston, Burritt stopped off at the *Emancipator* office and discussed with J. W. Alden, publisher of that Liberty Party paper, ways to expand the operations of the Party. Burritt returned to Worcester with a package of Liberty Party tracts to distribute. He and his close friend Julius Clarke met "to concoct some antislavery action," having resolved "to espouse the cause of the Liberty Party this fall." For several months Burritt had pondered this decision. To work actively in the antislavery crusade required a sturdy indifference to public opinion, which frowned on abolitionists. There was also the more serious danger of having to face physical intimidation—the kind that Theodore Weld and Henry B. Stanton had frequently been exposed to. Burritt expected "to lose some of my reputation," but he did "not wish to retain any of it that is based on my support of a slaveholder."[14]

It was a deep sense of outraged moralism that made Burritt decide to help the Liberty Party. Like most antislavery men, he attacked slavery on religious and moral grounds. Yet he saw nothing improper or inconsistent in joining moral with political suasion, so long as the latter did not compromise the former. By offering to aid the Liberty Party, however, he was forcing himself to play a political role which he disliked and for which he had had practically no experience.

Burritt's initiation into political activity of a sort had begun in 1840 when Samuel Hoar, acting in behalf of the

14. *Ibid.*, Sept. 23, 28, 1843.

Whig Committee of Concord, had invited him to participate in the Fourth of July celebration in that town, perhaps even to deliver a speech. Burritt had declined because he had already accepted a similar offer from the Whigs of Barre. These invitations came at a time when the political atmosphere in Massachusetts, like that throughout the nation, was charged with emotion over the approaching presidential election. This was the Log Cabin, Hard Cider campaign in which the Whigs had no platform other than that of a rustic democracy, and a splendidly misrepresented candidate in old William Henry Harrison. The Democrats, too, had a misrepresented candidate—but not so splendidly —in the incumbent President Van Buren, and there were silver forks and gold goblets to explain, not to mention a still depressed national economy.

In declining Hoar's invitation, Burritt revealed his Whig sympathies. He acknowledged that "tastes, habits, and pursuits have kept me aloof from any active participation in the political discussion of the day." But he was not heedless of what was going on in Washington, or at least of what Whig newspapers claimed was going on. They attributed the nation's economic plight to the moral bankruptcy of the Van Buren administration. Burritt swallowed their fanciful conclusion. He wrote Hoar that he had "long watched, with a painful interest the movements of the present government," and that he was "alarmed at the insidious inductions of principle which are expressly to sap the foundations of the moral & political virtue of the nation; —of the fearful an[d] increasing extent of executive patronage, and the more humiliating instances of executive *bribery*."[15] Later, Whigs at Worcester had invited him to address a local party conclave gathered in honor of Harrison's inauguration. What Burritt said is not known, but it was

15. Burritt to Samuel Hoar, Worcester, July 3, 1840, American Antiquarian Society.

reported that he "took the anvil and hammered out a well-wrought and impressive address, in which sentiment kept pace with manly style."[16]

Worcester was a Whig stronghold, as was most of Massachusetts, during the Jacksonian era. From the standpoint of political ideology there was no fundamental disagreement between Whigs and Democrats: both parties endorsed popular principles and "reached broadly similar class constituencies."[17] The Whigs, however, were generally accepted as a party of social refinement and economic solidarity, while the Democrats had found it difficult to shake off the epithet of "Locofocoism," which to many was synonymous with political radicalism and social heterodoxy. Burritt was a Whig more out of temperament than conviction.[18] His social aspirations dictated his brand of politics as much as anything else. He had attended a few Locofoco conventions in Worcester and was surprised that they were not so boisterous or disorderly as common Whig gossip had made them out. But he betrayed his social affinity for the Whig party when he attended its 1843 State Convention: he declared it "a noble sight to see the embodiment of old Massachusetts in the thousand delegates assembled to nominate a candidate for their governor."[19]

Burritt's political principles were so mixed that they fitted him for neither the Whig nor Democratic party. He believed in free trade and considered paper currency dangerous and undemocratic. Unlike most Whigs, he thought oc-

16. Worcester *Aegis*, March 10, 1841.
17. Marvin Meyers, *The Jacksonian Persuasion* (Stanford, 1957), p. 8.
18. Elijah Burritt had been a Democrat. In a letter to James K. Polk in 1834 Elijah had boasted that, as a Georgia editor, he had "performed no half-way part in promoting the 1828 presidential election and sustaining the administration" of Andrew Jackson. (Burritt to Polk, New Britain, Jan. 31, Mar. 14, 1834, Library of Congress.)
19. Journals, Sept. 2, 1841, June 7, 1843.

casional rebellions in defense of political liberties were justifiable. He sympathized with those Rhode Islanders who supported the Dorr Rebellion of 1842 in an effort to extend the suffrage. He had "no doubt but that the *people* were in the right, and took the only way to assert it." His politics, then and always, was essentially the politics of morality: whatever was morally right was *ipso facto* politically sound. Burritt had no taste for politics because it tended to align "the people not into a union but a kind of human avalanche." Listening to politicians, moreover, was "enough to give one an *ennui* of political life."[20] In 1842 he had not yet voted in a presidential election.[21]

Anxious to render immediate and significant service to political abolitionism, Burritt and Julius Clarke arranged a meeting of "a few friends of the cause" in Worcester. A plan to establish "a small antislavery paper" was rejected, but it was agreed to hire a man to solicit subscribers for the *Emancipator* and to distribute Liberty Party tracts and pamphlets. Six dollars was "raised . . . on the spot" to purchase copies of the *Emancipator* for free circulation. "Thus I have put my hand to a work which may seriously affect my standing," wrote Burritt, "but I will stand the hazard of the die." It was a modest beginning, but it was a start.

Burritt tried to interest several Worcester Liberty Party enthusiasts in establishing a correspondence with cohorts in the remaining fifty-four towns in Worcester County "to publish, issue & distribute whatever papers they might think adapted to the dissemination of light." Two committees were formed for this purpose, but the members seemed reluctant to support the proposal. Burritt and Clarke decided to go it alone. "We two," declared Burritt, "resolved ourselves into a *Voluntary Tract Association*." They drafted

20. *Ibid.*, Oct. 25, Nov. 10, 1842.
21. Burritt to Salmon P. Chase, New Britain, Oct. 2, 1862, in Curti, *The Learned Blacksmith*, pp. 143–144.

a circular to be sent throughout the county informing the towns of the new association and of the tracts it intended to circulate.

Burritt explained the association, which was now to embrace the whole of New England and New York, to J. W. Alden and Joshua Leavitt, the editor of the *Emancipator*, who approved the project and offered assistance. On taking leave of Alden and Leavitt, he reassured himself that he was doing the right thing: "I have put my hand to this work, and I shall not look from any motives of cuning [*sic*] expediency."

In Portland, Maine, Burritt talked with General James Appleton, the Liberty Party gubernatorial candidate in that state, about the projected tract association. "He feels with me," said Burritt, "that the cause of Antislavery must be invested with more dignity; that the means to promote it must be based upon the highest principles of truth & Christianity; that it must be divested of bombastic phraseology of florid, windy rhetoric, and presented in the language of calm reason & Christian philosophy." Appleton promised to write a tract.[22]

In less than a month from the time Burritt decided to help "the cause of freedom," he had formulated plans for a Worcester County Tract Association and then had enlarged it to include all New England. He was fast warming up to abolitionism, and he did not intend to take a subordinate position if he could help it. He was displaying the resourcefulness and organizational skills which would characterize all his reform enterprises. But he was also giving a preview of his lifelong tendency to jump into reforms with the unshakable conviction that a just cause need only be brought before the people to triumph. He really believed that "in less than five years . . . one great irresistible phalanx of

22. Journals, Sept. 30-Oct. 12, 1843, *passim*.

freeman . . . shall cut asunder the insidious ligaments which
connect them with the institution of slavery."[23]

Though he denied worrying about his reputation, Burritt
was concerned about "the imputation of fanaticism we may
incur." He was afraid Worcester Whigs would accuse him
of political apostasy. In a letter to a Liberty Party friend
he declared that

> the friends of humanity shall teach the Whigs in 1844 that
> it is too late in the history of the world to bring forth a
> *Slaveholder* [Henry Clay] as a candidate for the presidency
> of this enlightened republic. For I am still a Whig, as I
> have ever been; and in parting from that noble, though
> misguided party, I bid them no eternal adieu. We shall soon
> meet again; we shall not go to them, but they will come to
> us.[24]

Virtually all the leaders of the Whig party in Massachusetts
loathed slavery, but they were too realistic to think it could
be abolished immediately and too practical to abandon
their party for the Liberty Party.[25] Those who became political abolitionists were usually Whigs, and, like Burritt,
believed they had not really bolted their former party, but
that the party had deserted them.

Burritt set about "procuring men of political experience &
Christian philanthropy to write" for the New England Anti-
Slavery Tract Association. He wished the tracts would be
written, as he told the Reverend Frederic Hedge, "in language that cannot irritate or provoke any prejudice [and]
shall present lucidly & succinctly the dark institution of
slavery in all its moral, social, political & pecuniary bear-

23. Burritt to [J. G. Carter], Worcester, Oct. 5, 1843, Haverford
College Library.
24. *Ibid.*
25. David Donald, *Charles Sumner and the Coming of the Civil
War* (New York, 1960) pp. 131–134.

ings."[26] He spent nearly a month writing a long epistle to the Reverend John Angell James, of Birmingham, England, a distinguished Nonconformist minister. The letter, though verbose and effusive, shows the broad evangelism that had carried him into the antislavery movement and illustrates the fact that Burritt conceived evangelism and abolitionism as inseparably bound together.

The sin of slavery, he wrote to James, was a sin against the very essence of Christianity, the "one family circle in the universe, which, though as old as eternity, recognized no relations more distant than those of Father, sons & brethren." In such a circle of indissoluble Christian relationships "neither time, nor distance, nor color, nor language, nor nation, nor any adventitious circumstances of humanity, creates any distinction" among God's children.

> . . . the Christians of the two Anglo-Saxon nations have been elected as kings & priests unto God, to *cowork* with him in restoring the benighted race of man to a better destiny. How happy that in this blessed field of action, they may leave their *eagles* and *lions* at home and meet & march under the standard of Emmanuel! How pleasant that our obstinate nationalities may be melted down into Christian unity, and our Patriotism expand into philanthropy . . . to rescue millions from the bondage of sin and the yoke of slavery![27]

Charles Foster, in *An Errand of Mercy*, insists the evangelical united front between England and America for the purpose of evangelizing the world expired in 1837.[28] If it did, Burritt was not told of it:

26. Journals, Oct. 19, 1843.
27. Burritt to the Reverend John Angell James, Worcester, Oct. 25, 1843, Columbia University Library.
28. Charles Foster, *An Errand of Mercy* (Chapel Hill, North Carolina, 1960), pp. 249–274.

It would seem [he wrote to James] that the whole pagan world and all the dark regions of cruelty & oppression have been assigned to British & American Christians, not only as a field of *labor*, but as a field of union: where the lofty affinities of the Anglo-Saxon genius & blood may cooperate with their more exalted & intimate relation by *the blood* of the *Lamb*, to unite them in bonds of brotherhood more indissoluble than the common ties of nature. . . I rejoice that the providence and Gospel of God are bringing all these influences to bear, like mutual attraction, upon our two great nations, and that we are nearer together than at any period since we had a separate existence.

After further expatiation on the nature of evangelicalism, Burritt returned to slavery. He stated that abolitionism, once "regarded as a transient ebulition [*sic*] of fanaticism . . . has become the ebulition of a *Niagara*, due to the efforts of the Liberty Party." Unhappily, practically "all the northern churches, of all evangelical denominations, extend the hand of Christian fellowship to slaveholding ministers, while they disclaim all fellowship with Slavery." Equally insidious were those Northerners who had maintained "that we have no right to interfere with the *domestic institutions* of the South." Burritt scoffed at that "piously affected horror at bringing the subject of antislavery into politics."

The Reverends John Pierpont, Leonard Bacon, Calvin Chapin, and the eminent Scotsmen Dr. Thomas Dick and Thomas Chalmers, were among the distinguished people from whom Burritt solicited tracts. He told Bacon that the Tract Association wished "to secure, for the year, 52 of the best writers of the country, each furnishing the matter for one powerful tract" each week. With the Garrisonians in mind, Burritt informed Chapin that he was interested in engaging "those eminent & philanthropic men who have hitherto been driven from the cause by that ferocious fanaticism that would demolish all the hallowed institutions of religion in order to get at the evil of slavery.[29]

Burritt thought Longfellow's *Poems on Slavery* would make an admirable tract. "I have just learned with pious indignation," he wrote the Cambridge poet, "that your beautiful *Poems on Slavery,* which deserve to be republished and read in heaven—have been almost entirely suppressed from circulation by that pusilanimous [sic], dough-faced servility to Southern sentiment, which has enslaved the North with a meaner bondage than negros [sic] suffer at the South." Should Longfellow allow the Tract Association the use of his antislavery verse, Burritt promised to "set machinery upon it that shall exhale it & rain down again in dewdrops 'like orient pearls' over all the towns & villages of the free states."[30] Not only did Longfellow donate his poems; he paid for the plates as well.

Burritt placed great stock in the Tract Association because he believed in the efficacy of the printed word. "Such a phalanx of mighty minds appearing suddenly in the field at this crisis of the struggle," he had written Leonard Bacon, "would almost certainly ensure a conquest for humanity." He predicted that "200,000 human minds" edified by the Christian logic of antislavery tracts would assist in placing the quietus on slavery.[31] Once the people realized that slavery was sin, they would march righteously to the polls and cast their votes for the Liberty Party. To Burritt it was as simple as that.

29. Burritt to the Rev. John Pierpont, Portland, Maine, Oct. 11, 1843, Pierpont Morgan Library; Burritt to Dr. Thomas Dick, Oct. 30, 1843, New York Historical Society; Burritt to the Rev. Leonard Bacon, Worcester, Oct. 30, 1843, Yale University Library; Journals, Oct. 29, 1843.

30. Burritt to Longfellow, Worcester, Nov. 6, 1843, in Curti "Henry Wadsworth Longfellow and Elihu Burritt", *American Literature*, VII (1935), pp. 318–319.

31. Burritt to the Rev. Leonard Bacon, Worcester, Oct. 30, 1843, Yale University Library.

Of course he overestimated the effect of these tracts on the popular mind. Abolitionism had never lacked an adequate literature of exposure. Antislavery tracts, circulars, pamphlets, broadsides and newspapers examining every facet of slavery had inundated the country for years. The Liberty Party, moreover, had its own Tract Depository, and had been disseminating four- and eight-page tracts on such topics as *Right Sort of Politics, Influence of the Slave Power,* and *Don't Throw Away Your Vote.*[32]

Largely under Burritt's supervision the Tract Association made some progress. By November, 1844, twelve tracts were being distributed. "The interest in this movement thus far manifested," declared J. W. Alden, publisher of the tracts, "exceeds our most sanguine expectations. We are receiving orders from every free state in the Union."[33] General James Appleton submitted a forceful tract on *The Missouri Compromise, or the Extention of the Slave Power.* James C. Jackson, Liberty Party leader in central New York, wrote on *The Duties and Dignities of American Freemen;* William Goodell, New York Liberty Party champion, drafted *An Appeal to Professors of Religion, Ministers, & Churches, Who are not Enlisted in the Struggle against Slavery;* Richard Hildreth's polemic was entitled *What can I do for the Abolition of Slavery?* Alvan Stewart, Liberty Party gubernatorial candidate from New York, Theodore Weld, and the renowned British Evangelical Thomas Clarkson also contributed articles. Burritt was hopeful that Cassius M. Clay, who had just made his antislavery debut, would write a tract.[34]

In the Association circular sent to all the New England

32. *Emancipator,* July 6, 1843.
33. *Ibid.,* Feb. 8, 1844.
34. For a listing of these tracts, see the *Emancipator,* Nov. 3, 1844; Burritt to Cassius M. Clay, Worcester, Jan. 20, 1844, American Antiquarian Society. See Burritt's article on Clay in *Christian Citizen,* Jan. 13, 1844.

states, Burritt had emphasized that the organization "did not design to be identified with the *Liberty Party,* particularly." Tracts written by Liberty Party men "would not be likely to excite or irritate any prejudice of their political character." Two of the first five tracts were written by prominent Liberty Party leaders—James Appleton and Alvan Stewart—but neither was an apologia for the party. James C. Jackson's tract, however, was a mordant indictment of the Whig and Democratic parties for their alleged subserviency to slaveholders; it ended with a spirited defense of the principles of the Liberty Party.[35]

Jackson's failure to refrain from lauding his own party while lambasting Whigs and Democrats drew a hot rebuke from the *Kennebec Journal,* an influential newspaper published in Augusta, Maine. But it was Burritt, not Jackson, who was censured for allowing the tracts to advance "the obnoxious principles of the Liberty Party" through a "vile imposition."[36]

Burritt chided the *Kennebec Journal* for having paraded him "before the world . . . as a man of tainted honor and integrity." He denied that he had ever implied the tracts would avoid politics. To the *Kennebec Journal* and to several Augusta abolitionists who had criticized the political posture of the tracts he posed some questions meant to put them on the spot:

> Was it your covert design to insinuate your hand into the movement to confine it to a sphere as narrow as your views of policy? Was it an insidious scheme of yours to get control of every sentiment and thought upon the subject of slavery and modify or suppress their utterance? Or were you content to limit your philanthropic surveillance to that field of gladiators who, under the appellation of Whigs and Democrats, are fighting with each other for southern suf-

35. *Christian Citizen,* March 30, 1844.
36. *Ibid.*

frage, and sacrificing, with unscrupulous idolatry, the most sacred interests and principles of the free, upon the bloody altar of that cannibal deity, the SLAVE POWER?[37]

The Tract Association failed to supply a tract for each week of 1844. By January, 1845, only fourteen had been published. Half had been written by Liberty Party men and none by those ministers whom Burritt had hoped to engage. The Reverend J. A. James had declined to write because he claimed it would be "foreign interference"; Dr. Thomas Chalmers refused because "It is now more than 20 years since I directed my attention to slavery." Joel Hawes, Leonard Bacon, Justin Edwards, John Pierpont, and Calvin Chapin did not even bother to explain. Dr. Thomas Dick contributed an original antislavery essay which was too long for a tract. Since the tracts were published by Alden of the *Emancipator*, and since so many were written by political abolitionists, the notion that the Tract Association was an adjunct of the Liberty Party may have hindered the organization. Burritt himself had grown disenchanted with the tract system and now thought it "rather a slow and comparatively expensive process of dissemination."[38] By the end of 1845 the Tract Association ceased to exist.

Burritt's loss of interest in the Tract Association was partly the result of his preoccupations with the weekly newspaper he had begun publishing in Worcester in 1844. Called the *Christian Citizen*, the paper aimed "to develop the Christian citizen into the full stature of a perfect man, in the discharge of all his Religious, Social, and Political Duties. Avoiding all sectarian tenets and controverted points of religious belief, it will seek to extract from the spirit of the Gospel, a Practical Christianity, which shall pervade the heart and inspire all the actions of life."[39]

37. *Ibid.*
38. *Ibid.*, Jan. 18, 1845.
39. *Massachusetts Spy*, Nov. 8, 1843.

Liberty Party men in Worcester were chagrined that Burritt's proposed newspaper would not confine itself to political abolitionism. They were, according to him, "all on the qui vive to publish a paper somewhat in opposition to mine." Actually, they were considering publishing a newspaper not in opposition to his, but one that would be the official organ of the Liberty Party for Worcester County. The Reverend R. B. Hubbard, the party leader in Worcester, told Burritt "officially" that the *Christian Citizen* "would not be the *man* for the . . . party" unless it became "the battleaxe of partisan warfare."[40] Burritt was not averse to using his paper to endorse political abolitionism, but neither did he plan on making it a carbon copy of the *Emancipator*. He wished to give his paper a broader scope. Ever since his first peace lecture in June, 1843, his interest in that cause, though secondary to antislaveryism, had enlarged. And if his labors in the field of temperance had been haphazard, he nevertheless deemed that reform a primary one.

The first number gave promise that the *Christian Citizen* would be an articulate advocate of antislaveryism and of Liberty Party precepts. Burritt promised to "bestow special attention upon every social, political, pecuniary and physical bearing of the institution of slavory, with a freedom that shall never bend to the prejudices of popular opinion." He was also going to employ every conceivable argument to convince the reader "that the exercise of his political prerogative is one of the most serious and responsible duties that he is called to discharge in his life." The implication was clear: the Christian citizen was he who voted against slavery by voting for the Liberty Party. Nowhere did Burritt specifically refer to the party by name; but

40. Journals, Oct. 30-Nov. 1, 1843.

there were enough references to political abolitionism to appease Hubbard.[41]

Joshua Leavitt's *Emancipator* hailed the *Christian Citizen* "as a co-laborer in the Anti-Slavery cause," even though it was "not technically a Liberty Party paper." But Burritt, Leavitt added, "is a Liberty Party man, and we misjudge if his paper should not have a strong sprinkling of our doctrines and measures."[42] The veteran abolitionist William H. Burleigh, editor of the *Christian Freeman*, a Liberty Party paper published in Hartford, commended the early issues of the *Christian Citizen*. He was delighted by Burritt's open letter to ex-Governor Ellsworth of Connecticut which reprimanded Ellsworth for having written a letter deprecating antislavery extremism. Under the headline "A Blacksmith vs. a Governor" Burleigh summed up the way in which Ellsworth's letter "was pounded . . . to some good purpose" by Burritt.[43]

The *Christian Citizen* had some 1,800 subscribers, but that was far from encouraging. "I have put down my paper to such a low price [one dollar per year] that if I had 5000 paying subscribers, it would scarcely pay my board," Burritt lamented. Lecture fees enabled him to continue his paper on a tenuous financial basis. "Were it not that that *Citizen* swallows up all I can earn, even at this rate," he remarked after earning $75.00 for a week's work, "I might lay up something for 'the rainy day.' "[44] When Burritt was absent from Worcester, Julius Clarke, the Reverend George Allen, and Thomas Drew helped to prepare the paper for printing.

Garrisonians were quick to jump on Burritt and his paper.

41. *Christian Citizen*, Jan. 6, 1844.
42. *Emancipator*, Jan. 6, 1844.
43. *Christian Freeman*, Jan. 11, 18, 1844.
44. Journals, Jan. 31, 1844, Jan. 3, 1845.

Nathaniel P. Rogers, editor of the *Herald of Freedom*, published in Concord, New Hampshire, laughed at "the incongruity" of the title *Christian Citizen*, calling Burritt "a politician and an advocate of governmental force and coercion."[45] Burritt answered by writing an article on "Moral Suasion" to demonstrate its insufficiencies. Admitting that the "ballot-box has given the institution of slavery an almost overwhelming power in the Republic," Burritt asked, "But if this moral and political engine possesses such a giant capacity for evil, shall we throw it aside, as being impotent for good?" Unconvinced, Rogers reminded Burritt that "slavery is a moral evil" and had to be overthrown by a "Moral Revolution."[46]

Most of Burritt's antislavery pieces lacked the pithy eloquence of Garrison's and the harsh sustained logic of Leavitt's. The editorials were on a par with those found in the *Emancipator*. But many of them, such as "Who Shall Have Your Vote" and "Southern Policy", were written by Clarke or Allen or Drew. "The Land of the Brave, and Home of the Free" was a typical Burritt article—emotional, melodramatic, and stuffed with pious argot. It related the sordid side of America that the "bruised and hardened of every clime" had never heard about:

> They never listened to the half-smothered wailings of despair which God hears both night and day, ascending to his throne from human beings, bought, beat and bound in the very Capital of this boasting nation . . . They never heard the suppressed moaning of the little child, bought in its mother's arms and torn forever from her embrace . . . They never fathomed the despair of the mother's heart when her late-weaned infant was *knocked off* by the sheriff's hammer to some stranger, who tore it from her arms . . . They never saw how human nature, like a defenceless, unmurmuring

45. *Christian Citizen*, Mar. 2, 1844.
46. *Liberator*, June 28, 1844.

lamb, bled on the very steps of the Capitol, while the appointed champions of liberty were speaking long and loud within of the sacredness of human rights.[47]

"All Mortgaged" was an antislavery story by Burritt that Leavitt reprinted in the *Emancipator* with the observation that it came "from a man with a *heart* in him."[48] It was certainly written more from Burritt's heart than from his head. A "sable fugitive from slavery" had been given refuge by several New Englanders. "A slave in New England!", they queried, "is it possible that slaves can breathe here and not be free!" Calling for a copy of the Constitution, they read "among great swelling words about liberty . . . that there was not an acre nor an inch of ground within the limits of the great American Republic which was not MORTGAGED TO SLAVERY."[49]

In spite of the quiet role Burritt was playing in Liberty Party politics, he was one of five men nominated to run for the state senate from Worcester County. Burritt accepted the nomination, but his paper and Journal were strangely silent about it, and it is not clear that he attended the Liberty Party convention that nominated him.[50] Only a few Liberty Party men believed that James G. Birney had a real chance to be elected president, but many did expect to capture some state offices. In Massachusetts they were disappointed all around. Though Birney received over 10,000 votes in Massachusetts, more than the whole country had given him in 1840, no party candidate was elected to any state office. Burritt got fewer than one hundred and fifty votes. Party leaders interpreted the election results with their usual buoyancy. "The election of 1844," stated the

47. *Christian Citizen*, Feb. 10, 1844.
48. *Emancipator*, Jan. 15, 1845.
49. *Christian Citizen*, Nov. 30, 1844.
50. Worcester *Palladium*, Oct. 23, 1844.

Emancipator, "considered in all its bearings, is full of hope to the Liberty Party in Massachusetts!"[51]

For Burritt 1844 was not as promising a year as he had anticipated. "I feel," he wrote on January 1, 1845, "that I have done but little during the past year for the cause of humanity and God. My paper has dragged rather heavily on my hands; and the fact that I was not earning my bread from its income, has taken away some of my ambition." For the past six months he had felt beset by "an unnatural despondency." His mother had died in August, 1844, and he was deeply affected by her death. She had left a characteristic message for him: "be a useful man and do good in the world."[52]

Burritt felt uneasy over his irregular participation in antislaveryism. But rather than work more actively in the cause, he drew closer to the peace crusade. When the Reverend R. B. Hubbard at last established a Liberty Party paper in Worcester, Burritt became annoyed, especially when the paper, the *County Gazette,* took many of his subscribers. He was now against filling his own paper "with matter that smacks of party"; he would be his "own man the coming year, and go for *humanity* at large." It lightened his mind not to have to "cramp my soul to the narrow, cast-iron dimensions of party. I feel that I have dabbed a little too much in partisan politics during the past year, either for my own good or that of the public."[53]

The Liberty Party thought that he had not "dabbed" enough. Hubbard was right when he wrote that the *Christian Citizen* filled an "important sphere . . . somewhat different from that which we intend to occupy"; his was a straight party paper, and Burritt's was not. Hubbard's pre-

51. *Emancipator,* Nov. 13, 1844.
52. Journals, Jan. 1, 1845; Burritt to Elihu Burritt Lane, Birmingham, England, March 31, 1866, Swarthmore College Peace Collection.
53. Journals, Jan. 1, 1845.

diction that the two papers would not "come in collision" was borne out by the cordial relations they always enjoyed.[54] But Burritt must have breathed easier after reading several numbers of the *County Gazette*. In all ways his journal was much better.

From 1845 on Burritt's enthusiasm for abolitionism slackened substantially. He did not abandon the cause, but he put it in a new perspective—the perspective of peace. "Let every man who loves his race place upon the open record of the public mind his testimony against the sin-breeding custom of War, and this green world would soon be rescued from a burning curse, whose progeny—inheriting all the attributes of their parent—are Slavery, Anarchy, Piracy, Infidelity, and the whole legion of lust."[55] He had once considered temperance fundamental to all reforms; now it was peace.

The quantity of antislavery material in the *Christian Citizen* decreased after 1845, but the quality improved. Dr. Thomas Dick's treatise, written for the Tract Association, was chopped into several articles and printed in Burritt's paper. It was the sharpest arraignment of slavery ever to appear in the *Christian Citizen*.[56] Burritt himself wrote what was perhaps his finest antislavery article in scolding Garrisonians for preaching "No Union with Slaveholders." He had heard a resolution to that effect introduced by a Garrisonian at an Anti-Annexation of Texas rally in Boston's Faneuil Hall in January, 1845. Though Burritt branded the annexation bill as "one of the most stupendous schemes of iniquity ever concocted in this country," he detested Garrisonian anti-government principles. Out of "imperative necessity and religious duty" he apotheosized the Union.[57]

To Burritt the Union was "an institution of God" en-

54. Worcester *County Gazette*, Jan. 3, 1845.
55. *Christian Citizen*, March 29, Sept. 27, 1845.
56. *Ibid.*, Jan. 25, May 3, 1845.
57. Journals, Jan. 29–30, 1845.

dowed with the destiny of "making this hemisphere the *heart half* of the great system of humanity." Slavery, "the vicious offspring of circumstances contemporaneous with the formation of the American Union," would die all the sooner once the latent moral energies of the Union were directed against it. "The North may repudiate," he said, "but it cannot dissolve its connection with slavery by dissolving the Union." After all, "Northern distilleries furnished the red, burning currency that bought his spirit, flesh and blood on the African shore." The North and South had "sinned together . . . have suffered together . . . and . . . must repent together." And since it would "require the moral power of the whole Union to abolish slavery, then let Union be our cry-word—Union now and Union forever!"[58]

Devotion to the Union was a hallmark of the Whiggish mind, as well as of the political action abolitionists. But none of the prominent political abolitionists at this time talked or wrote so rhapsodically of the Union. Burritt did because he was an extreme Evangelical who seldom bothered to analyze his ideas, because he considered the Union a sacred compact for the promotion of liberty and brotherhood,[59] and because he overappraised the strength of disunionist sentiment. Like Webster fifteen years earlier, Burritt believed liberty and Union were inseparable and eternal.

The article, widely circulated by newspapers on his exchange list, was responsible for the invitation he received to address the great Southern and Western Liberty Convention to be held in Cincinnati in June, 1845. Salmon P. Chase was the chief organizer of the Convention.[60] The

58. *Christian Citizen*, Mar. 15, 1845.

59. See Paul C. Nagel, *One Nation Indivisible, The Union in American Thought, 1776–1861* (New York, 1964), pp. 69–209.

60. Dwight Dumond, *Antislavery, The Crusade For Freedom in America* (Ann Arbor, 1961), p. 303.

Boston *Morning Chronicle*, the Liberty Party daily edited by Leavitt, announced that "Burritt *must* go" and suggested that a purse of fifty dollars be collected for him to defray expenses. A Lowell factory girl had anonymously sent Burritt ten dollars to make the trip, and someone else contributed five dollars. But Burritt had agreed to lecture before two literary societies of Oberlin College in Ohio in August. He declined the Cincinnati offer because he said he could afford neither the money nor the time to make two trips West.[61]

In a lengthy letter to Samuel Lewis, an Ohio educator, political abolitionist, and chairman of the committee of arrangements for the convention, Burritt sent his apologies for being unable to attend: "Although I cannot be with you in person—or rather in body—I shall be present with every earnest sympathy of my soul, with every attribute of my humanity that can pray and hope for man, and labor to lift up my down-trodden brother the Slave." The letter stressed the majesty of the Union:

Dissolution of the Union?—What! cut in two the Mississippi, that jugular vein of the New World, and sever all the mighty arteries of the Union, and leave it to bleed to death in hostile segments, both writhing in the cauteries of mutual hatred! . . . Dissolve the Union! dissolve the moral power we have and need to abolish slavery! May God grant that your Convention banish that treacherous idea from every American heart. I trust that its Satanic lineaments will be detected and detested, should it surreptitiously enter your councils in the guise of an angel of light. No! You will not

61. Worcester *County Gazette*, May 14, 1845; *Christian Citizen*, June 14, 1845; Journals, April 26, 1845. Professor Louis Filler mistakenly declares that Burritt attended the Cincinnati convention. (Louis Filler, p. 187.)

meet to *dissolve*, but to *evolve* the Union; to renovate it on the basis of the fathers of the Republic.[62]

Burritt's letter was read before the convention of 2,000 abolitionists, as were communications from Cassius Clay, Seward, Greeley, William Jay, and others. It was printed in a pamphlet containing the convention's address to the public written by Chase. While the letter might not have enhanced his position as a political abolitionist, since it said little about politics and slavery, it helped restore his reputation as a Whig.

The Reverend Samuel J. May, a Garrisonian, thought Burritt's letter attacked disunionism "very sarcastically." Garrison wrote Burritt that his letter "astonished, shocks, appals me! If it be not used deceitfully—if it be not a mere flourish of rhetoric—if it means what the people in this land, what the people in other lands, will understand it to mean, without some new and extraordinary interpretation—then I am constrained to pronounce it in a high degree impious, and worthy of all condemnation." He explained to Burritt what the Union was and what it was not; it was not divinely inspired, but "the work of men's hands, and therefore may be imperfect, oppressive, or monstrous."[63]

Burritt was invited to address the Eastern Liberty Party Convention in Boston in October, 1845. It was the first major antislavery talk he gave, and it concerned the relation between "organic sins" and slavery. Burritt's theme came from the Reverend Edward Beecher's doctrine of organic

62. *The Address of the Southern and Western Liberty Convention Held at Cincinnati, June 11, 1845, To The People of the United States; Also, the Letter of Elihu Burritt to the Convention* (Cincinnati, 1845), pp. 14–15.

63. Samuel J. May to J. B. Estlin, June 30, 1846, Boston Public Library; *Liberator*, July 16, 1845; Walter M. Merrill, *Against Wind and Tide. A Biography of Wm. Lloyd Garrison* (Cambridge, Mass., 1963), p. 209.

sins. Beecher argued that, if a state sins, individuals within that state are not to blame; the state, not its citizens, will be punished by God. Burritt denounced Beecher's concept, though he conceded that the minister's "singular philosophy of moral responsibility seems to meet with great favor in this age and country of Carnal Policy."[64] By refuting Beecher's notion, Burritt was rejecting what might have been a kind of corollary of his own ideas on the Union. But as a reformer he could not accept a doctrine of "*incorporated or organized sins*" that absolved individuals from guilt.

Burritt's Cincinnati letter and his address to the Boston convention moved Liberty Party men to enlist him more directly in their cause. In a letter to Birney, H. B. Stanton declared that Burritt, along with Whittier, Longfellow, Richard Hildreth, and James Russell Lowell, would make excellent contributors to a new Liberty Party paper he proposed.[65] At the Massachusetts Liberty Party convention in October, 1845, thirty-one votes were cast for Burritt as the party's gubernatorial candidate, only twenty fewer than were received by the perennial candidate Samuel Sewall. He was nominated for lieutenant governor on the first ballot by a wide margin.[66]

Burritt declined the nomination. Because several Whig newspapers understood this to mean that he had quit the Liberty Party, Burritt wrote a letter to stop such rumors: "While I am as deeply affected with pleasure as surprise at such an unexpected and unmerited expression of . . . confidence and consideration, my relations to a collateral field of labor, and, I trust, of philanthropy, would render it em-

64. *Christian Freeman*, Oct. 9, 1845; *Christian Citizen*, Sept. 27, 1845.

65. Dumond, ed., *Letters of James Gillespie Birney* (2 vols., New York, 1938), II, 960.

66. *Christian Citizen*, Oct. 5, 1845.

barrassing, if not improper, for me to occupy a prominent political position." But the "principles, aim, and end of the Liberty Party," he went on, embodied "the sublimest morality that was ever 'brought into politics' in this fallen world."[67]

One of the few antislavery articles written by Burritt in 1846 described how the "ingenious wickedness of the American Constitution" compelled three million bondsmen "to vote to be slaves . . . to the last generation." He was referring to the three-fifths clause in the Constitution which, by counting three out of every five slaves for the purpose of congressional representation, gave the South twenty-one additional representatives "to denounce and vote down even the mildest petition for the abolition, or mitigation of slavery." And indirectly the slaves put them there: "Most subtle and astute of all human deviltries!"[68]

Garrison rejoiced that Burritt could write so darkly of the Constitution. He felt he had proselytized Burritt: "we trust Mr. Burritt is now prepared to reiterate the cry—'No Union with Slaveholders!' " But Garrison was wrong. He misinterpreted Burritt's moral indignation to mean that he had given up on political abolitionism. Edmund Quincy, Garrison's ally, was not fooled: "He is not exactly *New Organized* [Liberty Party] . . . having come into the field since those days, but he stands on the ground of the New Organization & his influence is on their side."[69]

Burritt always remained in good standing with political abolitionists. Even after his reform work had taken him to England, they did not forget him. Liberty Party men in New York, led by William Goodell, organized in 1847 a new national antislavery party, the Liberty League, and nomi-

67. *Christian Freeman*, Oct. 30, 1845.
68. *Christian Citizen*, Jan. 31, April 25, May 9, 1846.
69. *Liberator*, May 15, 1846; Edmund Quincy to Richard D. Webb, Dedham, Mass., May 23, 1846, Boston Public Library.

nated Gerrit Smith, the philanthropist-reformer, and Burritt, 3,000 miles away, as president and vice-president respectively.[70] Burritt declined the nomination, and some antislavery men were piqued by his refusal. Amasa Walker, Burritt's co-laborer in the peace cause, explained his position well:

> He is wholly absorbed in a great moral movement and although we know that he deeply sympathizes with the objects and aims of those who are acting politically for the redemption of the slave, he does not . . . feel that it is his mission to head a political party, for any purpose whatever. The moment he becomes a candidate for office, he loses all his moral power, especially in his own country.[71]

In 1843 Burritt was ready to enter the field of applied philanthropy; he had been moving in that direction ever since his labors in the Old South revival. The antislavery movement was the logical one to assist first—no one had to point out to him the need for benevolence there. Because he discerned no contradiction in carrying morality to the polls, he had supported the Liberty Party, had run for the state senate on its ticket, and had been nominated for lieutenant governor. These political accolades are surprising in view of his negligible contributions to the Party. But if he cautiously avoided any close connection with the Liberty Party, it was because partisan politics ruffled his evangelical disposition. Unquestionably he got more out of antislaveryism than he gave to it. That movement afforded him

70. The Liberty League was established by New York political abolitionists who wished to commit the Liberty Party to a more comprehensive program, or, as Burritt oversimplified it, "upon a Free Trade basis as well as Antislavery." William Goodell, *Slavery and Antislavery* (New York, 1852), pp. 475, 477, 481; Ralph V. Harlow, *Gerrit Smith, Philanthropist and Reformer* (New York, 1939), pp. 178–181.

71. *Christian Citizen*, Sept. 11, 1847.

his first protracted experience in benevolence. It introduced him to important philanthropists and reformers, and it gave him a chance to demonstrate his integrity and sincerity. Abolitionism sharpened his perception of the sin-infested world in which he lived. It was in the peace movement, however, that he saw the possibilities of expunging sin on a grand scale.

6

Apostle of Peace

Much of the peace sentiment in America in the early 19th century was in response to the War of 1812, itself part of the Napoleonic maelstrom that had kept a large part of the world in armed conflict for nearly twenty years. With England and America at peace in 1814, and Napoleon finally overthrown the following year, American pacifists sought to create positive instruments for peace. Their crusade began officially with the establishment of the New York and Massachusetts Peace Societies in 1815. David Low Dodge, a New York merchant, was the prime organizer of the New York Society, while the Reverends Noah Worcester and William E. Channing were chiefly responsible for the creation of the Massachusetts Society. Over fifty other state and local societies, as far north as Maine, as far south as Georgia, and as far west as Indiana, were formed within the next few years. Some of the societies corresponded with each other on a fairly regular basis, but from 1815 to 1828 the peace movement was unorganized.[1]

1. Merle Curti, *The American Peace Crusade, 1815–1860* (Durham, North Carolina, 1929), pp. 4–21; W. Freeman Galpin, *Pioneering For Peace, A Study of American Peace Efforts to 1846* (Syracuse, 1933), pp. 9–34.

The task of centralizing scattered peace societies into a national organization was largely the work of William Ladd, a Maine pacifist. Through his exertions the American Peace Society was founded in 1828. Ladd was not only the founder of the national society, but was also its chief benefactor and guiding light until his death in 1841. After Ladd's death the Reverend George C. Beckwith, secretary of the Society and editor of its monthly literary organ, the *Advocate of Peace*, became the dominant figure in the organization, though Samuel E. Coues, the president, Joshua P. Blanchard, the treasurer, and Amasa Walker, a member of the executive committee, were also active.[2]

Lack of money had always hindered the Society. It seldom realized the minimum $5,000 yearly revenue it deemed necessary to carry on operations—usually it managed on only $3,000. The Society issued numerous tracts, but their circulation was generally restricted to the northeast. The *Advocate of Peace* frequently came out bimonthly, rather than monthly as intended, because, its editor declared, "the slender income of our Society" was not enough.[3]

The American Peace Society did not suffer from a lack of would-be leaders. But after the death of Ladd there was no personality in the peace crusade comparable to Garrison or Weld in the antislavery movement. Of the major benevolent associations, the American Peace Society was the least energetic. In 1845 George Beckwith wrote, "The American Peace Society is engaged in a system of operations designed by the diffusion of light and love to produce a change of public sentiment respecting war, as shall lead nations to discard the sword as the arbiter of their disputes, and adopt in its place substitutes more rational, more Christian, and far more effective for all purposes of protection

2. Curti, pp. 42–60.
3. *Advocate of Peace*, Jan. 1845, p. 1.

and redress."[4] But these operations—tracts, meetings, petitions—were neither vigorous nor effectual.

The dispute within peace ranks over the question of defensive war did most to limit the effectiveness of the Society. In the early years of the crusade for peace the Reverend Noah Worcester refused to condemn defensive war. He believed the Scriptures sanctioned it. He also wished to enlist the services of those moderate pacifists who justified defensive war as necessary for the self-defense of a nation. The New York Peace Society, following the lead of David L. Dodge, opposed all war—defensive as well as offensive. The constitution of the American Peace Society purposely left the issue of defensive war unresolved, vaguely stating "We receive into our communion all who seek to abolish war." Dodge and others, especially Quakers, expressed dissatisfaction at the Society's glossing over such a vital point. Pressure from the opponents of defensive war increased until Ladd, at first reluctant to renounce all war, used his influence to commit the Society to such a course. In May, 1837, its constitution was amended so as to condemn defensive war. This action caused some conservatives to withdraw from the Society and others to complain. When in 1837 Beckwith became secretary of the Society and editor of its periodical, he sought the support of all peace men whatever their views on defensive war. Thus, in 1838 the Society, in a series of resolutions to clarify the amendment of the previous year, announced that the amendment was not intended to touch on "the right of private or individual self-defense, to a denial of which the Society is not committed."[5] For a while, harmony was restored among peace men.

But this proved ephemeral. There were extremists who desired more from the Society than just a disavowal of all

4. *Ibid.*, March, 1845, p. 25.
5. Curti, pp. 9–11, 66–90; Galpin, pp. 99–123.

war. Garrison, along with Edmund Quincy, Henry C. Wright, and the Reverends Adin Ballou and Samuel J. May, castigated the Peace Society "as radically defective in principle, and based upon the sand." These men, and their few but uncompromising followers, believed in non-resistance. They insisted on the inviolability of human life, denying that the government or any individual had the right to take a life for whatever reason. Garrison charged the Society with temporizing on peace principles in the same cowardly way the American Colonization Society dodged the slavery issue.[6] The Peace Society made an honest attempt to listen to, and if possible to appease, the peace extremists. All efforts failed, however, and peace extremists organized the New England Non-Resistance Society in September, 1838.

In a Declaration of Sentiments the New England Non-Resistance Society upheld the sacredness of human life and declared that, inasmuch as governments were "upheld by physical strength and its laws . . . enforced virtually at the point of the bayonet," non-resistants "cannot hold any office which imposes upon its incumbent the obligation to compel men to do right on pain of imprisonment or death." Non-resistants agreed to exclude themselves "from every legislative and judicial body, and to repudiate all human politics, worldly honors, and stations of authority." And, unlike the American Peace Society, this organization promised to link the peace cause to other reform projects.[7]

Though the New England Non-Resistance Society was always a small organization, many peace reformers were in general accord with its outlook. Amasa Walker agreed "with its members entirely in their leading principles,"[8]

6. F. J. and W. P. Garrison, *William Lloyd Garrison, The Story of His Life Told by His Children* (4 vols., New York, 1884–89), II, 222–235; Curti, pp. 75–80; Galpin, pp. 115–123.

7. Galpin, pp. 124–151; Curti, pp. 80–83.

8. Samuel E. Coues, MS Peace Album, Harvard University Library.

as did Ladd and Samuel E. Coues. But since these men would not become practicing anarchists, they steered clear of the non-resistants.

Elihu Burritt had become interested in peace inadvertently. In the summer of 1843 a Boston Baptist Society had invited him to give a series of lectures in the Tremont Theatre. The Baptists had just purchased the Theatre, and they hoped to pay for its renovation into a church by sponsoring public lectures.[9] Burritt began writing a scientific lecture on "The Anatomy of the Earth" for the engagement. He intended to show that nature, like the human body, was composed of interdependent parts, each indispensable to the proper functioning of the other parts and together forming an organic whole. While writing the lecture, he was "especially struck" by the marked variations in soil, climate, and topography even in those countries lying "within the same belt, and washed by the same sea." Such an arrangement was nature's way of binding "nation to nation . . . by the difference and the necessity of each other's productions." A "natural bond of peace and good neighborhood" existed to promote good will among men of all nations. Instead of writing a scientific lecture, he had written one on peace. He was then totally ignorant of the peace movement.[10]

Delivered in the Tremont Theatre on June 28, 1843, Burritt's peace lecture on the "Motives and Tendencies of International Peace,"[11] according to him, "chained the audience for 1½ hours"; some "of the first men of Boston . . . testified their gratification in a very excessive manner." He intended "to deliver it as often as opportunity opens" since "it may do good."

During the following year he gave numerous peace lec-

9. Journals, May 5, 12–13, 1843.
10. Burritt, Ten-Minute Talks, pp. 17–18.
11. Emancipator, June 22, 1843; Journals, June 26–29, 1843.

tures and made the acquaintance of many pacifists. In Portsmouth, New Hampshire, he met the president of the American Peace Society, Samuel E. Coues. Coues had heard much about Burritt, admired the straightforward peace principles of the *Christian Citizen,* and had contributed several articles to it. He was particularly pleased by the *Christian Citizen's* strong stand against defensive war. Burritt thought Coues "a man after my own heart; full of kindness and expanded philanthropy."[12] Coues brought Burritt into the small circle of peace radicals who like himself attacked the principle of defensive war: Amasa Walker, Joshua P. Blanchard, and the Reverend Aaron Foster.

From late 1844 until 1846 Burritt, aided by Walker, Coues and Blanchard, organized a series of peace conventions throughout Massachusetts for the purpose of promoting "the diffusion of correct sentiments on the subject of war." These conventions were neither authorized by the American Peace Society nor supported by its conservative members, since the principal question discussed was "whether all War is not inconsistent with the spirit of the gospel." Coues, among others, plainly spelled out the danger of justifying defensive war:

> If we may fight in defense of our lives, we may and must fight in defense of the lives of others; if we may fight in defense of others, we may fight in defense of our property; if in defense of our property, then we may fight in defense of political rights; if in defense of rights, then we may fight in promotion of our interests; next, in promotion of our glory and our crimes. The gradations by which we reach this climax are easy and inevitable.[13]

Though a minority in the American Peace Society, the anti-defensive war adherents were the most active peace

12. Journals, Oct. 13–14, 1844, Jan. 1, 1845.
13. *Christian Citizen,* Dec. 7, 14, 21, 1844.

workers and their influence belied their number. Their
strength and determination was evidenced when, at the
annual meeting of the Society in May, 1845, the executive
committee, appointed to manage the affairs of the organization for the coming year, was dominated by peace radicals. The committee proposed making Burritt the editor
of the *Advocate of Peace* "in order to lessen the expense
of publication and to introduce some salutary change in its
character." Beckwith, according to Burritt, "took the proposition very hard."[14]

Realizing the futility of trying to convince conservative
members of the Peace Society to espouse the abolition of
all war, Burritt and Amasa Walker established in 1846 the
Worcester County Peace Society. Its object was "the promotion of the cause of Peace and Universal Brotherhood;
and being founded on the principle that all war is utterly
inconsistent with the spirit of Christianity, will endeavor
to illustrate its baleful influence on all the great interests
of mankind, and devise means for insuring permanent and
Universal Peace"; Walker was president of the association,
and Burritt corresponding secretary. It was a very busy
radical peace society whose field of operations extended
beyond the boundaries of Worcester County and even
Massachusetts.[15]

The conservatives of the American Peace Society tried
not to get alarmed over the Worcester Society. Beckwith
welcomed the new peace organization, admitting that it
contained "able and devoted friends of peace."[16] But the
Worcester Society, in its stalwart condemnation of defensive war, was what it was intended to be from the start: a
rival of the American Peace Society.

14. Journals, March 25, May 31, 1845; Galpin, pp. 165–167.
15. *Advocate of Peace and Universal Brotherhood*, April, 1846, p.
101, May, 1846, pp. 127–128.
16. *Ibid.*, June, 1846, p. 145.

The national peace society refused to associate itself with any of the several moral reforms of the day. Burritt was not so scrupulous. He was prudent in not using the *Advocate of Peace and Universal Brotherhood*, as the Society's journal was now called, to champion any cause other than peace. But in the *Christian Citizen*, which by mid-1845 was the most powerful organ of American pacifism, he came close to interweaving the peace movement with temperance and antislaveryism. He also wrote convincingly against capital punishment, and there was no mistaking his interest in free trade.[17] The *New England Puritan*, a staid religious paper published in Boston, acidly asserted that the American Peace Society was "gradually falling into the hands of radical men, who have sought to subsidise it to purposes which nearly the whole Christian community regard with settled displeasure."[18] Beckwith, disquieted by such reports, denied that the Society was interfering "whatever with any other project or reform."[19]

At the 1846 annual convention of the American Peace Society the Burritt faction dominated the speechmaking. But the Beckwith group was able to control the nature of the resolutions introduced. Four resolutions were adopted which equivocated on defensive war and which demanded that the Society remain "distinct from anti-government, from the question of Capital Punishment, and all other extraneous subjects." The Society desired the support of all pacifists, "whatever their views respecting defensive wars."[20]

The position of the radicals in the American Peace Society steadily deteriorated after the conservatives pushed through their 1846 resolutions. Led by Beckwith, the conservatives considered devising a new constitution incor-

17. *Christian Citizen*, June 6, 13, 20, 1846.
18. Quoted *ibid.*, May 30, 1846.
19. *Advocate of Peace and Universal Brotherhood*, June, 1846, p. 142.
20. *Ibid.*, p. 137.

porating the resolutions. Burritt, who had sailed for England in June, 1846, was kept informed of the internal affairs of the Society. "Beckwith," he noted ominously in his Journal, "is working to reduce the moral basis of the A. P. Society to a lower standard to accomodate [sic] the peace advocates of *defensive war*." On December 3, 1846, he wrote his "farewell address to the Advocate and to the American Peace Society." He could not "remain connected with the society a moment after the prohibition of all war was taken out from its constitution and the lawfulness of defensive war was admitted."[21]

The December issue of the *Advocate of Peace and Universal Brotherhood* was the last under Burritt's editorship. Reviewing the progress the periodical had made while in his hands, he tried to restrain his anger at the Society. He harbored no grudge and trusted that "it may not prove detrimental to the cause of Peace, that our different roads have met and merged for the distance intercepted between the beginning and end of one year."[22]

Yet Burritt could not resist rebuking the narrow outlook of the Society. The radicals and conservatives, he declared, were "travelling, at least obliquely, in the same direction, though by different roads." The "one we have chosen leads through fields of broader and bolder enterprise; the one in which they prefer to walk . . . bends to merge with the easy highway of the multitude." The contemplated changes in the Society's constitution would "greatly facilitate the accession of numbers to the membership roll." There was "no disqualifying reason why the Mexican and American soldiers who stabbed at each other's hearts on the streets of Monterey, might not alternately subscribe to the highest article of faith remaining in the Society's creed, and that

21. Journals, Oct. 30, Dec. 3, 1846.
22. *Advocate of Peace and Universal Brotherhood*, Dec., 1846, pp. 273–276.

too, with the points of their bayonets newly dipped in human blood!" He ended on a note of eloquence and strength:

> Peace is a spirit, and not an intellectual abstraction: it is a life, not a theory. The separation to which we have alluded, and any other that may ensue in consequence of a change in the constitution of the American Peace Society, we devoutly hope will occasion no root, nor word, nor thought of bitterness or unfriendly controversy. In our own case they will not; and in the case of those who may withdraw with us we trust they will not; let us separate in *Peace*. Let no unkind thoughts mingle in the reminiscence of our union or disunion. The world is broad enough for us all; let there be no strife between us. The roads we are respectively taking diverge too far to bring us within the range of controversy.[23]

Having withdrawn as editor of the *Advocate*, Burritt quit the executive committee of the Society, to which he had been elected in 1845. Samuel Coues wrote a "manifesto to the public" announcing the resignation from the executive committee of himself, Burritt, Walker, Blanchard, and a few other radical pacifists. Though "a strict investigation" had exonerated the executive committee from having mingled other reforms with peace, Coues asserted that perhaps "the position of some of us as individuals, in regard to capital punishment, injures the Society."[24]

The American Peace Society did not draft a new constitution or amend the old one to appease the heavy preponderance of conservatives. To have altered the 1837 amendment condemning defensive war might have implied that the Society condoned the Mexican War. But Beckwith's influence and control became supreme.[25] The question of

23. *Ibid.*
24. *Ibid.*, 276–278; Journals, Dec. 17, 1846.
25. Curti, p. 96; *Christian Citizen*, June 5, 1847.

defensive war was conveniently overlooked as Beckwith
sought to restore harmony. The Peace Society, wrote a
bitter radical pacifist, had been "buried alive by the Jesuit-
ical maneuvres of [the] Rev. George C. Beckwith."[26] Those
who had relinquished their posts on the executive committee now looked to the multiple-reform association Burritt had organized in England in 1846 as the last best hope
for radical pacifism.

Though pacifists differed in their opinions as to what constituted war, and under what conditions self-defense was
proper for a nation or an individual, they were in unison in
attacking war as the greatest sin of mankind. The underlying consensus of pacifism was that war outrageously violated Christianity. If the Old Testament contained injunctions for war, the New Testament made war unnecessary
and unnatural: Christ was "the Prince of Peace." J. P.
Blanchard confessed "that in the history of the ancient Is-
raelites, there is much to countenance war in the directions
of God himself. But, he quickly added, "a new Gospel has
beamed upon the earth."[27] To Burritt "War and Christianity" was "the most stupendous incongruity that can be
found between the source of light and the center of utter
darkness."[28]

Burritt's peace postulates were akin to those advanced
by other pacifists. He dilated on old principles rather than
invented new ones. The *Kennebec Journal* was more impressed by the "enlarged and all pervading philanthropy"
of his first peace lecture than it was with its "over-sanguine"
ideas. It took notice of how Burritt disdained "all narrow

26. Frederic W. Holland, MS History of the American Peace Cause
(3 vols., compiled about 1865), I, 44–45, Boston Public Library.
27. *Christian Citizen*, Dec. 21, 1844.
28. Burritt, MS Lecture on the Constitutional Unity of Christians
and the Natural Bonds of Brotherhood, Connecticut Historical Society.

or national limits" and included "the whole family of man in his fraternal and cosmopolitan embrace."[29]

From the moment Burritt threw in with reformers, he fancied benevolence as a world-wide undertaking. "Our neighbor is Man!", he declared, "wherever he may be found, whatever may be the color of his skin, into whatever pit of misery and degradation he may have fallen." There were no limits to his conception of brotherhood. "Is your fellow-being of a skin not colored like your own; do you suspect him of poverty, guilt, or misery; is he a heretic, a Roman Catholic, an infidel or a pagan? He is your *brother* still; and no disparities of condition, character, or sentiment, will release you from the cardinal obligation of love." The "law of Love" was the "law of Gravitation in the moral world."[30]

Burritt's fundamental peace premise was the brotherhood of man and of nations. His excellent peace column in the *Christian Citizen* was capped by the words of St. Paul: "God Hath Made of One Blood All Nations of Men." He believed that peace was not only the natural condition of man but of nature as well:

> From the rain-drop world of the viewless animacule to the outer-most circumference of our solar system, reaching across the whole amplitude of mind and breathing and breathless matter, not even the archenemy of man himself could find a single *natural provision* for war: nor could an angel of light, following in his track, detect a single hieroglyphic that could show that the providence of God ever anticipated any other condition than *perpetual peace* among men.

The physical anatomy of the earth was meant for peace and brotherhood, he maintained, as God's purposeful con-

29. *Kennebec Journal*, Oct. 20, 1843.
30. *Christian Citizen*, Jan. 13, 1844; Burritt, *The Neighbors, or, The Samaritan Mirror* (Philadelphia, 1844).

struction of it indicated so clearly. Some observers might claim that the western and eastern hemispheres, because they varied so markedly in soil, climate and topography, were intended by God to remain aloof from each other. Burritt could not accept this view:

> Let me tell that anatomist to look again and see what St. Paul saw: let him trace the *effect* of this anomaly but a little way, and he will arrive at a glorious cause, a cause of causes, the very innermost divinity of the arrangement, which is nothing less than a physical provision to carry out the eternal truth, that 'God Hath made one blood of all nations of men,' and meant that they should feel and read it too in the unwritten statutes of nature. That every lack of physical correspondence between the two hemispheres, multiplies and subdivides necessities not only between different zones, but also within the same parallels of latitude all around the globe. It is the great sub-marine chain that connects China and Greenland, Siberia and Brazil; that chain whose links grow larger and larger as they approach the earth's extremes, and grapple together mutual antipodes with the hooks of steel. The Greenland hunter . . . wants *every thing* that the Chinese peasant can produce, and the New Englander wants *half* of the same productions; and that peasant wants everything that the arctic hunter can reach with his bow or harpoon, and *half* of what the New Englander can produce from his skill. So that the physical relations between different countries, increase in strength with their intervening distance. This arrangement to make one nation dependent on another is the primitive basis of international commerce and comity.[31]

Though most peace men refused to involve the cause in the other social crusades of the day, they admitted that peace was closely related to other reforms. Burritt thought it was the basic reform:

31. *Christian Citizen*, March 2, 1844.

War is a sin-breeding sin of sins, whose satanic progeny have filled the world with every form of violence, suffering, degradation, and misery, and preyed with their serpent teeth upon all the best interests of humanity. We despair of any permanent world-wide, transforming reform, until Christianity is divorced from its unnatural, ungodly wedlock with the spirit, the fiendish spirit of War.[32]

Political and economic injustices caused by war were standard peace arguments. Burritt's first peace lecture caricatured the War of 1812. For the "facts" on the war he had consulted Theodore Dwight's *History of the Hartford Convention* (1833), a book which seethed with New England's hatred of "Mr. Madison's War." Burritt averred that "there never was a war got up between two Christian nations upon such artificial and frivolous pretenses as our Last War with Great Britain." At a cost of 30,000 lives and $100,000,000 "the government invited the people to go into a jubilee of exultation over the brilliant exploits of our army and navy." This was all the nation got out of the war:

Not a principle had been established; not a question of controversy settled; not an inch of territory either gained or defined; nothing established but the solitary fact, that the Americans could fight and fight bravely, too, with or without a cause. The man that refused to exult at this fact, was suspected of treason and called a traitor.[33]

Burritt relished pointing out the financial waste of war. "The war-debts of the European nations amount to $10,000,000,000. It would require the labor of *four millions* of men, at $150 per annum for each man, to pay the *interest* of this sum at six per cent. To pay the principal, it would be necessary to levy a tax of at least TEN DOLLARS on

32. *Ibid.*, Jan. 18, 1845.
33. *Ibid.*, Jan. 13, 1844.

every inhabitant of the globe!" From 1789 to 1844 the United States had "expended on the War Department $663,438,851. The interest of this sum, at 6 per cent, would build Whitney's great railroad from the Lakes to the Pacific, of 2500 miles in length, at $15,000 per mile." Burritt liked to contrast arms expenditures in America with contributions received by benevolent societies. The federal government, he stated, "recently contracted with a private company in Connecticut for the supply of 30,000 pistols, at $6.50 each; or 195,000 dollars' worth of those weapons so much in vogue with duelists and assassins." The American Bible Society, on the other hand, "congratulates itself on receiving, the past year, $166,652, the aggregate of all that has been given through the Union for the dissemination of the Word of Life at home and abroad." Thus, "Christendom expends more in one year on the means and instruments of human slaughter, than has been given to the promulgation of the Gospel."[34]

He argued that it was the working class that shouldered the financial burdens of wars by being obliged to pay the military bills of earlier generations. A nation's war debt would always "be a great millstone about the neck" of future generations. Even if war debts were passed on from one generation to another, "we cannot get rid of the *interest* in this way." That had to be paid by the workingmen of each generation through "the purchase of every article of food and clothing, and, in some instances, for the very light of heaven through our windows."

For as long as he was engaged in the peace reform, Burritt pleaded with the working class in Europe and America to use its numerical strength to abolish war. First, he urged workingmen in America to vote only for those political leaders dedicated to peace principles. Then, a few years

34. *Advocate of Peace and Universal Brotherhood,* Jan., 1846, pp. 26–28; Feb., 1846, pp. 53–54.

after the establishment of the First International in 1862, he expressed the "hope" that "the working-men of Christendom will form one vast Trades Union, and make a universal and simultaneous *strike* against the whole war system." In an article on "The World's Working-men's Strike against War" he reached the conclusion that "the Great Powers" would be forced to maintain peace or else face "an organized strike" of all workers throughout the world.[35]

Through the "School Room" department of the *Christian Citizen*, Burritt informed children of the horrors of war. The column addressed the young as if they were adults, and on delicate matters pulled no punches:

> During all the ages of the human race, the People have not been the source nor the subject of Governments, but the victims of them, all bound like sheep for the slaughter, all ready to be immolated on what has been called, the *altar* of *National Glory*, and which has drunk more blood, both Christian and pagan, than all the Juggernauts of the world could have done, even had there been one of them in every neighborhood. Monstrous idolatry! Whose Christian name is *Patriotism*.[36]

Burritt devised peculiar arithmetical problems to impress juveniles with the "terrible vision and computation of blood" brought on by war.[37] Using Dr. Thomas Dick's estimate that 14,000,000,000 people had perished through wars, he posed two problems to the children: "Now, supposing that these men, women and children averaged 4 feet in length, and were placed along in a line on the ground, how many times would their bodies reach around the globe, admitting it to be 24,000 miles in circumference?" The other problem was

35. Curti, *The Learned Blacksmith*, pp. 36–37. *Bond of Brotherhood*, May, 1867, p. 79. *Fireside Words*, Oct., 1868, p. 159. Burritt, *Ten-Minute Talks*, pp. 265–266.
36. *Christian Citizen*, March 29, 1845.
37. Journals, Feb. 7, 1845.

just as ghastly: "The average weight of blood in a common-sized man is 28 lbs. and its quantity 3½ gallons. What would be the circumference of a circular lake, ten feet deep, which would hold all the blood of these fourteen thousand millions of human beings?"[38] One wonders how eagerly youthful readers awaited the next issue of the *Christian Citizen* to see if their answers matched Burritt's.

A major assumption of pacifists was that peace was practicable. They were not such visionaries that they did not think it imperative to construct a workable basis for world peace. The key to this basis was a Congress of Nations that would draft a body of international law, and a Supreme Court of Nations that would adjudicate disputes among nations according to such law.[39] Noah Worcester was the first American consistently to advocate the plan, but it was William Ladd's *Essay on a Congress of Nations,* published in 1840, that did most to stimulate pacifists. The nub of Ladd's scheme was simple:

1st. A congress of ambassadors from all those Christian and civilized nations who should choose to send them, for the purpose of settling the principles of international law by compact and agreement . . . and also of devising and promoting plans for the preservation of peace, and in meliorating the condition of man.

2nd. A court of nations composed of the most able civilians in the world, to arbitrate or judge such cases as should be brought before it, by mutual consent of two or more contending nations.[40]

38. *Christian Citizen,* Feb. 8, 1845.
39. For an excellent survey of the history of the movement for a Congress of Nations, see James B. Scott's "Introduction" to William Ladd's *Essay on a Congress of Nations* (New York, 1916), pp. ii–xiv.
40. William Ladd, *Essay on a Congress of Nations,* edited by James B. Scott, p. xxxix.

Burritt had not reasoned out the political and constitutional niceties of a Congress of Nations, but he stoutly defended the idea. "No political event," he wrote, "can transpire in the civilized world, which would so deeply affect the condition and prospects of mankind, as a Congress of Nations to form a code of International Law and a Supreme Court of the World, to which should be referred for final adjudication all questions of controversy which may arise between nations."[41] Amasa Walker and J. P. Blanchard agreed with Burritt.[42] At the peace conferences arranged by these three men the subject of a Congress of Nations was commonly discussed. Burritt would soon emerge as the world's leading champion of a Congress of Nations.

What was most remarkable about Burritt's contributions to pacifism was his uncanny knack for reaching a wide segment of the public with conventional peace notions. Believing that the success of the cause depended on the effectiveness of pacifists in bombarding people with the literature of peace, in 1845 he proposed to Walker and Blanchard "a plan of operations, which if adopted . . . will produce a salutary effect upon the public mind with regard to Peace." He urged that twenty-six peace reformers write a short article each week for the entire year; twenty-six newspapers, one from each state, could then be supplied with a weekly article. No newspaper would have the same writer furnish more than one article. "The public," explained Burritt, "would soon be impressed with the idea that there was a great change come over the press [as] our pens . . . circumscribe the Union."[43]

41. *Christian Citizen*, Oct. 25, 1845.
42. William Garrison to the Rev. Samuel J. May, Boston, Jan. 4, 1839, Boston Public Library; see Blanchard's article on a Congress of Nations in the *Advocate of Peace and Universal Brotherhood*, Feb., 1846, pp. 39–42.
43. Journals, Jan. 11, 31, 1845.

Walker, Blanchard, and Coues thought the idea too burdensome. Burritt, "disheartened" that his "magnificent system of effort" was passed over for "one of boyish expansion," was forced to find a method of reaching the public
that did not involve so much work. He initiated an ingenious plan which he called the "Olive Leaf Mission." He
"wrote a short [peace] article of about the length of a third
of a column of common newspaper, and printed it on a
small slip of paper, surmounted by a dove with an olive leaf
in its bill."[44] To a dozen newspapers he sent printed copies
of his first Olive Leaf, and was gratified that six published
it. This encouraged him to print more Olive Leaves and to
send them to more newspapers.

Within a month's time thirty newspapers on his exchange
list printed his Olive Leaves as regularly as he despatched
them. He guessed that "at least 100,000 minds" were being
reached by his articles every week. "I know not why I may
not put an article upon the subject of Peace into every
paper in the Union," he wrote, "and have it appear as
original." Soon he was transmitting 200 and then 1,000
Olive Leaves to various newspapers, "two hundred of which
gave them insertion." By 1846 he estimated that two million people read his Olive Leaves.[45]

The dove with the Olive Leaf in its bill became a familiar
messenger of peace throughout America. People read such
articles by Burritt as "War Must Cease If Christians Will
Not Fight", "The British Navy", and "A Word to American
Christians About War." He appraised their effect inordinately: "I believe the press throughout the free states has
been affected by operations in the cause of peace," and that
"my . . . plan has done more to disseminate its principles
than all that has been done by the Peace Society since its

44. Burritt, *Ten-Minute Talks*, p. 19.
45. Journals, March 17-April 26, 1846, *passim*. Burritt to George
Bancroft, Paris, April 21, 1849, Massachusetts Historical Society.

organization." His efforts required a sixteen-hour working day, but he was "in a state of moral exhilaration under the influence of my operations in the great reform." Though his funds were low, he reasoned that God would not allow a humanitarian to go hungry: "I have labored for months without the slightest reference or hardly provision for what I should eat or drink or wear, trusting that if my labors were such as God would approve, he would feed me on the same footing as the ravens." Coues, "from the spontaneity of his munificent heart," offered to accept Burritt's draft on him for any reasonable sum. To Burritt this was a sign of God's providence.[46]

Under Burritt's temporary aegis the *Advocate of Peace* was a much better periodical than it had been under Beckwith's management. He enlarged the journal and filled it with original material. Dr. Thomas Dick and the Reverend J. A. James furnished stimulating articles, as did Dr. Eliphalet Nott. Burritt appealed to Longfellow for an article after having published a few of his poems in the journal.[47] Garrison spoke highly of the "new dress" of the *Advocate* and with "all our heart" wished it success.[48]

Since Burritt wanted the most "gifted pens" to write for the *Advocate*, he sent a request to Charles Sumner. After July 4, 1845, the most talked-about peace man in America and England was Sumner, who "for years . . . had had an active, though quiet, interest in the peace movement."[49] Sumner's Fourth of July peace oration in Boston on "The True Grandeur of Nations" was a magnificent display of

46. Journals, April 2-May 17, 1845, *passim*. The entire cost of printing 1,500 Olive Leaves was five dollars. Burritt, *Thoughts and Notes at Home and Abroad* (London, 1868), p. 195.
47. Burritt to H. W. Longfellow, Worcester, April 27, 1846, Harvard University Library.
48. *Liberator*, Feb. 6, 1846.
49. David Donald, *Charles Sumner and the Coming of the Civil War*, p. 107.

eloquence if not of originality of profundity. Almost overnight the address thrust him to the head of the peace ranks.
With characteristic hyperbole Burritt wrote that Sumner's
speech "will be more read, will have a greater influence on
the Christian world, than any other which has been delivered since the [D]eclaration of [I]ndependence."[50] He told
Sumner that, "as the cause of Peace dates principally from
your oration, it becomes a 'Young America' of yours, and
you must in a degree father it."[51] Sumner obliged Burritt
by writing a short article for the *Advocate* entitled "The
Word 'Honorable'."

The most distinctive change introduced by Burritt in the
Advocate of Peace was broader coverage of peace activities
in Europe, especially England. Even before he assumed
editorial charge of the Society's journal, he had begun corresponding with British peace reformers. He sent many
copies of the *Christian Citizen* to England, as well as Olive
Leaves to British newspapers. He kept the Reverend John
Jefferson, secretary of the London Peace Society, informed
of the progress and plans of American pacifists and stressed
the need for closer international ties.[52]

Forces were at work which soon brought American and
British pacifists into each other's arms. America in the
forties was in an expansionist mood. Polk had been elected
president in 1844 on a platform which called for the "re-
occupation of Oregon" and the "re-annexation of Texas."
It was a slogan quite congenial to a restless America whose
people for over half a century had been rapidly spilling into
the West, but it was also one which frightened pacifists.
The annexation of Texas was closely followed by the outbreak of war with Mexico in 1846. There was also the threat

50. *Advocate of Peace*, Sept. & Oct., 1845, p. 98.
51. Burritt to Charles Sumner, Worcester, Nov. 19, 1845, Harvard
University Library.
52. Journals, April 26, 1846.

that the United States and Great Britain would go to war over the Oregon boundary dispute.

Burritt was disgusted by the Mexican War, of course, but he was appalled at the possibility of war with England. It "would be the greatest curse that has visited this world since the fall of man!", he wrote. "If this world is ever to be redeemed from the tyranny of darkness and despotism of sin, it will, it must be done through the Anglo-Saxon race."[53] The American Revolution, he had earlier written to the English minister J. A. James, "when it dissolved our political connection, severed the weakest tie that bound us to our mother land."[54]

British Quakers originated a program they hoped would avert war between Great Britain and the United States. Joseph Crosfield, a Manchester Quaker and devoted peace man, drafted an *Appeal to the Merchants of the Realm* of Great Britain which implored them to urge American merchants to demand arbitration of the Oregon controversy. Crosfield sent Burritt a copy of the *Appeal* and asked him to have it inserted in American newspapers, explaining that he had singled him out because "thy name is quite familiar to us."[55] Crosfield hoped that the *Appeal* would lead to an exchange of similar declarations of peace, or "International and Friendly Addresses," as he called them, between the two countries.

Burritt converted the *Appeal* into an Olive Leaf and printed 1,500 copies.[56] He sent a copy to 800 American newspapers, to every member of Congress, and to 200 newspapers in Great Britain; the rest he intended "to address to eminent merchants in different parts of the Union, so that

53. *Christian Citizen*, Feb. 15, 1845.

54. Burritt to the Rev. J. A. James, Worcester, Oct. 25, 1843; Columbia University Library.

55. *Advocate of Peace and Universal Brotherhood*, March, 1846, pp. 69–72.

56. For a copy of that Olive Leaf, see *ibid.*

they may be prepared to receive and answer the communications which the next steamer will probably bring over." Burritt was "grateful," as he wrote the New York merchant William E. Dodge, "that the cause of peace has such eminent friends among those who guide the Commerce of the world."[57]

The *Appeal* was almost as much a plea for free trade as it was for peace. Many British pacifists, including Crosfield, Joseph Sturge, William Cunningham, and George Bradshaw, were backers of the Anti-Corn Law League which for seven years had been working to undo the remaining props of England's protectionism. They contended that free trade would advance the cause of peace. Both Richard Cobden and John Bright, leaders of the fight for cheap bread, "considered freer trade not an end in itself but chiefly a means by which to promote international peace."[58] Burritt believed "FREE TRADE, the Commercial Harbinger of the Millennium . . . is crossing the threshold of this hate-seared world, to fuse the nations into one peaceful and happy brotherhood."[59] But he was a pacifist first, and a free trader solely as it pertained to international peace and brotherhood. His understanding of the connection between peace and free trade came from his association with Amasa Walker, one of America's best known economists.

Burritt wrote Crosfield that "the prospect of unrestricted Social and Commercial intercourse makes my heart palpitate for joy; especially in view of the interesting and intimate union in which it will merge our two great nations." He suggested that English towns and cities exchange

57. Burritt to William E. Dodge, Worcester, Feb. 13, 1846, American Antiquarian Society.

58. Herman Ausubel, *John Bright, Victorian Reformer* (New York, 1966) p. 114; J. A. Hobson, *Richard Cobden, the International Man* (London, 1918), p. 37.

59. *Advocate of Peace and Universal Brotherhood*, March, 1846, pp. 79–80.

Friendly Addresses with their "namesakes" in America: "a Boston for a Boston; a Rochester for Rochester; New London for London; Worcester for Worcester; Norwich for Norwich." He recommended that each Address be signed by as many citizens of each town as possible. The idea fascinated Crosfield.

Burritt became the agent in America and Crosfield the agent in England for the distribution of Friendly Addresses. There ensued a brisk exchange of these messages. The New York Address to the residents of York, England, was signed "by 400 most respectable and influential citizens." The Friendly Address from New England's Boston to Old England's Boston was signed by Josiah Quincy, Jr., the mayor, and George Hillard, president of the city's Common Council. Burritt had asked Sumner to write the Address and to "get it subscribed to by one or two hundred of the leading citizens of Boston."[60] The most interesting Friendly Address from England came from the National Association for Promoting the Political and Social Improvement of the People. Written by William Lovett (the founder of that society and one of the principal leaders of the "moral force" Chartists during the late thirties and early forties), it exhorted American laborers not to be deluded into thinking that war promoted prosperity.[61]

English ladies wasted no time getting into the act. Almost 1,700 signatures of females were affixed to the Address sent from Exeter, England, to the women of Philadelphia and the United States generally. Burritt entreated Mrs. Sigourney "to write a response . . . to this love-breathing message from your English sisters." Her "genius" in the movement, he told her, "would mark a new era in Woman's

60. *Ibid.*, pp. 123–124; Burritt to Charles Sumner, Worcester, Feb. 23, 1846, Harvard University Library.
61. *Advocate of Peace and Universal Brotherhood*, April, 1846, pp. 91–95.

influence on the destiny of the race."[62] Mrs. Sigourney wrote an *Address From Many Ladies in New England to those of Great Britain*. Burritt arranged an Address from Philadelphia ladies; Lucretia Mott headed the committee which secured 3,000 signatures for that Address.

About thirty Friendly Addresses were exchanged between Great Britain and America during the Oregon controversy. The most effective was that sent from Edinburgh, Scotland, to Washington, D. C. Burritt personally showed the Edinburgh Address to numerous congressmen in Washington, including Calhoun, "who read the address, and looked at the signatures with much interest." Calhoun informed Burritt that he "cordially approved of the expression of such sentiments in direct communications between the people of one country and the citizens of another, on questions of such vital importance to both"; the Senator promised to use his influence "to effect an amicable arrangement of the existing difficulty."[63]

Lewis Tappan wrote Joseph Sturge, an outstanding Quaker philanthropist and reformer from Birmingham, England, that the "peace addresses . . . are producing a most beneficial effect in the United States." Sturge testified to their authority in Great Britain.[64] When the Oregon controversy was finally settled in June, 1846, peace reformers on both sides of the Atlantic congratulated themselves. It is impossible to gauge the role of Friendly Addresses and other forms of peace propaganda in cooling off national

62. Burritt to Mrs. Sigourney, Worcester, June 1, 1846, Boston Public Library; Burritt to Mrs. Sigourney, New Britain, June 11, 1846, Klingberg Collection.

63. Burritt, *Ten-Minute Talks*, p. 20; Burritt to Samuel S. Green, New Britain, April 16, 1874, in *Proceedings* of the American Antiquarian Society (Worcester, 1905), Vol. XVI, p. 280.

64. Henry Richard, *Memoirs of Joseph Sturge* (London, 1865), p. 405. Sturge to Burritt, Birmingham, Mar. 3, 1846, Central Connecticut State College Library.

tempers, but their influence was probably negligible. The most significant achievement of Friendly Addresses was that they drew American and British pacifists closer together.

While editing the *Christian Citizen*, the *Advocate of Peace and Universal Brotherhood*, supplying weekly Olive Leaves to 200 newspapers and carrying the brunt of the American end of the Friendly Address movement, Burritt was still not convinced that public opinion was surfeited on the subject of peace. He decided to issue "a little way messenger of peace, under the title of 'The Bond of Brotherhood.' " This was a small four-page sheet filled with "short spicy articles . . . on the subject of Peace and War." He thought the *Bond* ideal for free distribution at railway stations and other thoroughfares of travel. The Reverend J. W. Walker took charge of distributing the *Bond* in Cleveland, and the Reverend Samuel J. May supervised circulation in the railroad cars and canal boats that passed through Syracuse. Burritt hired "six bright lads" to hand out the small sheet at several railroad depots in Massachusetts.[65]

Most of the material in the *Bond* was written by Burritt, but occasionally it included articles from other peace men, such as Charles Sumner. Assorted anecdotes and epigrams relating to war and peace made the publication quite lively. A typical barb was: "A Qualification for the Presidency: The scalp of an Indian Chief shot by a common soldier."[66] Large numbers of the *Bond* were forwarded to England, particularly the issue which contained extracts from Calhoun's Senate speech in favor of an amicable adjustment of the Oregon boundary dispute. "However obnoxious the sentiments of Calhoun may be with regard to slavery,"

65. *Advocate of Peace and Universal Brotherhood*, April, 1846, p. 104, May, 1846, p. 128, June, 1846, p. 132, 143; *Christian Citizen*, June 13, 1846.

66. *Bond of Brotherhood*, June 10, 1846.

Burritt wrote, "still those which he uttered in the senate
on the subject of Peace & War, are certainly generous and
enlightened, and I think they will do a great deal of good
if read and published extensively in England."[67]

The American Peace Society had been busy in 1846.
George Beckwith lectured on peace, wrote many articles,
and was engaged in drumming up sales for a volume of
peace tracts he had printed at his own expense.[68] These
tracts, over sixty in number and written over a period of
years by eminent peace men, were not widely circulated.
Burritt considered the *Bond* "more happily adapted to
gratuitous distribution than mere tracts." The Peace Society
was moving ahead, but Burritt was moving faster. It is fair
to say that by 1846 he was the most dynamic figure in the
American peace movement. Certainly he was the hardest
working, and this is what impressed fellow pacifists, even
those who were not opposed to defensive war. He had not
added much to the ideology of peace, but he had given
the reform a new élan, a sense of action and direction. Not
since William Ladd's death had pacifists, conservative and
radical alike, seen such propulsive leadership.

In the spring of 1846 Burritt made up his mind to visit
England for a few months. He planned to make a foot tour
of England, as he stated in his autobiography, and perhaps
to write a book on his travels. He also wished to meet the
British peace reformers with whom he corresponded.[69] Burritt knew he would be welcomed in Great Britain. Douglas
Jerrold, the popular British journalist, had praised his Olive
Leaves and published in his *Shilling Magazine* the letter
he had written to Burritt. Jerrold's letter established in

67. Burritt to [?] Worcester, March 30, 1846, Boston Public Library.

68. George Beckwith, ed., *The Book of Peace: A Collection of
Essays on War and Peace* (Boston, 1845).

69. Burritt to [A. Southall], London, June 11, 1851, Friends House
Library, London.

Great Britain the sentimental stereotype of Burritt so well known in America:

> It's a fine thing to think of you, Elihu Burritt, Blacksmith. To see you, working all day—making your anvil ring again with glorious labor (how I should like just a set of shoes for my mare of your own making), to see you forging anything but swords and bayonets—and when *that* work is over, to think of you sitting down, with your iron pen in your hand, working away, to weld men's hearts together—to make the chain of peace, as your own Red Men say, between America, and England—and to keep it bright for ever. When I think of this work of yours I'm pretty sure that your true-hearted countryman Longfellow must have had you in his brain, when he painted the pictures of *his* blacksmith.[70]

The *Christian Observer*, the journal of the Religious Tract Society in England, publicized the news of Burritt's expected sojourn and acknowledged the favorable reception in England of both his Olive Leaves and the *Bond of Brotherhood*. His "zealous exertions to suppress slavery, to promote temperance, and to blunt the appetite of nations for war have been honorable to his character as a philanthropist and a Christian; and his labors have produced a considerable effect in his country, and have elicited many friendly memories from ours."[71]

Such British esteem for Burritt was shared by most reformers and philanthropists in America. But there were a few detractors. Cornelius Felton, a Harvard professor, cautioned Charles Sumner not to associate with the "one-idead enthusiasts" because, though "amiable and philanthropic," they were "flat." "Burritt," Felton remarked, "is silly. He

70. *Advocate of Peace and Universal Brotherhood*, May, 1846, p. 117.
71. Reprinted in *Littell's Living Age*, X (Sept. 1846), pp. 486–488.

and the rest of them write about you and talk to you like sentimental idiots."[72] Edmund Quincy said Burritt lacked "moral courage" and was "fitted for the caliber of the Peace Society and for the Third [Liberty] Party." Quincy "never heard of any warrior or slaveholder, or proslavery or fighting person that was offended by anything he has said."[73]

With considerably more in mind than just making a pedestrian tour of England or meeting peace correspondents Burritt decided to visit England. His "principal object was to associate, or to organize into a union, the friends of peace on both sides of the Atlantic."[74] He went to England with a definite plan, for which Amasa Walker was largely responsible. After reading Burritt's article in the *Christian Citizen* suggesting an "Anti-Slavery League of the World," Walker adumbrated a master plan of universal reform. He recommended

a *league*, not only against Slavery, but against war, intemperance, restrictions upon the trade of nations, and everything injurious to the universal interests of man; a league that could unite all hearts, all sects, all parties, all religions; one which might include Cobden and his associates who are struggling to abolish the Corn Laws of England, and give free trade to the world; O'Connell and his co-laborers, who are peacefully battling for Ireland's emancipation; Joseph Sturge and his friends who raise the banner of Universal Suffrage; Father Mathew and every Teetotaler on the

72. Cornelius Felton to Charles Sumner, n.p., n.d., Harvard University Library. This letter was written very soon after Sumner's memorable 1845 Fourth of July peace oration. At one of the peace conventions in Massachusetts sponsored by Burritt in 1844, Felton arose from the audience to speak in favor of defensive war. *Christian Citizen*, Dec. 21, 1844.

73. Edmund Quincy to R. D. Webb, Dedham, May 23, 1846, Boston Public Library.

74. Burritt to George Bancroft, Paris, April 21, 1849, Massachusetts Historical Society.

Globe; the great anti-slavery host on both sides of the Atlantic; the Peace men of all nations; in short, all who, in any department of moral effort, are striving for the elevation and improvement of man; a LEAGUE OF UNIVERSAL BROTHERHOOD.[75]

Evangelicalism had utterly intoxicated Burritt with the sublime vision of universal brotherhood. As he had outgrown the narrower spheres of temperance and antislaveryism, so he began to feel somewhat confined by the peace crusade. Now he was for universal brotherhood immediately achieved. Having borrowed money from Joseph Sturge and Lewis Tappan, and having made arrangements for the continuation of the *Christian Citizen* during his absence, he departed for England aboard the *Hibernia* on June 16, 1846.[76] Ironically—Burritt would have said providentially—also traveling aboard that ship was official news of the settlement of the Oregon controversy.[77] About a month after he sailed from America, he established in England the League of Universal Brotherhood. His attempt at the evangelization of the world was under way.

75. *Christian Citizen*, Feb. 7, 1846.

76. Joseph Sturge to Burritt, April 3, 1846, Swarthmore Friends Historical Library; Burritt to Lewis Tappan, Worcester, May 1, June 11, 1846, Library of Congress.

77. Burritt, *Ten-Minute Talks*, p. 20.

7

The League of
Universal Brotherhood

No mere whim induced Burritt to select England as the country in which to establish the international humanitarian society he had in mind. There was a long tradition of philanthropy and reform in England, and Burritt was well-acquainted with the good works of the Evangelical Churchmen and the Dissenters. Since the early 1800's Protestants in England and America had formulated an ideology of Evangelical Protestantism to redeem a wicked world and had established numerous benevolent societies as instruments of that redemption. A thriving Anglo-American community of humanitarian endeavor existed throughout the first half of the 19th century. British and American reformers continually travelled the Atlantic to aid, advise, and comfort one another. Moreover, they had organized in London "World" conventions on antislavery (1840, 1843) and peace (1843), and planned an international temperance convention for 1846.[1] Thus, when Burritt arrived in England in the summer of 1846, he knew he would be at home among his evangelical cousins.

Neither Dissenters nor the evangelical party within the

1. Frank Thistlethwaite, *America and the Atlantic Community, Anglo-American Aspects, 1790–1850* (New York, 1963), pp. 76–150.

Anglican Church monopolized the humanitarian and moral reform projects that abounded in 1846. The Quakers had been, and still were, active in antislavery work, but the same was true of Evangelical Churchmen. Temperance "was not in fact necessarily either a sectarian or a party agitation."[2] The leadership of the peace movement was not confined to any sect. Charity for the poor and destitute, agitation for prison reform and against capital punishment, the establishment of "ragged" schools, were but a few of the many benevolent activities preoccupying humanitarians of nearly every religious denomination.[3] Sectarianism remained strong, but it was no necessary barrier to benevolence.

Burritt lost no time getting to work once he reached England. He traveled widely, meeting peace reformers and urging the international reform society he was about to establish.[4] In Worcester, England, in July he wrote the pledge for the League of Universal Brotherhood he hoped to establish:

Believing all war to be inconsistent with the spirit of Christianity, and destructive to the best interests of mankind, I do hereby pledge myself never to enlist or enter into any army or navy, or to yield any voluntary support or sanction to the preparation for or prosecution of any war, by whomsoever, for whatsoever proposed, declared or waged. And I do hereby associate myself with all persons, of whatever country, condition, or colour, who have signed, or shall hereafter sign this pledge, in a "League of Universal Brotherhood"; whose object shall be, to employ all legitimate and moral means for the abolition of all war, and all the spirit and all the manifestations of war throughout the

2. G. Kitson Clark, *The Making of Victorian England* (Cambridge, 1962), p. 199.

3. David Owen, *English Philanthropy, 1660–1960* (Cambridge, 1964), pp. 134–181.

4. Burritt to Henry C. Wright, Liverpool, July 4, 1846, Boston Public Library.

world; for the abolition of all restrictions upon international correspondence and friendly intercourse, and of whatever else tends to make enemies of nations, or prevents their fusion into one peaceful brotherhood; for the abolition of all institutions and customs which do not recognize and respect the image of God and a human brother in every man of whatever clime, colour, or condition of humanity.[5]

The League of Universal Brotherhood got its start in the village of Pershore shortly after Burritt wrote the pledge. William Conn and George-Cross, both woolstaplers from Pershore, had heard Burritt lecture on peace in nearby Worcester. When they saw Burritt walking in their village a few days later, they invited him to tea. Conn and Cross, local temperance advocates, discussed peace with Burritt. They told him that the English government would experience difficulty filling militia quotas because of the widespread peace sentiment among the people, and that, if their own names were drawn for militia duty, they would refuse to serve. On hearing this, Burritt shouted, "That's just what I want! and if I could find only half a dozen men on this side the water, who would band themselves together, declaring that they would have nothing to do with war, and would sign a pledge," then the League of Universal Brotherhood would become a reality. He recited the pledge from memory to Conn and Cross, who stated that signatures could be secured in Pershore. On the evening of July 29, Burritt read the pledge from a "little clasped-book" to twenty laborers who had gathered in Conn's house. He explained its meaning and implications along with the aims of the League of which they would be the first members. Eighteen persons signed the pledge, including Burritt. The group then knelt in prayer. "It was a solemn moment," reported Conn, "and never will the scene be effaced from

5. Burritt, *Ten-Minute Talks*, p. 21; Journals, Dec. 25, 1847.

my memory." As for Burritt, he knew that "Providence" had "detained" him in Pershore "for some great purpose."[6]

Admittance into the League was simple. Upon signing the pledge, any male or female over twelve years of age became a member. The pledge not only proscribed all war, but committed the signer to total abstinence from military service and bordered on non-resistance. It was ambiguous, however, in commanding individuals not "to yield any voluntary support or sanction to the preparation for or prosecution of any war." Technically, as some of the critics of the pledge pointed out, it forbade the paying of taxes, since much of any government's tax revenue was used for military purposes. Burritt ignored this interpretation, paid taxes, and believed the word "voluntary" allowed a Leaguer to pay taxes in good conscience.

The pledge was as broad as it was bold. Its essential premise was the literal understanding Burritt had of the Biblical statement, "God Hath Made of One Blood All Nations of Men." For Burritt this justified the formation of a benevolent society on the widest possible basis—one that recognized and accepted, in the words of the pledge, "a human brother in every man, of whatever clime, colour, or condition of humanity." Burritt explained to Garrison, who was in England, that the League "would be to Slavery, War, Intemperance, Ignorance, Political & Social Inequalities what the Anti-Corn League was to Monopoly in this country."[7]

Joseph Sturge, a Birmingham Quaker and an early signer of the pledge, was one of the League's chief supporters. Sturge had been an heroic figure in the British antislavery movement which had led to the Emancipation Act of 1833.

6. See William Conn's letter relating the incidents of the birth of the League in the *Christian Citizen*, Dec. 11, 1847.
7. Burritt to W. L. Garrison, Frome, Sept. 8, 1846, Boston Public Library.

In 1841 he had organized the Complete Suffrage Union to unite Chartism with middle-class radicalism. Sturge had been willing to endorse the Six Points of political democracy found in the People's Charter, but he had insisted upon giving them another form and the Charter another name. The "moral force" Chartists had objected to the proposed change, and on this point the Complete Suffrage Union had foundered. Sturge had also been active in the Anti-Corn League movement; but his conviction that free trade could not be won until the Charter, or its equivalent, was accepted by the government, as well as his advocacy of the exclusion from British ports of slave-grown produce, had alienated him from the Anti-Corn Law League. By 1843 he had "retreated from politics to crusading for the causes in which he had a purely moral faith."[8]

Sturge introduced Burritt's League to prominent British philanthropists and reformers. At a social gathering of the delegates of the World's Temperance Convention in London, on August 5, 1846, he spoke generously of it. Burritt, who had attended the Temperance Convention, talked to the delegates about its purpose. They seemed interested, and he passed around a few copies of the pledge. About seventy persons signed, among whom were some of Great Britain's better known humanitarians: James Haughton, a Dublin Unitarian involved in temperance, antislaveryism, and peace; Thomas Harvey, a Leeds Quaker and antislavery associate of Sturge; the Reverend John Jefferson, secretary of the London Peace Society; the Reverend John Campbell, an influential Congregationalist editor of the *Christian Witness* and the *Christian's Penny Magazine*; and Lawrence Heyworth, a wealthy Liverpool philanthropist and free trader.[9]

8. G. D. H. Cole, *Chartist Portraits* (London, 1941), pp. 163–186.
9. *Advocate of Peace and Universal Brotherhood*, Oct., 1846, pp. 244–245.

Burritt went "from place to place on foot, holding special meetings in private houses and trying to interest people" in the League. He "succeeded," he wrote Garrison, "beyond all my expectations."[10] Lecturing on "The Elements and Agents of Universal Brotherhood", he explained why the League coincided with the main social currents of the day:

> No one who keeps his eye out upon passing events can fail to observe and admire the social tendencies of the times. No philanthropist can contemplate their silent and peaceful influence, without being inspired with the hope of a better day for his race. The social principle has been operating upon human nature on a small scale up to the present day. It has been at work for ages, linking hearts into small societies. The boundary of a nation has hitherto been the limit of its attraction. But the world has just entered a new period of its centralizing power. It began with associating two hearts; and then went on associating hamlets, towns, counties, states and provinces into a nation. It has now become an irresistible force of centripetal attraction, drawing nations together toward the Sun, Source, and Centre of Universal Brotherhood.

The social principle, Burritt declared, begins to operate when two individuals band together for some moral purpose. Their efforts will lead to the creation of a local reform society which will in time expand into a county association. Eventually there will emerge a national and finally a world's reform society. Burritt cited the temperance and antislavery movements as proof of the irresistible force of the social principle. In addition "to all this centripetal attraction of the social principle in the moral world," there existed several "agents" of universal brotherhood: first, commerce was "weaving the nations together in the hempen web of coarser interests"; second, the steam engine was

10. Burritt to W. L. Garrison, Frome, Sept. 8, 1846.

"reducing oceans to a river's width, bringing the compass of a continent within the travel of a day, compressing sea-divided nations into immediate neighborhood"; and fourth, through the telegraph "man has webbed the whole earth with a network of his magnetic wires, so that in the twinkling of the eye, he could thrill all that dwelt thereon, with an unwhispered thought of his heart." Should Christianity keep pace with mechanical progress in drawing together all men and nations, then universal brotherhood, "a nice family circle of mankind," would be achieved.

But who was going to capitalize on these social elements and mechanical agents for the promotion of universal brotherhood? "Why, who else . . . but that wonderful Anglo-Saxon race, that is diffusing itself and its genius over the world? . . . If British and American Christians do their duty, the boy is at school who will live to see half the human family speaking the English language, and half the habitable surface of the globe covered with the Anglo-Saxon race, and blessed with its civilization." But how was the Anglo-Saxon race to accomplish this exalted mission? Through the League of Universal Brotherhood, of course.

In September, 1846, Burritt called the attention of Americans to the League through the *Christian Citizen*. Two clasped hands surmounted the pledge, beneath which were the names of 160 Britishers who had signed. Burritt announced that the League was "something more than a mere *peace* society." Most of its operations would "be more remedial, educational, and upbuilding, than destructive in their character." This was because the League was "based upon the whole compass of the principle, that every man is bound to be as much a brother as God is a father, to every human being, however deep may be the moral darkness and degradation of that being."[11]

11. *Christian Citizen*, Sept. 12, 19, 1846.

Having introduced the League to Britishers and Americans, Burritt set out "to get up little conversational meetings" throughout Great Britain for the purpose of organizing local League branches. He began publishing the *Bond of Brotherhood*, which became the official organ of the League, to assist in advertising his benevolent society. But the *Bond* did not spare him from the arduous task of travelling far and wide in search of pledge signatures.

Scarcely a day passed when he was not lecturing on the League or on peace, explaining the League to small, informal groups, writing for the *Christian Citizen* and the *Bond*, and dashing off as many as fifty letters. His daily routine is fairly illustrated by the way he spent September 25, 1846, in Exeter. Though "in a state of nervous debility," he lectured on peace to 1,200 people. Then he presented to the ladies of Exeter from the ladies of Philadelphia a Friendly Address which, to accommodate the more than 3,000 signatures appended to it, was nearly fifty feet long. Next he read Mrs. Sigourney's *Friendly Address from the Ladies of New England*, "and made some remarks upon the interesting interchange of kind and pacific sentiments which had been elicited during the past year." Finally he returned to the residence of his wealthy Quaker host John Dymond "about 11 P.M. in a wretched condition, to which I became insensible about 4 in the morning."

Burritt had his first opportunity in November to broach the League to a London audience. When he completed his talk by reading aloud the League pledge, "the whole house echoed and resounded with the most enthusiastic acclamation of applause. Men swung their hats and ladies waved their handkerchiefs in token of their approbation of the principle." Many from the audience came up to shake his hand, and several people asked for his autograph.

British Quakers were by far the strongest supporters of the League. Without their encouragement, assistance, and money the League would not have progressed much beyond Pershore. Sturge put £100 at Burritt's disposal "to aid in the promotion of the . . . League." But more important, he introduced Burritt to the right people and allowed him to use his name as a sponsor. Quakers from all over Great Britain contributed large and small sums of money. Burritt's "Three Manchester Friends"—Joseph Crosfield, William Cunningham, and George Bradshaw—gave considerable time and energy in publicizing the League. James Clark, a wealthy Quaker manufacturer, "secured nearly 100 names to the pledge, embracing some of the most respectable members of English society." Female Friends too were very helpful in getting pledge signatures. A Quaker meeting house was the easiest place for Burritt to get an audience and signatures.[12]

Burritt had outgrown his earlier disdain for Quaker meetings. He attended many and seldom missed the Yearly Meeting. "In the evening," he recorded in his Journal in 1847, "I attended another silent service, which I begin to enjoy." Four years later he wrote, "I like the simple worship of the Friends, and feel myself surrounded with the most precious influences when in their midst."[13] He was "deeply indebted to the kindness of Friends for admitting me to privileges which are very rarely accorded to those from without their communion."[14] His letters to Quakers were usually interspersed with "thee's" and "thou's".

It was the earnest social conscience of British Quakers, rather than their mode of worship, that endeared them to him. He could never fully appreciate Quaker silent services. He thought it "a pity that the Friends eschew reading the Scriptures in the Meetings. This would tend to concentrate

12. Journals, Sept. 25-Dec. 23, 1846, passim; May 28, 1847.
13. Ibid., July 27, 1847, May 25, 1851.
14. Burritt to [Southall], Ackworth, July 6, 1851, Friends House Library.

their thoughts upon a certain train of meditation and furnish matter for exhortation . . . I like their simple way of speaking when the spirit moves, but believe the spirit would move more frequently if they would read aloud a few chapters."[15]

The Unitarians were useful during the early stages of the League, though they were much less central than the Quakers. Mary Carpenter, who was engaged in reform work among delinquent children, assisted in the formation of a League branch in Bristol, as did Dr. J. B. Estlin, a prominent surgeon and philanthropist. William Rathbone, a Liverpool philanthropist who had once been a Quaker, contributed money to the League; Richard Rathbone, William's brother, never signed the League pledge, but he admired Burritt and gave money for League operations.[16]

Burritt's relationship with the Unitarians was actually never close. It seemed intimate, however, when in October, 1846, a memoir written by the popular Quaker journalist Mary Howitt appeared in the *People's Journal*, to which the Unitarians were "principal contributors."[17] Sturge advised Burritt against "identifying" himself with that sect. Other Quakers told him "to adopt non-intercourse with the Unitarians, and not salute them as neighbors." Burritt was surprised that pacifists in Leeds, most of whom were Quakers, frowned on the "idea of associating with a Unitarian even in a work of mercy." "Sectarianism," he observed, "is exceedingly alert in this country, and bitter in its manifestations." He wrote to Sturge "expressing pretty fully

15. Journals, May 2, July 16, 1852. Burritt found American Quakers more "exclusive" than those he met in Great Britain and "less disposed to unite with other denominations." Yet they were "more prepared than any other class in America to assist the League."
16. Journals, Sept. 30, Oct. 9, Nov. 28, 1846; June 7, 1847.
17. Mary Howitt's *Memoir of Elihu Burritt* is in Burritt, *Thoughts and Things*, pp. v–xxvi; *People's Journal*, Oct. 31, 1846, pp. 239–246.

my view of the spirit of sectarianism."[18] And he never refused aid from the Unitarians.

Many free traders who had been associated with the Anti-Corn Law League, including the president, George Wilson, signed the League pledge. Free traders had been exponents of peace for many years and following the repeal of the Corn Laws they became more active in peace work. Joseph Crosfield and William Cunningham helped to establish a large League branch in Manchester, and they made arrangements for Burritt to address free-trade gatherings throughout England. Burritt foresaw a day when George Wilson would "become President of the League of Universal Brotherhood, when its circumference shall embrace thousands of every civilized nation on the globe."[19] But while free traders had respect for the League, most of them preferred to work with the London Peace Society.

Burritt's organizational work for the League was hampered by the numerous social calls he received and by those he was expected to make. He did not fully anticipate the great fuss Britishers made over him. Dr. J. B. Estlin remarked that Burritt had "occasioned much interest" in Bristol. On the day Burritt gave a peace lecture in Bristol, men and boys were "parading the streets with placards announcing the 'American Blacksmith.'" John Wigham, a Scottish Quaker reformer, witnessed the rousing success Burritt enjoyed in Scotland.[20]

His reputation as a profound scholar of languages had

18. Journals, Sept. 21–22, Oct. 26, 1846, Sept. 6, 1847, Sept. 12, 1851. About five years after Burritt's *Memoir* appeared in the *People's Journal*, he was told of one lady who thought he was a Unitarian and therefore refused to read his writings "lest they should be dangerous."

19. Journals, Oct. 12, Nov. 18–19, 1846.

20. J. B. Estlin to Samuel J. May, [Bristol], Sept. 3, 1846, Boston Public Library; Journals, Sept. 30, 1846; John Wigham to Maria Weston Chapman, Jan. 4, 1847, Boston Public Library.

preceded him to England.[21] Burritt sensed the fact that many people attended his lectures to see what a self-taught blacksmith looked like. "They do not hesitate," he wrote, "to put me in the position & character of Tom Thumb and to make me feel that I am to be seen and heard for a shilling." Practically every day during his first few weeks in England, people, "losing a delicate sense of propriety in their overweening curiosity, question me in public and private on the subject of my philological attainments."[22] Some skeptics thought him a fraud. Richard D. Webb, a Dublin Quaker reformer whose letters frequently appeared in Garrison's *Liberator*, described how British crowds "stare" at Burritt in awe over his reputed mastery of fifty languages. He told Edmund Quincy that Burritt was "the least distinguished man" he had ever met. Burritt's "conversation," declared Webb, "is poor and limited and I can't observe a trace of the 50 languages. . . Nobody in England wᵈ make the least account of him if it were not for the preposterous reputation he has got of knowing fifty languages." Quincy agreed. The sharp-tongued Garrisonian was "sure that he is an unmitigated *Humbug*. As to his knowing 50 languages, I don't believe he knows *one* well." Burritt would "be found out, if he gets into the company of men competent to test his acquirements."[23]

In the summer of 1847 Burritt issued a call for a London meeting of League secretaries which would formally establish the British League. Forty League sympathizers and secretaries, mostly Quakers, met in London on July 13 and heard Burritt announce that, "as the representatives of the various local Leagues in Great Britain, we now assume a

21. *Manchester Guardian*, July 3, 1846.
22. Journals, Dec. 5, 1846.
23. R. D. Webb to Maria W. Chapman, Dublin, July 16, 1846, Boston Public Library; Webb to Edmund Quincy, Dublin, March 2, 1847, *ibid.* ("An hour of Garrison is worth a year of Burritt", Webb remarked.) Quincy to Webb, Dedham, March 28, 1847, *ibid.*

national organization." He recommended that quarterly meetings of the secretaries be held in London. To centralize League activities, he suggested that Great Britain be divided into twelve districts. Each would be the responsibility of a member of the standing committee of twelve which would take charge of holding a public League meeting once a year. District meetings were to be rotated, so that one would be held every month.[24]

By the time of the first quarterly meeting in London in October, 1847, League membership had risen to nearly 15,000. Approximately 130 League branches, varying in size from twenty-five members to 2,500, had been established. The board of officers had been filled. No president or vice-president was ever elected, but executive authority was instead vested in a National Committee whose number varied from fourteen to sixteen members. Charles Gilpin, a Quaker publisher from London, was treasurer. Burritt held the demanding office of corresponding secretary until 1849, when Edmund Fry, a Quaker, replaced him. Most of the members of the National Committee were Quaker philanthropists and reformers.[25]

Funds were especially needed for the publication and circulation of the *Bond of Brotherhood*. In 1846 over 100,000 copies of that monthly had been distributed in Great Britain and the British colonies—almost the same number had been sent to America. Burritt was fortunate that "good Joseph Sturge," his unfailing benefactor, thought highly enough of the *Bond* to pay the deficits it regularly incurred.[26]

The League was anything but cohesive. It lacked funds, organization and sustained executive leadership. Most of the members of the National Committee belonged to other

24. Journals, July 13, 1847.
25. *Christian Citizen*, Dec. 18, 25, 1847.
26. Journals, Oct. 6, 1846, June 25, 1847, Feb. 21, 1848.

reform associations whose work the League reduplicated. Additionally, the League was so all-comprehending in its emphasis that some reformers were puzzled over what it intended to do. When Burritt began charting a series of sweeping programs, many of them shied away from the League. Because of its great size, decentralized organization, and incredibly broad goals, the League could easily have ended before it started. That this did not happen was due to Burritt. In a real sense, Burritt was the League and the League was Burritt. Headquarters were wherever he hung his hat.

To Burritt the pledge was "founded upon the expanding obligations of that broad commandment: 'Thou shalt love thy neighbor as thyself.'" But to many Americans and Britishers it seemed a perplexing oath to uphold ambiguous and ill-defined principles. A correspondent for the American *Christian Reflector* asked, "did you ever know such a farce as this before, in a great moral movement?—a pledge without a fixed meaning?—a pledge accommodated to contradictory views?" George Beckwith voiced the majority opinion of American Peace Society members: "I hardly know what it means. It is a fine conception, but altogether too vague and broad for any specific purpose."[27] Even J. P. Blanchard had begun to harp "upon the despotic pledge." He failed to see why the League could not operate "without a written contract."[28] Richard Rathbone had written Sumner that he could not sign the pledge. "The practice of *signing pledges at all* is, with me, a question of doubt." Rathbone feared the pledge would bind him "*not only* never to volunteer into [the] Army or Navy, nor to take up the sword in any cause,

27. Quoted in *Christian Citizen*, July 19, 1847; *Advocate of Peace*, May and June, 1847, pp. 52–53.
28. Journals, July 30, 1847; see Blanchard's article attacking the pledge in *Christian Examiner*, XLIV (May, 1848), pp. 356–366; extracts of Correspondence between Burritt and J. P. Blanchard, 1851, Central Connecticut State College Library.

(which I could sensibly promise) but also never to contribute to warlike expenses, while, at the same time, I am constantly paying my share of Taxation, an immense proportion of which *I know* is conclusively appropriated to warlike purposes."[29]

Charles Sumner refused to sign the pledge for much the same reason as Rathbone. Burritt had counted on Sumner to influence important Bostonians to join the League. He wrote Sumner that he realized "the pledge is exceeding[ly] broad, & radical, involving the basis of more than a peace society. But it should be broad, deep and strong to meet the necessities of coming generations."[30] Sumner suggested that Burritt replace the pledge by the one he himself had drafted. Burritt let Rathbone know how exacerbated he was that Sumner "has conceived that the great movement of the League is susceptible of a new basis, at this stage of its existence and progress." Rathbone regretted being unable to sign the pledge, "for it would be *very grievous* to me not to cooperate . . . in his holy League and publicly and gladly to own him as my leader."[31] It was easier to reject the pledge than to deny Burritt.

There were people who chuckled at Burritt and his League. *The Times* derisively styled him "the *Yankee Cobbler*." The *Gloucester Journal* wrote a "severe critique" of one of his peace lectures. *Blackwood's Magazine* ridiculed the "new Peter the Hermit" America had sent England in

29. Richard Rathbone to Charles Sumner, Liverpool, Nov. 26, 1846, Harvard University Library; Burritt to Richard Rathbone, July 6, 1846, Klingberg Collection.

30. Burritt to Charles Sumner, Gloucester, Aug. 15, 1846, Harvard University Library; *ibid.*, Mar. 31, 1847. (The pledge, Burritt told Sumner, "is the platform on which I am planning world-wide measures for the fusion of nations into one peaceful brotherhood. . . It is strong, it precludes all war; it associates all who sign it in one energetic unity, in spirit, aim & effect.")

31. Richard Rathbone to Charles Sumner, Liverpool, April 2, 1847, Harvard University Library.

the person of Burritt, who with a "gang of itinerant lecturers . . . turn a questionable penny by holding forth to ignorant audiences upon subjects utterly beyond their own contracted comprehension." In the *Liberator* Edmund Quincy assessed the League as nothing more than a grotesque fantasy. "We never joined it ourselves," he wrote, "simply because of the fatuity it bore in its countenance, and the absurdity that was written in its very face. We thought it simply an honest humbug, well devised to enable gentlemen to think they were doing a great deal when they were doing nothing."[32]

These critics were a tiny minority. William Chambers, editor of the influential *Chambers's Edinburgh Journal*, was dubious about pacifists; but, himself an apostle of self-improvement, he admired Burritt and sympathized with his cause. "By all means let Elihu alone, and see what he will do in his own way," Chambers urged. "Who knows but this wandering blacksmith may, after all, do more to disseminate ideas of peace among foreign nations, than any ambassador . . . or other accredited functionary."[33] Henry Vincent, a former Chartist leader turned temperance lecturer, became one of Burritt's closest associates. Vincent declared in 1848 that "the League of Universal Brotherhood must not be laughed at because it propounded what practical people call a Utopian idea. If we laughed at this principle, we laughed at Christianity."[34] At the time of Vincent's remarks the League had established some 400 branches in Great Britain, America, and the British colonies, with a total membership of over 30,000.

Mary Carpenter was angered by Quincy's diatribe in the

32. Journals, Dec. 14, 1848, Oct. 28, 1846; *Blackwood's Magazine*, LXVI (Nov., 1849), p. 583, and LXXII (March, 1853), pp. 373–378; *Liberator*, Aug. 20, 1847.

33. *Chambers's Edinburgh Journal*, XV (March 29, 1851), pp. 193–195.

34. *Christian Citizen*, July 15, 1848.

Liberator against the League. She wrote Maria Weston Chapman, an American abolitionist, that she "regretted" Quincy's article because it threw a "stigma on a man who is devoting heart and head to the interests of humanity." Several months later she again wrote:

> If you knew him, you would I think understand him better & admire with us the devotedness with which he gives his heart & powers to the cause of human brotherhood. I have seen nothing in his writings of a compromising character. I have heard nothing from him but the breathings of a most Christian spirit. I cannot call him vain or inflated. If he gives in milk & not strong meat, he but follows the apostolic example in administering food to babes in Christ. I quite agree with him in not understanding that the peace of Christ is a sword.[35]

Burritt was a knight-errant of benevolence forever on the alert for any act of philanthropy that might cast a favorable light on the League. His search involved him in the episode of "The Little Nailer." Josiah Banner, or "Jemmy Stubbins" as Burritt nicknamed him, was an unlettered Bromsgrove lad who toiled most of the day alongside his father making nails. Burritt, who had "accidentally" met Jemmy while walking through Bromsgrove, wrote a sentimental narrative of his "Hour with the Nailer" for the *Christian Citizen*. He suggested that American children contribute nickels for

35. Mary Carpenter to Maria W. Chapman, Oct. 31, 1847, Boston Public Library; *ibid.*, March 19, 1848. (The Quaker diarist Caroline Fox thought Burritt was "a natural gentleman, and seems to have attained the blessed point of self-forgetfulness, springing from ever-present remembrance of better things." The Swedish author Fredrika Bremer noticed in Burritt "the expression of singular mildness and human love which marks his countenance." Horace N. Pym, ed., *Memories of Old Friends, Being Extracts from the Journal and Letters of Caroline Fox, of Penjerrich, Cornwall* (Philadelphia, 1883), pp. 266–267. Adolph B. Benson, ed., *America of the Fifties: Letters of Fredrika Bremer* (New York, 1924), pp. 41–42.)

Jemmy's education.[36] From all over New England children sent nickels to the office of the *Christian Citizen*. Burritt made arrangements for Jemmy's schooling and outfitted him with a new suit of clothes. The townspeople, having read Burritt's article about Jemmy in an American newspaper, also rendered some financial assistance.

But the nickels which had been sent to the *Christian Citizen* never reached Burritt because Thomas Drew, the assistant editor, appropriated them for the paper's expenses. Burritt had therefore to pay for Jemmy's school and clothing bills; he complained that "nearly all the philanthropic enterprises I have set on foot, have devolved upon myself." Still, his philanthropy had cost only a few pounds, and the publicity he received was worth much more. Furthermore, he published in America in 1850 a little pamphlet on *Jemmy Stubbins, or The Nailer Boy*, which he sold for a nickel.[37] By 1848 Jemmy had acquired enough schooling to write several letters of gratitude to American children who had donated to his school-purse.

The Irish famine diverted Burritt from the "plight" of Jemmy Stubbins. Toward the end of 1846 the famine had reached disastrous dimensions. Burritt acted quickly and with his wonted optimism. "I am on the eve of leaving for Ireland to fathom the cause, extent & cure of its misery," he wrote to a League member.[38] Arriving in Ireland, he was overpowered by the squalidness and misery of the people. He spent two weeks visiting those parts of the country where famine was most acute:

36. *Christian Citizen*, Sept. 12, 1846.

37. Journals, Dec. 22, 1846, June 24, Dec. 26, Mar. 31, 1850, Dec. 24, 1851; Burritt, *Jemmy Stubbins, or The Nailer Boy* (Worcester, 1850). (For part of the story of Jemmy, see *Thoughts and Things*, pp. 168–173.)

38. Quoted in Curti, *The Learned Blacksmith*, p. 45; Burritt to [?], Birmingham, Feb. 6, 1847, Swarthmore College Peace Collection.

Skibbereen, Feb. 20, [1847]. This morning the Reverend Mr. Fitzpatrick, with several gentlemen of the town, called and I accompanied them in my first walk through this Potter's Field of destitution and death. As soon as we left the house a crowd of haggard creatures pressed upon us, and, with agonizing prayers for bread followed us to the soup house. One poor woman, whose entreaties became irresistibly importunate, had watched all night in the graveyard lest the body of her husband should be stolen from its last resting-place, to which it had been consigned yesterday. She had left in her hovel five children, sick with the famine fever, and she raised an exceedingly bitter cry for help. A man with swollen feet pressed closely upon us, and begged for bread most piteously. He had pawned his shoes for the last morsel of food he had eaten. . .[39]

The League published his poignant *Journal of a Visit of Three Days to Skibbereen, and its Neighborhood.*[40]

Before he had left for Ireland, Burritt had written an *Olive Leaf for the American People*, asking them to aid the starving Irish: "Farmers, Mechanics, Merchants, men of the United States, children, wives and mothers will you let thousands of your kind be thrown uncoffined when two cents of Indian meal a day will save a life." Writing from Skibbereen, he sent an appeal to the people of Worcester County, Massachusetts, to supply food and clothing on a quota basis: "we should have about 60,000 pounds of provisions to begin with, in the town of Worcester." He wrote Lord John Russell, the Prime Minister, to ask whether England would pay the freight charges for food and clothing he was planning to have sent from the United States to Ire-

39. Quoted in full in C. Northend, *Elihu Burritt. . .* pp. 41–52.
40. Burritt, *Journal of a Visit of Three Days to Skibbereen, and its Neighborhood* (London, 1847). In an "Introduction" to the *Journal*, Joseph Sturge wrote, "A single individual is reported to have given £1000 for Skibbereen," implying that this philanthropist had done so because of Burritt's moving narrative.

land;[41] Russell replied that the government was prepared to do so.

Burritt appealed to members of the Boston Relief Committee, which was already at work sending aid to Ireland. The *Jamestown*, a warship loaned by Congress, was loaded with supplies and sailed from Boston harbor to Cork under the command of Robert B. Forbes, a Boston merchant, and other gentlemen who volunteered their services. Irishmen greeted the ship with jubilation. Cork and Dublin newspapers carried detailed accounts of the errand of brotherhood. The Dublin *Nation* wrote, "America needs friends in Europe, and our relations have always been of a friendly kind; *but from this year forth no Irishmen will willingly draw a trigger against her*."[42]

While Burritt may not have been indispensable in getting provisions from America, his graphic description of Irish distress and urgent appeals undoubtedly activated many individuals and organizations that might otherwise have extended only sympathy.[43] The Boston Relief Committee showed its appreciation for his labors by authorizing Forbes to offer him free passage to America aboard the *Jamestown*.[44] Burritt declined. In a letter to a member of the Boston Relief Committee he profusely assessed the significance of the *Jamestown* voyage:

> My soul is full of deep emotion for what you are doing and have done for humanity . . . The Jamestown has arrived at Cork, and probably ere this has opened her butteries upon

41. *Christian Citizen*, Feb. 27, March 27, 1847.

42. Quoted *ibid.*, May 15, 1847.

43. Cecil Woodham-Smith, in her study of the Irish famine, makes no reference to Burritt; see her account of the Jamestown relief voyage in *The Great Hunger* (New York, 1962), pp. 243–244.

44. Sarah Forbes Hughes, *Letters and Recollections of John Murray Forbes* (2 vols., Boston, 1899), I, 120–121. For a brief reference to Burritt and the Irish famine, see Merle Curti, *American Philanthropy Abroad* (New Brunswick, New Jersey, 1964), p. 52.

the famished populace. No naval enterprise ever exceeded this in true moral grandeur. It opens a new chapter of promise and progress in the history of nations. It is one of the first conquests in the reign of Peace & Universal Brotherhood. It will stand out in illustrious contrast with the dark deeds of blood in Mexico which men profanely call victories —splendid victories. My heart is full to overflowing—full of gratitude to God and to the men and women of America touched to benevolence by [H]is finger. I never loved old Massachusetts so well, so profoundly. . . Her children, wherever scattered around the globe, will rise up and call her blessed for this great act of philanthropy.[45]

Burritt's Irish relief work was more a personal triumph than a League accomplishment. But the League was not lacking reform enterprises. By September, 1846, Burritt had already hatched plans for free-labor produce, emigrant-aid to America, and ocean penny postage. He soon added Friendly Addresses, Olive Leaves, and international peace congresses to his swelling list of benevolent projects.

Friendly Addresses and Olive Leaves were in many ways the central part of the League's work. At the first annual meeting of the British League in London, in May, 1848, Burritt declared that the association did not aim at the "mere abstinence, or cessation from war, slavery, violence and oppression." It would try "to displace the malevolent spirit which inspires these bloody and hateful systems, by the spirit of good will and fraternal concord among men."[46]

In 1847 the League, assisted by the London Peace Society, arranged for the exchange of Friendly Addresses between British and French towns. Addresses, usually forwarded to the mayor of the town, were sent from Manchester to Lyons, Liverpool to Marseilles, Birmingham to

45. Burritt to James Warren, London, April 18, 1847, Boston Public Library.
46. *Christian Citizen.* July 8, 1848.

Bordeaux, Leeds to Lille, Bristol to Brest, Southampton to Havre, and Sheffield to Strasbourg. "Nearly a score of other English towns," wrote Burritt, "paired off with towns in France, and sent them right brotherly letters." French towns reciprocated. The Liverpool to Marseilles Address contained 25,000 signatures, while that from Bordeaux to Birmingham was signed by 1,700 Frenchmen. After the overthrow of Louis Philippe in 1848, Burritt wrote a Friendly Address to the people of Paris from the people of London. Joseph Sturge headed a deputation to Paris to convey the Address to the new French government. The poet-statesman Lamartine, in accepting the Address, declared that "it would be laid up in the archives of the nation as the bond of fraternity between the two peoples." It was translated and published in French newspapers under the direction of the government.[47]

Burritt believed Olive Leaves were more effective than Friendly Addresses in spreading the glad tidings of peace and brotherhood. In Hamburg, in 1849, he originated a plan for the systematic insertion of Leaves in leading European journals and newspapers without cost to him or the League. He established Olive Leaf Societies to raise money to supply European journals with a monthly Olive Leaf.[48]

He was "never . . . more sanguine in reference to an enterprise"[49] than he was about the Olive Leaf Society project. During the early 1850's he travelled throughout

47. *Bond of Brotherhood,* July, 1851, p. 158, Nov., 1852, pp. 52–56; Journals, March 3, 7, 14, 1848. (For some samples of British Friendly Addresses to France, see *Thoughts and Things,* pp. 334–364.)

48. Burritt to [A. Southall], Hamburg, Sept. 5, 1853, Friends House Library; Burritt to Edward Ashly, London, Aug. 21, 1851, Klingberg Collection.

49. Burritt to A. Southall, London, Jan. 18, 1851, Friends House Library; Burritt to the Reverend Jabez Burns, London, July 12, 1851, New York Public Library.

Great Britain in an effort to interest small groups of females in his scheme. In 1850 he sent by almost every steamer bound to America "10 to 25 letters to persons in different states," asking them to establish Olive Leaf circles.[50] Whenever he returned to America, he personally tried to form such societies. Not many American or British groups to whom he explained the plan failed to establish a Society. "In almost every case, after such an explanation, the ladies formed themselves into an association which was called an 'Olive Leaf Society', which met once a month, corresponded with similar societies, and raised a certain amount to pay for the insertion of the Olive Leaves in Continental journals."[51] The entire project was conducted by British and American ladies.

The first Society was set up in Southampton in 1850. Two years later, more than 100 societies had been created. The majority were in Great Britain, in most cases begun by Quaker ladies. Occasionally ladies of other denominations extended a hand. In Burnley, rejoiced Burritt, "25 ladies came together and formed a Society, nearly all of whom belong to the Established Church! Is not this a victory?" American Olive Leaf Societies were organized in New York, Brooklyn, Philadelphia, Wilmington (Delaware), Baltimore, Cincinnati, Boston, Roxbury, New Britain, Berlin (Connecticut), and elsewhere.[52] Two thriving Societies were established in Hamburg and Altona, Germany, by ladies brought together by the Reverend Adrian Van Andel, whose

50. Burritt to [Gerrit Smith], Hamburg, December 28, 1850, Massachusetts Historical Society; Burritt to [?], London, October 3, 1851, Central Connecticut State College Library.

51. Burritt, *Ten-Minute Talks*, p. 39; Burritt to Catherine Ireland, London, September 1, 1851, Klingberg Collection.

52. Burritt to [A. Southall], London, April 22, September 8, 1851, Friends House Library; *Bond of Brotherhood*, April 1, 1851, p. 118; Burritt to Elizabeth Stanley, London, January 19, 1855, New Britain Public Institute.

acquaintance Burritt had made in 1849. Many Olive Leaf groups, particularly those in America, disbanded soon after inception. By 1858, however, Burritt, who was "tempted" by then to regard most League enterprises "as failures," was proud to report that the Olive Leaf Mission "still retains its vitality in the spirit which it seems to have quickened into life in the hearts of hundreds."[53]

Olive Leaf Societies were amply rewarded for their contributions. By the beginning of 1851 Olive Leaves were regularly published in journals and newspapers in Paris, Berlin, Hamburg, Frankfort, Augsburg, Leipsig, Bremen, Cologne, and Vienna. Later that year, when a St. Petersburg paper had been reached with Olive Leaves, Burritt triumphantly announced "that cold and despotic Russia has opened her iron portals to our gentle dove." In 1852 about twenty European journals included a monthly Olive Leaf in their columns.[54]

Olive Leaves and Friendly Addresses fell woefully short of creating the kind of international climate for peace that Burritt desired. Their appeal was bound to be limited, and

53. Forty Olive Leaf Societies had disbanded by 1853. Journals, July 6, Aug. 8, 1852, Aug. 18, Nov. 15, 1853; Burritt to Mrs. Merriam, Washington, D.C., April 27, 1854, Historical Society of Pennsylvania; Burritt to [an English Quakeress], New Britain, June 27, 1858, Historical Society of Pennsylvania.

54. Bond of Brotherhood, Feb., 1851, p. 77; August, 1852, pp. 2–3. Some of the European journals and newspapers which printed monthly Olive Leaves were: Hamburger Nachrichter (Hamburg); Constitutionelle Zeitung, Vossiche Zeitung, National Zeitung (Berlin); Illustrirte Zeitung (Leipsig); Weser Zeitung (Bremen); Frankfurte Journal (Frankfort); Schwabischer Merkur (Stuttgart); Berlingske Tidende, Foedrelandet (Copenhagen); L'Evenement (Paris); El Clamor Publico (Madrid); El Barcelones (Barcelona); L'Opinione (Turin); Il Corriere Mercantile, (Genoa); Handelsbad (Amsterdam).; L'Independence Belges (Brussels). Longfellow wrote Burritt that he was happy to see that Olive Leaves, "which like the tongues of Pentecost . . . [were] now speaking in various dialects to various nations." Quoted in Bond of Brotherhood, Sept., 1851, p. 24.

their influence was trivial. It is unlikely that most pacifists took them as seriously as did Burritt. He believed Friendly Addresses to be a meaningful sort of "people-diplomacy."[55] But, like Olive Leaves, they were no more than a clever way of keeping peace propaganda before the public. Both techniques represented not so much the typical *modus operandi* of peace reformers as they did Burritt's immeasurable self-satisfaction in knowing that people in various parts of the world were reading about peace.

Believing it was absolutely essential to bring "the young . . . into pleasant communication on things that make for peace," Burritt promoted peace societies for juveniles in Great Britain and America and established an International Sunday School Association. He asked Lewis Tappan, Samuel Coues, Longfellow, Mrs. Sigourney, and many other influential Americans to form juvenile peace societies in their respective towns. By 1848 a dozen societies were operating in Great Britain, but none could be sustained in America save a small one in Lancaster, Massachusetts. He arranged for a few American Sunday Schools, including one in Peoria, Illinois, to correspond with some in England, but the correspondence did not last long.[56]

Burritt also hoped to instruct the youth of both countries in the principles of peace and brotherhood through his *Waterloo Series*. Issued in pamphlet form, these moralistic tales told of *Hannibal, or the Story of a Wasted Life, The Man that Killed his Neighbors, Soldiers and Citizens,* and *The Story of Oberlin*. He edited a series on *Illustrations of the Law of Kindness*, "designed for circulation among children in Sunday Schools and Common Schools" in Great Britain and America. Burritt could not neglect "children just beginning to read." For them he wrote four-page *Leaflets*

55. Burritt, *Thoughts and Things*, pp. 329–333.
56. Christian Citizen, Dec. 12, 1846, May 1, July 6, 1847; Journals, July 6, Dec. 5, 29, 1847.

of the Law of Kindness.[57] He found it difficult to coax Leaguers to write some of the pamphlets, but he had even more trouble trying to get children to read them.

While breezily evolving humanitarian schemes in England, Burritt kept an eye on League developments in the United States. The League had begun well there. By 1847 15,000 Americans had joined. In the reform-minded town of Oberlin, Ohio, Amasa Walker, a professor of political economy at Oberlin College, campaigned vigorously for the League. Amos Dresser, a rabid Oberlin pacifist, reported that over 700 signatures had been secured in the town.[58] State branches were established in Maine, New Hampshire, Rhode Island, Massachusetts, Vermont, Ohio, Illinois, and Michigan. The Philadelphia Methodist Conference had "recommended that the pledge be presented to their respective churches for signatures." The New England Conference of Wesleyan Ministers adopted a resolution favoring the presentation of the pledge "to all our Churches." Five hundred ministers had signed the pledge by 1847, including the renowned Unitarian Theodore Parker.[59]

In May, 1847, a large number of Leaguers from all the New England states and from several of the western convened in Boston to form the American League. Amasa Walker presided over the meeting, at which it was resolved

> that we feel perfect confidence in the truthfulness and power of the principles upon which the League is founded, as embodied in the pledge, and in their final triumph. And while we have a deep sense of the magnitude of the work,

57. *Bond of Brotherhood*, Feb., 1851, p. 88, Aug., 1852, p. 6; Journals, March 14, 31, 1848.

58. Robert S. Fletcher, *A History of Oberlin College* . . . , I, 271–289.

59. Journals, June 23, 29, 1847; MS Lecture on the League of Universal Brotherhood, American Antiquarian Society; *Christian Citizen*, June 19, 1847.

we feel encouraged that we are acting in harmony with the advancing spirit of the age.[60]

Burritt was elected president of the American League, since it was assumed that he would return shortly. Coues was one of seven vice-presidents, as was Gerrit Smith, in 1848; Walker was corresponding secretary, and the Reverend E. W. Jackson was treasurer. These officers, plus the executive committee of six and the recording secretary, formed the Board of Managers which handled League national affairs.

By 1850 the American League existed in name only. Walker, despite his blanket approval of the pledge, was chiefly interested in the League's peace operations. He and Coues were nettled because Burritt had committed himself to so many reforms. J. P. Blanchard complained about the pledge and merely went through the motions of backing the League. Burritt was continually advised to return to America to take charge of the organization. Coues, disgusted by Burritt's prolonged stay in Great Britain, stopped writing him;[61] Walker warned that Burritt was "ceasing to be an American." In 1849 Burritt was "disheartened that *I* must do all that is done in America" for the League; in 1851 he had "fears that all was dead there"[62]—fears soon justified.

More discouraging to Burritt than the collapse of the American League was the demise in 1851 of the *Christian Citizen*. Thomas Drew, the assistant editor, had been derelict in his editorial duties and had mismanaged the paper's funds. Owing over $3,000 in *Christian Citizen* debts, Burritt was forced into bankruptcy. The paper was "my first-born

60. *Christian Citizen*, June 5, 1847.
61. Charlotte Coues to Amasa Walker, March 29, 1848, Massachusetts Historical Society.
62. Journals, Jan. 28, April 22, 1851.

. . . bled to death by those in whom I reposed unbounded faith."[63]

The British League was also falling apart. District and quarterly meetings were held infrequently, and the annual meeting was poorly attended. Most of the local branches were dormant. Burritt did not seem to notice that the structure of the League was beginning to melt away. He continued directing reforms. He still believed that in time the League would encircle the globe.

Burritt had founded the League on Christian love and brotherhood, and he nurtured it with unwavering fidelity. Despite the nice reasons of some Britishers and Americans for not signing the pledge, there was really little in it with which any Christian could find fault. Given the active Anglo-American community of benevolent endeavor, it is not difficult to understand why the League had appeal. Yet given the improbability of the task, success could only have been marginal. Much of its early popularity was the result of novelty. Still, many plain people in Great Britain and America, as their letters in the *Christian Citizen* attested, signed the pledge with the conviction that it embodied a moral prescription for a better world. The League was undeniably visionary and utopian, but that was because Burritt had created it in his own likeness.

63. Burritt, a few months before he departed for England in 1846, had made T. W. Butterfield, publisher of the Worcester *Aegis*, a partner in his paper. Drew and Butterfield absorbed most of the profits in their salaries and sent practically nothing to Burritt, who in 1848 finally bought out Butterfield's share. But Burritt made the colossal mistake of retaining Drew as assistant editor and then compounded the error by sending the Scottish poet-pacifist J. B. Syme to America to help Drew. Once in America Syme forgot about the League and together with Drew converted the paper into an organ of the Free Soil Party. Drew, meanwhile, continued to saddle the paper with heavy debts. Journals, Dec. 31, 1846-Nov. 15, 1851, *passim.*

8

International Peace Crusader

By 1840 the peace crusade was scarcely an international movement. Pacifism was organized in only four countries—the United States, Great Britain, France, and Switzerland. In France *the Société des Amis de la Morale Chrétienne et de la Paix* had been established in 1821 by the Duc de Rochefoucauld-Liancourt with the help of British and American pacifists. The Society of Christian Morals was interested in peace, but was never strictly a peace society. Its purpose was "to recall continually to the human mind the principles of Christianity." The Geneva Peace Society had been founded in 1830 by the Comte de Sellon expressly to promote peace. The French and Swiss organizations maintained a fairly regular correspondence with the British and American national societies, but were not nearly so active as the latter groups. Not until 1867 was another national peace organization created. There were of course many professing pacifists scattered throughout all of Europe. Though unorganized, they had been reached by the tracts, circulars, and pamphlets distributed by the American and London Peace Societies.[1]

1. A. C. F. Beales, *The History of Peace* (New York, 1931), pp. 51–55.

When Burritt joined the cause, even the national movements in Great Britain and the United States had lapsed. Peace reformers had talked about the necessity of establishing a cooperative transatlantic peace venture more ambitious and effective than a mere exchange of salutations and local progress news. They believed that international steps to end war were a logical sequel to national peace campaigns.

In 1843 an international peace congress was held in London to integrate national movements. Joseph Sturge had suggested the meeting during a visit to the United States in 1841. For two years British and American reformers worked sedulously to make the proposed convention a success. Pacifists from almost every nation in Europe were invited. But out of a total of over 300 delegates chosen to attend the London Peace Convention, not quite half appeared. Just six non-British European delegates, including Rochefoucauld-Liancourt, were in attendance, and the American contingent was embarrassingly outnumbered by the one from Great Britain. Practical peace measures dominated the discussions and speeches of the three-day Convention. Resolutions were adopted favoring arbitration clauses in treaties, restrictions on the sale of munitions, and a Congress and Court of Nations.[2]

Three years after the London Peace Convention, however, there was no serious probability of holding another. The interest it had generated in practical international peace plans rapidly subsided. The American Peace Society was languishing as a result of the factional feud over defensive war. British peace reformers (most of whom were opponents of defensive war) had no desire to summon another world conference that would again be comprised almost exclusively of London Peace Society members.

The Friendly Address movement and the Olive Leaves

2. Curti, *The American Peace Crusade*, pp. 136–141.

Burritt dispatched in 1846 acted as a tonic to British and American pacifists. One peace reformer credited Burritt with "the idea of bringing English friends into hearty co-operation with American peace-men, instead of an irregular exchange of letters & papers."[3] The idea for closer international ties was definitely not "peculiar" to Burritt, but he did succeed in making it more of a practice than a gesture. With the cooperation of several British pacifists he organized international peace conventions in Brussels, Paris, Frankfort, and London, from 1848 to 1851.

Burritt and George Bradshaw, a Manchester Quaker philanthropist and a Leaguer, conceived the idea of holding a peace congress in Paris in 1848. Five years had elapsed since the London Peace Convention, and they felt it was incumbent on the League to organize another meeting. Burritt was sure the League was capable of carrying it off. Sturge agreed and recommended that Burritt go to Paris to make the necessary arrangements.[4]

The aim of the proposed peace conference was to start a world-wide movement in favor of a Congress and Court of Nations. Burritt wanted "no measure short of [the] creation of a High Court of Nations . . . discussed" at Paris.[5] Before he left for Paris, he sent League secretaries a circular declaring that

> the great object of the Convention will be to discuss and develop some rational, practical and efficient substitute for War, in settling the disputes which may arise between nations. It is very probable that no other substitute will be proposed or discussed than the creation of a HIGH COURT OF NATIONS, and a code of International Laws, by which all cases of international controversy shall be adjudicated.[6]

3. F. Holland, MS History of the American Peace Cause, p. 51.
4. Journals, Feb. 23, 1848.
5. Burritt to John Bowring, London, Aug. 10, 1848, American Antiquarian Society.
6. New York *Tribune*, Oct. 19, 1848.

There was little that Burritt could say or write about a Congress and Court of Nations that British and American pacifists did not already know. They were conversant with the arguments in its favor. Having read William Ladd's classic *Essay on a Congress of Nations*, the last major treatise on the subject, they were familiar with the proposed machinery of such an international body. Yet this did not prevent Burritt from telling British and American Leaguers that the time was at hand to demonstrate for a Congress of Nations, and that the League was just the organization to mastermind public discussion. He spoke about a Congress of Nations as if only hard work and a little luck were necessary for its fulfillment. He vowed to employ every resource of the League to publicize the proposition "for the coming year and for all the years it may require to secure its adoption by the people and Governments of Christendom." The peace gathering in Paris was in his mind merely "preparatory" to "an ultimate Congress of Nations."[7] Burritt appointed himself chief steward of that farsighted project. He was positive that it was the open-sesame to world peace.

Plans to hold a congress in Paris in 1848 were ironic in view of the revolutionary movements breaking out in all parts of Europe. These revolts for constitutional government and national independence met with surprising initial success. The overthrow of Louis Philippe in February had stimulated similar outbreaks throughout the continent. The polyglot Austrian empire appeared on the verge of dismemberment as Prince Metternich fled; Mazzini in Italy and Kossuth in Hungary were spearheading bloody movements for independence and constitutional government in their respective countries, and the Frankfort Assembly was nobly endeavoring to make Germany something more than a geographical expression. By late 1848, however, except for

7. Journals, April 13, 1848.

some constitutional victories in the small states of Denmark, Holland, Belgium, Switzerland, and Sardinia, the liberal uprisings had misfired and severe political reaction had followed.

Burritt construed these political upheavals as signs of the new times to come. He deplored the bloodshed, but could not conceal his sympathy for the apparent gains of liberalism. He applauded the overthrow of the Orleanist monarchy in France and mocked the furtive flight of Metternich, the "prince regent of all despots." He exulted that "Every potentate is trembling upon his throne; the people everywhere are demanding constitutions, concessions and reforms . . . one result of these popular agitations and overturnings will be, a reconstruction of nationalities in Europe, according to social, religious and political affinities. At least it may be predicted that all who speak the same language on the continent will resolve themselves into one nation." Yet the attempt by British Chartists to get the People's Charter adopted by the House of Commons frightened Burritt. He saw justice in Chartist demands but danger in their open threats of violence. Should England escape "this terrible catastrophe," he declared, "it will be from the interposition of Divine Providence."[8] Burritt's aversion to physical-force Chartism was inconsistent with his stand on the European liberal insurrections. Nor was it congruous with his earlier position in favor of the Dorr Rebellion in Rhode Island in 1842. At that time he had seen nothing wrong with the use of force to win political rights.

Burritt thought that the revolutionary tumult of 1848 would make a Congress of Nations more attainable. Critics of the plan had often charged that republican and monarchical governments represented in a Congress would engage in bickering sufficient to nullify any efforts to promulgate an acceptable international code of laws. But with

8. *Ibid.*, March 18, April 7, 1848.

monarchs on the run during the early phase of the liberal
revolutions, Burritt forecasted "that absolute monarchies
will never be in the majority again in this world; and that
all governments in Christendom are converging to one common basis, the *universal suffrage* of the people." Because
of the unification movements in Germany and in Italy, "the
nations to be represented in such an International Assembly
would be fewer in number, and more equal in size and
population, than at any previous period in modern history."[9]

That this solution involved force did not at first trouble
him. As a radical pacifist, he was in theory absolutely opposed to physical force. But like most republican-minded
peace men, Burritt overlooked a little bloodshed when
Liberty was besting Despotism. He had not started the
liberal revolts of 1848, nor could he stop them. He was
optimistic enough to think that a political basis for peace
might issue from the uprisings. He was for peace, but he
was for liberty too. Unable to reconcile the practical relationship between liberty and revolution, but gladdened
by liberal triumphs, he declared innocently, "If Universal
Suffrage in France, Germany, Italy, and Great Britain,
crowns the history of 1848, it will constitute a memorable
year in the life of mankind." Three years later, however,
when the forces of liberalism had been thoroughly routed,
he concluded that "the true freedom of a people can never
be acquired and permanently maintained by the sword."
Only "the moral resistance of a people to despotism will
ultimately secure their rights, without perpetrating a single
crime, or shedding a single drop of human blood." He wrote
Charles Sumner that he hoped "no other power than that
of truth and right will be arrayed even against the despotisms of the Continent."[10] Never again was he ambivalent

9. *Christian Citizen*, July 15, 1848.
10. Journals, June 24, 1848, Nov. 5, 1851; Burritt to Sumner, London, July 2, 1852, in Curti, *The Learned Blacksmith*, p. 96.

about non-resistance. Shortly after writing Sumner, he published luminous articles on "The Power of Passive Resistance", "The Dignity of Passive Resistance", "The Patriotism of Passive Resistance", and "The Economy of Passive Resistance."[11] Nothing that he ever wrote on peace surpassed these essays in clarity and cogency.

When Burritt went to Paris to prepare the way for the 1848 peace convention, he evoked the suspicion of various government officials whose nerves were frayed by the recent June revolt in Paris. He was hard put to convince them that the convention was to be "neither a 'red republican' nor a 'legitimist' demonstration." The noted free trader Horace Say told Burritt of several "insuperable" barriers blocking a peace conference in Paris. Burritt decided that the convention should be held in Brussels.[12] Two League members went to Brussels to help him.

The Belgian government was not opposed to a gathering in Brussels. The secretary to the Minister of the Interior assured Burritt "that foreigners had the same privilege of holding public meetings in Belgium as the subjects of the realm themselves." Letters of introduction from the British and American ministers to Belgium were all that were necessary. The Minister of the Interior, wrote Burritt, "cheerfully accorded all we could ask," even going so far as to procure a hall for the conference. "Thus our way has been opened . . . as manifestly here by Providence as it was hedged up in France," he exclaimed.[13]

The three-day session of the Brussels Peace Convention began on September 20 in the *Salon de la Grande Harmonie*. Over 150 British delegates were on hand, as were small deputations from France, Germany, Holland, and Italy. Auguste Visschers, Belgian Councillor of Mines and

11. Burritt, *Thoughts and Things*, pp. 269–281, 282–288.
12. Journals, July 11-Aug. 30, 1848, *passim*.
13. *Ibid.*, Sept. 4–5, 1848.

philanthropist, was elected president of the Convention; Burritt was one of four vice-presidents, who included Francisque Bouvet, a member of the French National Assembly and an officer of the Society of Christian Morals, and William Ewart, M.P. Delegates were treated to a daily round of peace orations. Visschers, Bouvet, Henry Vincent, and Burritt gave the principal speeches; impressive letters from Richard Cobden and John Bowring were read, commending the aims of the Convention.[14]

The first resolution introduced censured the war system and recommended that the "civilized world . . . adopt proper measures for bringing about the entire abolition of war." Resolutions advocating the insertion of arbitration clauses in international treaties, "a general and simultaneous disarmament," and a Congress and High Court of Nations were overwhelmingly adopted.[15]

The subject of a Congress and Court of Nations came up repeatedly. Burritt had invited the German liberal Arnold Ruge, a member of the Frankfort Assembly who had espoused a Congress of Nations before that body, to come to Brussels.[16] Ruge was unable to attend the Convention, but Francisque Bouvet spoke at length on the necessity of such a world organization. It was Burritt, however, who had the most to say about its virtues.

Burritt's Congress of Nations speech followed closely the principles which had been advanced in William Ladd's *Essay on a Congress of Nations*. "The first object," Burritt began, "which is sought to be obtained by a Congress of Nations is a well-defined Code of International Law." He praised the contributions of Grotius, Pufendorf, and Vattel, but declared that their combined efforts constituted "not law, but arguments; not decrees, but rules; not a code,

14. *Christian Citizen*, Nov. 4, 1848.
15. *Ibid.*, Nov. 4, 18, 1848.
16. Journals, July 31, 1848; *Christian Citizen*, Aug. 26, 1848.

but a treatise." Their "maxims, opinions, and precedents" needed to be embodied in international statutes. A Congress of Nations, in effect, "an International Legislature," would transform that amorphous body of opinions and precepts called international law into "solemn forms of legislation," which would be ratified by all the legislatures of the nations belonging to the Congress. The task was difficult, but not impossible: "Is there anything Utopian, visionary, or impracticable in the supposition that such a task might be satisfactorily performed by a body containing, we might assume, the aggregate wisdom of the world?"

Burritt demonstrated that an international Congress would be a manageable body. On the basis of one representative for every million inhabitants, the Congress would number "about three hundred and fifty members." The Congress would meet in some convenient European city and appoint "a Committee of International Law, composed of the most profound statesmen and jurists from the different countries." After sifting through all that had ever been written on international law, the Committee would draft statutes based on that law. In time, "six months, perhaps," there would emerge "a fixed well-digested code, created, sanctioned, and solemnized by all the moral prestige and authority that can be acquired from human legislation."

Having prepared an international code of laws, the Congress "enters upon the second department of its labors, and provides for the erection of a Grand International Tribunal, or permanent High Court of Nations, which shall decide all serious questions of controversy between the nations represented, according to the code thus adopted." The Congress would eventually disband after the High Court was fully assembled and ready to go to work. A parting act of the Congress could be to deliberate on "minor matters of International interests," such as the establishment of a universal system of weights and measures and the removal of all "obstructions to International trade and intercourse." Burritt concluded by saying that the Court "would be to the great orbit of humanity what the sun is in the solar system; if not in the quality of light, at least in that of attraction."[17]

Professor Giuseppe Bertinatti of Turin, a scholar of law, also addressed the Convention on the urgency of a Congress of Nations. His speech was so much like Burritt's that it struck many delegates as "a copy of the other." Burritt and Bertinatti had not compared notes beforehand, and the former was flattered by the similarity. The Turin professor had written his speech and invited himself to the Convention after having read in a circular that the proposition of a Congress of Nations was to figure conspicuously in the proceedings. The coincidence, together with the sympathetic reception shown by the delegates to the resolution calling for a Congress of Nations, made Burritt feel "that the grand idea . . . had taken a deep hold of the public mind on the Continent."[18] This was surely not a sound observation, but Burritt was always inclined to think his own sentiments represented those of the public.

The Brussels Convention was a memorable event. Newspapers throughout Europe and America were generally kind. "There was very little verbal parade" at Brussels, a foreign correspondent for the New York *Tribune* reported, "but a great deal of sterling thought" and common-sense peace plans.[19] Burritt, of course, thought the entire affair an unqualified success. The Convention, he wrote Charles Sumner, had "quickened the cause of Peace into a *movement*, which must take all the force and impetus of the Anti-Corn Law League." A Congress of Nations "I verily believe . . . will be possible in four or five years, if the

17. Burritt, *Lectures and Speeches*, pp. 193–202.
18. Journals, Sept. 21, 1848; *Christian Citizen*, Nov. 4, 1848.
19. New York *Tribune*, Oct. 19, 1848.

friends of peace . . . will unite their efforts."[20] The Brussels delegates, before they adjourned, had agreed to another conference the following year. There was not a shred of doubt in Burritt's mind that 1849 would witness an even more successful meeting.

No one disputed Burritt's primacy in organizing the Brussels Convention. The *Christian Citizen* gave an accurate and detailed description of the obstacles he had to surmount in order to arrange it. The New York *Tribune* commended "this clear-sighted, noble-hearted man who conceived the idea." John Greenleaf Whittier paid homage to Burritt in his poem on "The Peace Convention at Brussels." Charles Sumner dubbed the Convention "inspired" by Burritt "an epoch" in the international peace movement.[21]

Many members of the London Peace Society, however, sulked because they had modestly participated in the Brussels Convention. Several complained cryptically to Sturge that they were not satisfied with Burritt's methods of operation. They questioned his competence "to lead a great movement" and resented his and the League's aggressiveness in leading the peace reform. Sturge made a special trip to London to try to mollify them. Some Society officers proposed a merger with the League that would have put the reins in their hands. Sturge dissented, but an agreement was reached whereby both organizations would jointly sponsor the next convention.[22]

At the suggestion of the Reverend Henry Richard, the new secretary of the London Society, a Peace Congress Committee made up of members of the Society and the League was formed. Paris had been selected as the site of

20. Burritt to Charles Sumner, London, Nov. 8, 1848, Klingberg Collection.

21. New York *Tribune*, Oct. 19, 1848; *Christian Citizen*, Jan. 6, 1849; Charles Sumner, *Works* (Boston, 1870), II, 250–251.

22. Journals, Oct. 30–31, 1848.

the 1849 gathering and this Peace Committee was responsible for all the arrangements. The Committee voted to raise £5,000 to finance the public meetings which would be held to popularize the convention. The sum was unusually large —the League had carried off the Brussels Convention on £200. Burritt was encouraged by this "spirit of liberality" and was delighted that the Quakers, who dominated the Committee, acted as if "the Peace cause had become one of the *movements* of the day." He was hesitant about accepting the post of joint-secretary of the Committee because he felt acceptance would "absorb my individuality, or prevent my instituting and carrying forward operations connected with the League."[23] But he could not decline the office without offending the London Society.

The Reverend Henry Richard was an eloquent speaker and a competent writer. He understood the problems of peace far more realistically than Burritt, and he was not in Burritt's hurry to resolve the moral injustices of the world. He believed that the establishment of a Congress of Nations would require many years of careful planning and that an international peace convention would accomplish more if it concentrated on less idealistic goals. Richard and Burritt worked well together, but each was wary of the other. Burritt felt that Richard did not always work fast enough, while Richard thought Burritt too precipitate. Richard did not think it right for Burritt to conduct other reform enterprises while preparing for the Paris conference; Burritt harbored the suspicion that Richard was trying to subordinate the League to the London Society.

The only consequential peace reformer in Great Britain or America who believed that a Congress of Nations had a promising future was Burritt. The rest, their feet more firmly planted on the ground than Burritt, sought more

23. *Ibid.*, Nov. 1–16, 1848.

practicable solutions. The most popular peace plan in both countries was international arbitration treaties. In America William Jay, renowned lawyer and judge, had developed the most persuasive argument for arbitration treaties in his book, *War and Peace, The Evils of the First, and a Plan for Preserving the Last*, published in 1842. Joseph Sturge, Henry Richard, and Richard Cobden were enthusiastic supporters of arbitration treaties. Not long after the Brussels Convention Burritt was one of a deputation visiting Lord John Russell, the Prime Minister, to enlighten him on arbitration. Burritt referred to the precedent for the practice set by the United States and Mexico in the treaty of Guadelupe Hidalgo of 1848. Russell declared that should the United States initiate a move for an arbitration agreement with Great Britain, "it would be taken into their most serious consideration."[24]

Undoubtedly Russell realized that the United States would never instigate an arbitration treaty with Great Britain. But Burritt and other members of the deputation interpreted his cautious words as a virtual pledge that the British government wished to arrange arbitration treaties with other nations. "From the manner in which Lord John Russell replied the other day to Elihu Burritt," Sturge wrote to Lewis Tappan, " . . . we think it not at all improbable that he will not oppose such a measure, if he does not positively support it."[25]

Richard Cobden, an intimate friend of Sturge and Henry Richard, was preparing to introduce a motion in the House of Commons in favor of arbitration treaties. The Peace Congress Committee organized giant arbitration rallies to publicize Cobden's intended resolution. About 150 demonstrations were held, and some thousand petitions were sent

24. *Ibid.*, Oct. 30, 1848; Henry Richard, *Memoirs of Joseph Sturge*, pp. 430–431.
25. Quoted in Richard, p. 430.

to Parliament. Burritt spoke at approximately fifty of these meetings. Almost alone he arranged a rally at Exeter Hall in London on June 11, 1849, attended by 3,000 persons. When introduced in the Commons on June 12, Cobden's resolution was defeated by a vote of 176 to 79. But the proponents of arbitration were surprised at the support given it.[26]

Burritt believed arbitration was a useful method for settling international disputes. But he did not consider that it could produce enduring peace—only a Congress of Nations had that potential. When Richard and other pacifists, including League officers, recommended emphasizing arbitration and de-emphasizing a Congress of Nations at Paris, Burritt objected. He argued that Americans, "decided in their preference for a Congress of Nations," would be indifferent to the forthcoming convention unless the subject of a Congress was a salient issue. Sturge sharply informed Burritt that arbitration was "the first measure to be pressed." Cobden, who had no faith in a Congress of Nations, told Burritt that the subject was too "impracticable" to be discussed at the convention.[27] Burritt was hopeful that American pacifists would strenuously endorse the plan at Paris. He was not going to allow the subject to "be thrust into the background."

The glow of the Brussels Convention had been somewhat dimmed by the failure of American peace men to send delegates. Though they had not had much time to prepare for the Convention, Burritt had expected that the first world's peace conference since 1843 would draw at least a few American pacifists. After Auguste Visschers confided to

26. Hansard's *Parliamentary Debates*, CVI, 1849, pp. 54–121; Journals, Dec. 7, 1848, June 11, 1849; Curti, *American Peace Crusade*, pp. 192–193.

27. Journals, Dec. 7, 1848, Feb.-March, June 22, Aug. 15, 20, 1849; *Christian Citizen*, April 28, 1849; J. A. Hobson, *Richard Cobden, The International Man*, p. 52.

him that the success of the 1849 convention would depend on whether Americans "rather lead the way," Burritt personally took charge of telling the Americans that it was their sacred duty to be in Paris. "All are agreed," he wrote to Charles Sumner, "that America should lead the way in this work . . . Now do you not think it possible to get 50 or 100 of the right men from the United States to come over to attend the next Congress at Paris? including 15 or 20 members of our U. S. House of Representatives & Senate?" He tried to prod Sumner into action with the declaration, "The day has come for you to move in this great work, as a leader. You, for the United States, Cobden for England, Lamartine for France—what could you three not do for humanity, if met in such a Congress." Gerrit Smith was also wheedled: "If there be one man in America above any other, who ought to be present at that august demonstration, *thou art the man.*" Burritt sent a honeyed letter to Longfellow, as well as to many other Americans who he thought would add lustre to the Paris convention.[28]

Peace reformers in the United States laid elaborate plans to ensure a substantial deputation at Paris. Members of the League and the American Peace Society organized an American Peace Congress Committee to supervise the widespread publicity they intended to give the convention and to nominate delegates. An American Committee for a Congress of Nations, including Charles Sumner, John Tappan, Amasa Walker, and Joshua P. Blanchard, was also established. At a large demonstration in Boston, in March, 1849, peace men of both organizations were extravagant in their encomiums on the approaching convention and on the bright star that seemed to be shining over a Congress of

28. Burritt to Charles Sumner, London, Nov. 8, 1848, Klingberg Collection; Burritt to Gerrit Smith, May 19, 1849, New Britain Public Institute; Burritt to H. W. Longfellow, London, May 18, 1849, Harvard University Library.

Nations. Peace meetings honoring the convention were held
in many New England towns and cities. Ohio pacifists, led
by the antislavery Congressman Joshua Giddings, clamored
for solid American support of the convention and commended "the successful efforts of our distinguished coun-
tryman, Elihu Burritt, in the cause of Peace."[29] The Committee for a Congress of Nations had nominated over
seventy delegates, including Samuel G. Howe and William
Cullen Bryant. In January, 1849, Congressman Amos Tuck,
a New Hampshire pacifist, had introduced in the House of
Representatives a resolution requesting the Secretary of
State to correspond with foreign governments on the subject
either of arbitration "or for the establishment, instead
thereof, of a Congress of Nations, to determine International
disputes."[30] For the first time since 1841, pacifists seemed
ready to embrace "the American plan," as the subject of a
Congress of Nations was sometimes called out of deference
to William Ladd.

Burritt and Henry Richard worked diligently in Paris
trying to get persons of note to act as officers of the convention. Lamartine declined to serve as president, as did the
Archbishop of Paris, but Victor Hugo agreed to accept the
job. Hugo did not need much prompting. He had a true
passion for peace and was on close terms with leading
French and British pacifists. Such influential free traders
as Emile de Girardin, Frederic Bastiat, Horace Say, Joseph
Garnier, and Michel Chevalier also offered to help. Garnier,
editor of the *Journal des Economistes*, was an active mem-

29. *Christian Citizen*, Jan. 20, April 7-June 30, 1849, *passim*.
30. *Congressional Globe*, 30 Congress, 2 Session, Jan. 16, 1849,
p. 267. In March, 1849, Francisque Bouvet introduced an unusual
resolution in the French National Assembly, suggesting the immediate convocation of the major world powers at Constantinople, on
May 1, 1849, to discuss steps leading to "proportional disarmament" and international arbitration treaties. (*Christian Citizen*, May
5, 1849.)

ber of the Society of Christian Morals, while Girardin, publisher of *La Presse*, impressed Burritt with his genuine peace convictions. Bastiat, Say, and Chevalier were only mildly interested in the peace movement. They agreed to participate largely because Richard Cobden was at the head of the British delegation. The French government was not so suspicious as in the previous year of the intentions of pacifists. Alexis de Tocqueville, Minister of Foreign Affairs, assured Burritt and Richard that there would be no difficulty in securing the government's authorization. He himself did not believe that the time was right for arbitration treaties or a Congress of Nations and advised them "not [to] expect too much."[31]

The Paris Peace Convention, which convened in the Salle de Ste-Cécile on August 22, was larger than that at Brussels and more truly international in composition. Over 700 British delegates were in attendance, and "a very fair sprinkling of Germans, Dutch, and Russians."[32] Approximately 1,500 delegates and spectators all told attended the three-day Convention. Twenty-one American delegates appeared, including Amasa Walker, Charles Durkee, a Wisconsin member of the House of Representatives, and the presidents of Oberlin and Bowdoin. It was a smaller and a much less distinguished group than Burritt had anticipated. Several of the American delegates were advocates of defensive war who would, said Burritt, "add but little strength to the demonstration."[33] But a host of reputable Europeans were there: Victor Hugo, the president of the Convention, Athanase Cocquerel, a leading French Protestant minister, the Abbé Deguerry, curé of the Madeleine, Richard Cobden, Joseph Sturge, Emile de Giradin, Horace Say, Michel Chevalier, and Francisque Bouvet.

31. Journals, July 6–15, 1849.
32. *The Times*, Aug. 21, 1849.
33. Journals, Aug. 19, 1849.

Victor Hugo delivered the opening address. It was a brilliant and moving discourse on the bestiality of war and the favorable prospects for international peace. He announced to the delegates that they "turn[ed] over, as it were, the last page of the gospel—that page which imposes peace on the children of the same God." Peace was not only practicable, "it is inevitable and its execution is only a question of time, and may be hastened or retarded. The law which rules the world cannot be different from the law of God. But the divine law is not one of war—it is peace. Men have commenced in conflict, as the creation did in Chaos. Whence do they proceed? From war, that is evident. But whither do they go? To peace, that is equally evident." Hugo predicted that the day would come when

bullets and shells shall be replaced by votes, by the universal suffrage of nations, by the venerable arbitration of a great sovereign senate, which shall be to Europe what the parliament is to England . . . A day will come when a cannon shall be exhibited in public museums just as an instrument of torture is now, and people shall be astonished how such a thing could have been. A day will come when those two immense groups, the United States of America and the United States of Europe, shall be placed in presence of each other, extending the hand of fellowship across the ocean . . . Nor is it necessary that 400 years shall pass away for that day to come. We live in a rapid period, in the most impetuous current of events and ideas which has ever borne away humanity; and at the period in which we live, a year suffices to do the work of a century."[34]

Hugo's speech elevated the tone of the Convention; no subsequent address compared with it either in poetic eloquence or fervor. Most revolved on the resolutions favoring disarmament and arbitration treaties. Girardin, Bastiat, Cob-

34. *Christian Citizen*, Sept. 15, 1849.

den, and others attacked the high costs of standing armies and the hostility engendered among nations by an arms race and its baleful effect on the world economy. Peace and plenty as opposed to war and destitution was the leading motif in their addresses. Resolutions were passed enjoining the members of the Convention to influence the youth of the world in peace principles, to do the same "to ministers of religion" and "to the various organs of the press," and to work "for the extension of postal reform, for the universal adoption of weights, measures, and coinage, and for the multiplication of peace societies."

A resolution dealing with a Congress of Nations was not adopted until the final session. Had it not been for the pertinacity of Burritt and Amasa Walker, the resolution might not have been introduced, so strong was the opposition to it from Richard, Visschers, and Cobden. Burritt's essay on a Congress of Nations, which was read for him in French, preceded the resolution. The paper covered roughly the same ground as that at Brussels. One difference, however, was that it tried to show that a Congress would not "pretend to exercise any jurisdiction over the internal affairs of a country, or exert any direct political influence upon its institutions." The Abbé Deguerry said that a Congress was the surest way to achieve arbitration, disarmament, and lasting peace, although he realized that "such a step—such a congress—could not be arrived at all at once."[35] Burritt was disappointed that his favorite peace nostrum had not monopolized the proceedings.

At the Brussels Convention many delegates, especially Burritt, had been apprehensive over the possibility that they might fail. At Paris, they were gay and at ease, confident that the world anxiously awaited their dicta. Though the Paris Convention was not, as Burritt wrote years later,

35. *Ibid.*, Sept. 22, 29, 1849.

"the most remarkable assembly that had ever taken place
on the continent of Europe," it was an extraordinary feat
for the pacifists to have gathered together some of the
world's outstanding men to talk on peace. And there was
indeed for Burritt "something of a Pentecost in that three
days' experience."[36] The Convention encouraged pacifists
to believe they had captured the interest of people in all
countries. It motivated previously inactive pacifists to think
and act sanguinely. Burritt thought the Brussels and Paris
assemblies had presaged a new era in the peace movement:
"Contrast the progress of [the] last eleven months with that
of the preceding eleven years, and see if it has not proved
that we are reaching onward to the grand consummation
of the cause."

Henry Richard and the London Peace Society had been
of inestimable help in arranging the Convention. But in
the minds of most pacifists the Paris Convention had been
spawned by the Brussels Convention, and the latter had
been organized by Burritt. Victor Hugo had introduced Burritt to the delegates as "the real founder of the Peace Congress." When Burritt made his first official appearance before the Congress, "Nearly the whole assembly arose" and
applauded wildly; "for two minutes I was unable to speak
an audible word."[37] Before Burritt returned to America, in
October, 1849, a dinner was held in his honor in Manchester; many of Great Britain's most noteworthy humanitarians
and reformers attended. George Wilson and John Bright ex-
tolled his peace work. Wilson proclaimed that "the bar of
public opinion" in England had "decided that he shall take
his place with the Clarksons, and Howards, and Frys of our
native country." Bright admitted that he was "much surprised at the results" of Burritt's visit, and called the peace
conferences at Brussels and Paris "events of no ordinary

36. Burritt, *Thoughts and Notes*, p. 93.
37. See Hugo's remarks in *Christian Citizen*, Sept. 29, 1849; Journals, Aug. 21, 1849.

kind." Though Burritt was not returning to the United States as "Envoy Extraordinary and Minister Plenipotentiary from the Court of St. James to the capitol at Washington," Bright continued, he was nonetheless "an envoy from the people and the hearts of the people of this country to the peace-loving people and the hearts of the people in the United States."[38]

Frankfort was to be the scene of the 1850 convention. Burritt returned home to procure a huge American delegation and to show his comrades that he had not expatriated himself. He was ashamed that fewer than twenty-five Americans had attended the Paris Convention and that none was of the stature of Cobden or Hugo. The unconcern of the Paris delegates for a Congress of Nations, he thought, was due to the small American representation.

In the United States, Burritt conducted an extensive five-month campaign. His search for delegates took him to Virginia, Kentucky, Missouri, Ohio, Michigan, Illinois, and to practically all the northeastern states. He lectured on peace and on a Congress of Nations in crowded auditoriums, halls, and churches. "I have spoken nine nights in succession," he wrote in the midst of his tour, "and traveled about 1,000 miles during that space of time." He addressed large gatherings on "A Society of Nations" in Henry Ward Beecher's Brooklyn Church, in the Broadway Tabernacle, and in the Boston Tremont Temple. In Washington he discussed the peace congresses with Horace Mann, Joshua Giddings, George Julian, and Vice-President Millard Fillmore. So great was the demand for his appearance in the western states that he could not fulfill all the speaking engagements which had been arranged for him.[39]

38. Burritt, *Lectures and Speeches*, pp. 143–163.

39. Burritt, MS Lecture on International Law, Chicago Historical Society; Journals, Jan. 16 to May 13, 1850, *passim*; Charles W. Hunter to Zebina Eastman, Alton, Illinois, May 25, 1850, Chicago Historical Society.

Burritt returned to England, in May, 1850, convinced that his country would be ably represented in Frankfort. In late June, together with Henry Richard and Auguste Visschers, he proceeded to Germany to begin preparations. Burritt had made a few acquaintances in Germany when he spent two weeks there in 1849 trying to encourage attendance at the Paris Convention. Many German scholars, businessmen, and lawyers whom he had invited to Paris had declined because of their disillusionment over the failure of the Frankfort Assembly to create a unified Germany. But they had talked so approvingly of peace congresses that Burritt was certain "a large number of earnest and eminent" Germans would cooperate "when we come to Germany to hold a Congress." By 1850, however, German nationalists had begun to view unification as essentially a military problem. Several told Burritt that war appeared to be the only alternative left to bring about a unified Germany. The venerable Baron von Humboldt, interviewed by Burritt, Richard, and Visschers in Potsdam, was disappointed by the collapse of the Frankfort Assembly. Humboldt had seen "too many congresses to expect any practical result from them." He offered to endorse the convention, but excused himself as "too old and decrepit" to attend personally.[40]

The Frankfort Convention met from August 22–24, in St. Paul's Church. More European nations were represented at this congress than at either Brussels or Paris. Forty American delegates had arrived, almost twice the number that had gone to Paris. Delegates from many German and Italian states were there. Heinrich Jaup, former Prime Minister of Hesse-Darmstadt, was the presiding officer.

Burritt did not plan to address the Convention, but Cobden insisted that he "make a short speech to gratify the curiosity of some of the Germans." His speech was a "re-

40. Journals, July 8–22, 1850.

chauffé" of his two previous Congress of Nations essays. He was at first "disinclined to present a subject so unpopular with the English members" of the Convention, but he felt obligated since no other speaker had talked about a Congress. He was also upset by the "rambling declamations" delivered by two American delegates. A resolution was adopted urging "the convocation of a congress of the representatives of the various states, with a view to the formation of a code of international law." The resolution, which did not refer to a Congress and Court of Nations, was passed. No one except Burritt seemed to care. He was painfully coming to realize that a Congress of Nations might take a little longer than "four or five years."[41]

The Frankfort Convention indirectly entangled Burritt in a unique kind of diplomacy. Dr. Arthur Bodenstedt, a Berlin scholar and pacifist, suggested that the Convention attempt to settle the discord between the duchies of Schleswig-Holstein and Denmark. The duchies belonged to Denmark; but, demanding constitutional concessions and aspiring to ultimate independence, they had rebelled in 1848. An uneasy truce had been reached after some brief, bitter fighting. German nationalists, particularly those in Prussia, envisaged their eventual incorporation in a unified Germany. Dr. Bodenstedt had in his possession a document signed by Berliners and two Schleswig-Holstein envoys which stipulated that they were willing to submit the dispute with Denmark to the arbitration of a committee appointed by the Frankfort Convention. Jaup immediately reminded Bodenstedt of the Convention rule that forbade discussion of current political events.[42]

Joseph Sturge was enthralled by the rare opportunity for peacemaking. After further communications from Berlin sources verified the duchies' desire, he approached Burritt

41. *Ibid.*, Aug. 22–24, 1850; *Christian Citizen*, Sept. 21, 28, 1850.
42. *Christian Citizen*, Sept. 21, 1850.

and Henry Richard with the proposition of acting as quasimediators in the dispute. Richard declined because of his obligations to the London Peace Society, but Burritt was willing. Frederic Wheeler, an English Quaker, agreed to take Richard's place. In a letter to the contending parties they explained that their mission was merely to entreat them "to refer the whole question to the decision of enlightened arbitrators" who would not, however, be themselves.[43]

Burritt in Copenhagen and Sturge and Wheeler in Kiel acted as messengers for the exchange of dispatches between the duchies and Denmark. Baron von Reedtz, Danish Minister of Foreign Affairs, told Burritt that his government would entertain any plan of arbitration drawn up by the duchies. When a rapprochement seemed near, Sturge and Wheeler returned to England, leaving Burritt in Hamburg to continue in the capacity of a human telegraph between the disputants. For three months he played the role of diplomatist-extraordinary. For a while he thought progress was being made. But then von Reedtz peremptorily declared that Denmark would not continue to negotiate because it was tantamount to a recognition of the independence of the duchies. Outraged, Burritt threatened to expose Denmark by proclaiming through the European press its unwillingness to seek a peaceful solution.[44] Naturally this failed to frighten Reedtz. Austria shortened Burritt's stay in Hamburg by marching into Schleswig-Holstein and crushing the rebellion.

Nothing better points out Burritt's limitations as a pacifist than his experience in Copenhagen. His mission could hardly have resulted in anything but failure, but he never seemed even partially aware of this. He was optimistic that

43. Journals, Aug. 30, 1850; Richard, pp. 435–438.
44. Journals, Sept. 13 to Nov. 23, 1850; *Bond of Brotherhood*, Dec., 1850. pp. 49–51.

reason and good sense would resolve the crisis. At any rate, he should have learned how exceedingly difficult it was to negotiate a satisfactory peace. Yet be believed that his effort "would probably have succeeded had it not been interrupted by forcible interference."[45]

Burritt helped to organize three more peace conventions in London (1851), Manchester (1853), and Edinburgh (1853). Only the London Convention was an international gathering. The other two were British peace meetings convened to counteract the war hysteria in England which followed Louis Napoleon's dramatic transformation of the Second French Republic into the Second French Empire in 1851. The Paris Convention had been the apogee of the international peace movement. After that, the glamour of peace congresses had started to wear off. The London Peace Society considered it imprudent to hold yearly conventions, and American pacifists agreed.[46]

Burritt himself became less enthusiastic about peace conventions the more he began to realize how few were the supporters of a Congress of Nations. William Ladd and the American Peace Society had given the matter tremendous publicity from 1837 to 1841, but thereafter not many American pacifists were willing to promote a Congress. Although intrigued by its possibilities and fond of calling it "the American plan," they in fact thought it too unrealistic. Burritt continued to view a Congress "as the end and aim of . . . [peace] operations." It is to his credit that he became the prime exponent of a Congress because, improbable though it may have been, no other single plan contained such complete machinery for the maintenance of peace.

For the most part the peace congresses formulated sensible solutions for the settlement of international disputes

45. Burritt, *Ten-Minute Talks*, pp. 35–37.
46. Christina Phelps, *The Anglo-American Peace Movement in the Mid-Nineteenth Century* (New York, 1930), pp. 55–59.

among nations. The proposals were widely circulated, both favorably and unfavorably, by numerous American and European newspapers and journals.[47] They made up the stock of peace principles and arguments used by later-day pacifists. The congresses had succeeded in giving organized pacifism its first full-dress international hearing. Not many people may have believed that the goal of world peace was realizable, but few denied that the abolition of war was one of mankind's direst needs. On the whole, the peace conventions provoked sympathetic opinion because people liked to think that war was not inherent in the nature of man.

Yet the congresses created only a temporary impulse in the international peace movement. No new national peace societies were established and there was no significant clamor in Europe for peace. By 1850 many romantic European intellectuals and political idealists had seen attempts to fashion liberal governments by open public debate and constitutional procedures smashed by repressive governmental reaction. Some, like the embittered German nationalists of the ill-starred Frankfort Assembly, came to accept war as the last means to political freedom and national unity.

In the flurry of international peace agitation from 1848 to 1851 Burritt and Henry Richard towered above all other pacifists. But Burritt, more than Richard, was the central force behind the transatlantic movement. He believed that he had a messianic role in the cause. Writing to his sister Almira in 1849, he declared, "I am sure that none of you have ever felt that I was not called to occupy this great field of labor & duty, and that you have been reconciled to my long absence in view of the work which I have been called to."[48] His basic working principle was that the per-

47. *Ibid.*, pp. 180–185.
48. Burritt to Almira Burritt, London, June 29, 1849, New York Historical Society.

petual reign of peace on earth was just around the corner. Such unbridled faith infused the movement with high hopes. The practical Richard Cobden now and then was rankled by Burritt's ignorance of the political and economic aspects of peace. "Perhaps with more knowledge of the practical affairs of government," Charles Sumner wrote Cobden in reference to Burritt, "he would necessarily lose something of that hope which is to him an unfailing succor."[49]

The quixotic foreign policy of Napoleon III and the outbreak of the Crimean War in 1853 and the American Civil War in 1861 shattered the international peace crusade. Even before then, Burritt had grown stale: "I have now written upon almost every point and principle involved in the subject of Peace," he pompously wrote in 1852, "and . . . [it] is difficult to find a phase or feature to develop."[50]

If it was becoming a chore for Burritt to develop new insights into peace, it was the result of his having few insights outside those the Gospels provided him. His stand against war had been based almost entirely on the ethics of the New Testament and had been enunciated in the idiom of evangelicalism. On these grounds he had managed to make a pretty good case, but it was, nevertheless, a case that lacked sufficient solidity and credibility because it did not recognize that men and nations do not live by the Gospels alone.

The Crimean War gave Burritt another opportunity to put his peace principles to practical use. The London Peace Society was directing all its efforts against the war. Henry Richard suggested to Senator Charles Sumner that the United States offer to mediate between Russia and Turkey. Burritt, by now back home, wrote President Franklin Pierce that the United States was "the only power in Christendom

49. Quoted in Edward L. Pierce, *Memoirs and Letters of Charles Sumner* (Boston, 1887), III, 74.
50. Journals, June 22, 1852.

whose status and position would inspire confidence in the justice and impartiality of its arbitrament." He told Pierce how he and Cobden had personally requested the American minister to Great Britain, J. R. Ingersoll, to offer Russia and Turkey the mediation of the United States.[51]

On April 4, 1854, Burritt and Sumner called on Pierce to discuss the President's reactions to Burritt's letter. Pierce said he agreed with its spirit and principles but believed that the United States was not "in a position to deal competently with the merits of the question, and might embarrass the powers, without preventing a collision." Burritt asked Pierce for permission to inform Cobden that the United States might, if all other expedients failed, offer to act as mediator. Pierce refused to commit the country to such a course. A few days after the conference Sumner told Burritt he had again pressed Pierce with the question of mediation, but that the President's "chief objection seems to be that such an offer would give these powers an opportunity to step in between the U. S. & Spain in the matter of Cuba." Since the Pierce administration was agitating for the acquisition of Cuba, Burritt believed that there was "a good deal of reason" for Sumner's "conclusion."[52]

Great Britain and France had come to the aid of Turkey when the Crimean War started. Burritt was convinced that Great Britain, with a vital stake in the Near East, desired war with Russia. He was also certain that the British press, "cater[ing] to national prejudices," was "mainly responsible for this calamitous war with Russia." In the new monthly periodical he began editing in the United States in 1855, he accused British newspapers, especially *The Times*, of having "wrought immense mischief in Europe." He maintained that Russia had been duped into war to appease the imperialistic ambitions of Great Britain. He was hostile

51. *Ibid.*, March 24, 29, 1854.
52. *Ibid.*, April 3–7, 1854.

toward Turkey, and thought "the Turkish dynasty must ere long die." European Turkey was an anachronism which "must escheat to existing powers." He announced that Russia, because of geographic position, a similar religious faith, and a largely Slav population, was the logical successor to Turkish possessions in the Balkans.[53]

Burritt sided with Russia because he believed that her expansion into eastern Europe was not "antagonistic to the progress of civilization." Christian Russia was morally superior to Islamic Turkey. The "Turkish system, by a probation of centuries, has proved that it must die, that its territory in Europe should be divided between Austria and Russia; that England might properly have Egypt and Syria, and France, Algeria and Asia Minor."[54]

In a series of articles on "Nationalities" Burritt sketched a plan for a political reorganization of Europe which would insure peace and brotherhood. He suggested that all the countries of continental Europe be organized into three confederations under the leadership of France, Germany, and Russia. The "sentiment and dignity of nationality" would "be elevated and enlarged by the union of conterminous States under one government." Since France, Germany, and Russia were the "only *three* Nationalities in Europe possessing and exercising all the prerogatives of complete independent sovereignty," a fusion of nationalities into three great nation-states would result in "a vast political gain . . . to each and all." This amalgamation would "give to the confederate nations thus constructed the elements of new political life and progress."[55] Burritt also "admitted the probability of the whole continent of North America becoming

53. *Citizen of the World*, Feb., 1855, pp. 17–21, June, 1855, pp. 81–85.
54. Journals, Jan. 3, 1855.
55. *Citizen of the World*, Oct., 1855, pp. 145–148.

absorbed into the Union" of the United States on a confederative basis.[56]

Burritt's articles on the Crimean War and on nationalities reveal his profound misunderstanding of international politics. They also indicate an incredible inability to discern the drift of specifically European politics. He propounded a bizarre internationalism at a time when nationalism was rampant, and he naively believed the civil and political liberties of Europeans would be enhanced simply through the formation of three all-embracing nation-states. His arguments he based not on realities but on the frothy notion that the "social tendencies" of the age pointed to increased international cooperation, which he thought could be extended into political and constitutional realms so as to create a brotherhood of nations. Because society was beginning to integrate at least economically, through the general acceptance of the principle of free trade, he was absolutely certain that political and social integration would follow.

If Burritt's international peace pronouncements had been too optimistic, his prophecy of a new international political order was chimerical. Constantly on the lookout for "signs of the time," he generally misread them. His ingrained moralistic view of international affairs, both political and economic, was at once his weakness and his strength, for while it made him a poor judge of current events, it supplied the motive for his continuing search for universal peace.

56. Journals, Jan. 3, 1855.

9

Ocean Penny Postage

From peace to postage was an easy and logical step for Burritt. The League pledge urged "the abolition of all restrictions upon international correspondence and friendly intercourse." This declaration was based on the belief that the success of League operations depended "upon the facility and freedom of international intercourse, or upon a perfect free trade in thought and opinions, between the people of different nations." Cheap international postage would be "an inestimable instrumentality in the diffusion of knowledge and the Christian Religion" and in the promotion of world peace.[1]

In 1846 Burritt originated a plan to facilitate the exchange of letters among nations. He proposed that postage for the ocean transit of a letter be established at the uniform rate of one penny, or two cents, to which charge would be added the inland postage of the countries at each end of the journey. He called his plan "ocean penny postage." At first he desired that inland postage in all countries be reduced to a penny, so that the total cost of an overseas letter would be three pennies, or six cents. This would

1. *Christian Citizen*, Oct. 10, 1846.

have required a substantial reduction in existing rates, since
the minimum rate of a letter between Great Britain and
the United States was a shilling, or twenty-four cents. But
since Great Britain alone had domestic penny postage, Burritt thought it would complicate his plan if he insisted that
all nations adopt the same low inland rate.[2]

Great Britain's adoption of domestic penny postage in
1840 had stimulated movements in Europe and America for
the reduction of postage, but no country approached the
British standard. Domestic postage in the United States, for
example, was extremely high: letter rates depended upon
the number of sheets per letter and the distance it travelled.
The 1816 postal law fixing letter charges, which remained
virtually unchanged for almost thirty years, suggests that
letter-writing was a luxury in which the poor could hardly
often indulge. The rates were:

> For every letter composed of a single sheet of paper, con-
> veyed not exceeding 30 miles, 6 cents; over 30 miles, and
> not exceeding 80 miles, 10 cents; over 80 miles and not ex-
> ceeding 150 miles, 12½ cents; over 150 miles and not ex-
> ceeding 400 miles, 18½ cents; over 400 miles, 25 cents; and
> every double letter or two pieces of paper, double said
> rates; every triple letter, or three pieces of paper, triple said
> rates.[3]

Despite these rates, the Post Office ended each fiscal year
with a deficit: from 1837-1845 postal expenditures exceeded
revenues by nearly $2,000,000.[4] Owing chiefly to increased
agitation by postal reformers, who argued that high postage
discouraged letter-writing and helped create postal deficits,

2. *Ibid.*

3. *Postage Rates, 1789–1930, Abstract of Laws Passed Between
1789 and 1930, Fixing Rates of Postage and According Free Mail
Privileges* (Washington, 1930), p. 3.

4. Daniel C. Roper, *The United States Post Office* (New York,
1917), p. 62.

Congress in 1845 reduced domestic postage. Letters weighing under half an ounce could be sent within a distance of
300 miles for 5 cents and beyond that for 10 cents.

Whereas an inland letter carried under 300 miles cost 5
cents, Burritt's proposed rate for the same letter sent across
the seas was only two cents. Burritt knew very little about
postal matters and conditions at the time he began to formulate his scheme. During his early reform career in America, he began to complain about high postage when his
humanitarian ventures had turned him into a prolific letter-
writer. With satisfaction he noted in his Journal the 1845
reduction in postage; but before he drafted the League
pledge, nothing indicates that he planned to take up cheap
ocean postage as one of his reform enterprises. Yet he was
"exceedingly anxious to bring forward some great measure
on the platform of the League."[5] Ocean penny postage was
just the reform with which to begin.

Burritt believed that "Great Britain, under the accumula-
ting impetus of progress, which she cannot resist, might be
impelled to take another long step in advance, and establish an *ocean penny postage*." With movements underway
in Europe and the United States "for cheap postage to conform to the English system," he thought 1846 a propitious
year to commence agitation for his plan. In the first of a
multitude of Olive Leaves he was to write on this reform,
he disclosed the "magnificent sense in which Britannia may
'rule the waves.'" Through the genius of her free-trade principles England had showered on the world the marvels of
science and technology; England's "coal and iron are the
spirit, bone, and muscle of the socializing agencies now
working to bring the world's extremes into amicable neighborhood." Great Britain, because of a superior mentality
and finely-developed humanitarian instincts, had become
"the heart of the world, in every sense of moral, intellectual,

5. Journals, Feb. 10, 1845, Nov. 9, 1846.

and physical existence, and location." By establishing ocean penny postage Great Britain "would bring all nations of men within the range of the vital functions of that heart-relation which she sustains to the world."[6]

Burritt's second Olive Leaf on the subject generalized why "England alone" was capable of such a reform:

> The nation that shall work out this desideratum of the age must be singularly qualified for the undertaking, by the conformity of the genius of its population to the physical constitution of its territory; both of which must distinguish it from any other race and country. It is not enough that it be planted in the sea, upon a small island, and apparently compelled to provide for its wants by a commerce with distant and continental countries: nor is it enough that its population should increase by a ratio unparalleled in the propagation of the human species . . . A commercial necessity does not create a commercial genius. A sea-girt country does not, in itself, make a seafaring people.

Not only Great Britain's insular position alone had made her the commercial power of the world; it was also the "constitutional · genius" of the English race. That inherent quality of moral and intellectual brilliance had blended with "the physical constitution and condition of the island of Great Britain" to create a "gigantic ability" to institute ocean penny postage.[7]

The article omitted any trenchant analysis of the practicability of ocean penny postage because it had not yet occurred to Burritt to inquire whether the reform was feasible. But he felt strongly enough about the plan to inform American readers of the *Christian Citizen* that he intended "to bore John Bull until he will agree to convey letters across the ocean for a penny each." So confident was he

6. *Christian Citizen*, Oct. 10, 1846, Mar. 20, 1847.
7. *Ibid.*, April 3, 1847.

that the reform would be quickly enacted that in 1847 he vowed before several public meetings not to return to America until Great Britain adopted his postage program. The fact that about forty British newspapers had published his first two Olive Leaves was to him an affirmation that the scheme had blossomed into a movement. He was also "sure all the Leaguers in America will coincide with their brethren in England in the appreciation of Ocean Penny Postage, as a great instrumentality in 'fusing the nations into one peaceful brotherhood,' and in diffusing the principles of freedom, civilization and Christianity through the world."[8]

In 1847 Burritt undertook to learn something about postal affairs. He wrote Rowland Hill, Secretary to the Postmaster-General, introducing his plan and soliciting advice and assistance. Hill had been chiefly responsible for Great Britain's adoption of domestic penny postage in 1840. His pamphlet *Post Office Reform: Its Importance and Practicability*, published in 1837, was an incisive examination of the policies of the British Post Office. It had exposed the confused and contradictory rates on various forms of mail. Hill had emphasized the necessity of a uniform rate on inland letters and had demonstrated statistically that penny postage would pay. His ideas were adopted by British reformers of the Manchester School until eventually the government consented to initiate penny postage. A cardinal argument advanced by Hill in favor of the reform had been that postal revenues would not be significantly reduced by lowering the letter rate to a penny. He had predicted that penny postage would in time increase the number of letters five-fold, which figure, he had estimated, would offset the lower rate of postage. But Hill had miscalculated on how soon the five-fold increase would be achieved; not until 1851

8. *Ibid.*, May 15, 29, 1847.

did the gross postal revenue reach the sum brought in by the last year of the unreformed rates and even then the net revenue was only two-thirds of the 1839 figure. It required an additional three years for the volume of letters to increase sufficiently to approximate the 1839 net income. Hill himself later admitted that he had been "over-sanguine" in anticipating only a slight and "temporary" reduction in revenue from penny postage.[9]

In a conversation with Burritt in June, 1847, Hill acknowledged the importance of ocean penny postage, but revealed his sensitivity on the matter of revenue by declaring that the project "was impracticable on account of the diminution of the revenue which would ensue." Hill gave Burritt a pamphlet containing postal statistics. "Thus ended," wrote the undiscouraged Burritt, "my first interview with the Napoleon of cheap postage." Shortly afterwards Burritt wrote Hill to "expect to see & hear the proposition agitated during the coming winter, both through the press & public lectures."[10]

Burritt wrote several Olive Leaves to prove that cheap postage "would pay." He pointed out that the present minimum shilling rate drastically diminished the number of letters exchanged between Great Britain and the United States. Excessive amounts of mail lay "dead" in the British Post Office because the postage was so high that persons to whom letters were sent refused to accept them. Ocean penny postage would eliminate this nuisance and waste. Clandestine devices used to avoid ocean postage would also be checked. It was common procedure for people to give friends or even strangers crossing the Atlantic unsealed letters (sealed letters could not be privately carried) which the voyager would seal and mail at the end of the journey. "If every passenger should thus convey in his pocket twelve

9. Howard Robinson, *The British Post Office, A History* (Princeton, 1948), pp. 258–288, 321–324.
10. Journals, June 11, August 26, 1847.

letters," Burritt estimated that "1,000 [letters] crossed the ocean in every mail steamer, for which the English Government received not a single farthing. Allowing fifty transits a year, 50,000 letters would annually cross the Atlantic, outside of the English mail, and on the very steamers paid to convey it."[11]

Great Britain's adoption of his proposal, Burritt wrote, would give her a monopoly over "all letters from America directed to France, Germany, and the rest of the continent, and *vice versa* [making] English penny postage stamps a kind of international currency, at par on both sides of the Atlantic, and which might be procured without the loss of a farthing by way of exchange." This would allow small sums of money in the form of postage stamps to be conveyed between Great Britain and America "at less cost . . . than the charge upon money orders."[12] He referred to the popular practice of writing overseas letters on a special paper called "foreign post". Foreign post paper was tissue-thin and allowed a person to send in an envelope weighing under half an ounce over a dozen communications for the price of one. Burritt himself made frequent use of this practice.[13]

Burritt pointed out that the postal arrangements Great Britain concluded with steamship companies did not specify the "fixed price of postage on letters or newspapers transmitted in its mails." Great Britain could set any rate for overseas letters. Further, the Cunard line, which was paid a £145,000 yearly subsidy by the government to carry the mail, was obligated to convey mail irrespective of volume.[14]

Burritt attempted to establish the actual cost of an over-

11. *Christian Citizen*, July 24, 1847.
12. *Ibid.*, July 31, 1847.
13. Burritt to Mrs. Merriam, London, Sept. 1, 1854; Burritt to Elias Lane, London, March 22, [1847], Swarthmore Friends Historical Library.
14. *Christian Citizen*, Dec. 25, 1847.

seas letter on the basis of the three postal functions defined by Hill: collection, transmission, and delivery.[15] Using Hill's figure of one thirty-sixth of a penny for the cost of transmitting a letter, Burritt assumed that "collection costs twice as much as the transmission, or a penny for eighteen letters." Hence, if 30,000 letters were carried to America by every steamship leaving Liverpool, the expense of collecting and distributing the letters, at the assumed rate, would be less than £12. Allowing the Post Office £6 for sorting the letters in Liverpool and getting them aboard a steamer, the total cost of conveying the letters to America would have been £18. By charging only a penny for the ocean transit of each letter, the Post Office would have received £125 for an expenditure of £18.[16]

Burritt's profit analysis was a gross exaggeration. For one thing, it relied too heavily on Hill's conjecture that the average cost of transmitting a letter in Great Britain was one thirty-sixth of a penny; for another, it did not take into consideration the huge subsidy paid Cunard, which in 1845 came to roughly £12,000 a month. (This enormous sum was expended not only for the sake of mail service, but also because the government desired the construction of a large private merchant marine that could provide ships to meet various national needs.[17]) The fact that the 1848 net postal revenue was less than half of what it had been in 1839 was proof that Hill's one thirty-sixth figure was unreliable. Burritt was so anxious to prove that ocean penny postage would pay that he applied a convenient arithmetic to a complex problem and came out with a foolish answer. As a reformer who liked to show the fiscal common sense of his reforms, Burritt always made figures square with his preconceived notions.

15. Robinson, p. 266.
16. *Christian Citizen*, Feb. 12, 1848.
17. Robinson, p. 388.

From 1847 to 1849 Burritt continued to disseminate his ideas on ocean postage through Olive Leaves, occasional lectures, and talks with small groups of businessmen. The *Daily News* and *Nonconformist* in London, the *Manchester Examiner*, Preston *Guardian*, Leeds *Mercury*, Plymouth *Journal*, and *Chambers's Edinburgh Journal* were but some of the British newspapers and journals to endorse the project.[18] Ocean penny postage placards were displayed in public places throughout Great Britain. George Bradshaw, Burritt's Manchester friend, arranged for a special print to be inserted in his railway guides.[19] Envelopes bearing various designs and slogans were printed and sold. The design was usually a ship whose foresail or topsail carried such slogans as "THE WORLD'S WANT AND SHOULD BE BRITAIN'S BOON—AN OCEAN PENNY POSTAGE"; "BRITAIN! BESTOW THIS BOON AND BE IN BLESS-ING BLEST—OCEAN PENNY POSTAGE—WILL LINK ALL LANDS WITH THEE IN TRADE AND PEACE." League paper was headed by a picture of a ship on whose foresail were the words "OCEAN PENNY POSTAGE"; beneath the engraving was the rhyme:

"Fair speed thee ship whose signal is unfurled,
An 'OCEAN PENNY POSTAGE' for the world."[20]

After the Paris Peace Convention Burritt decided to make ocean penny postage the "chief operation" of the League. But his journey to the United States to enlist a large dele-

18. Journals, May 29, July 3, Sept. 4, Nov. 20, 1847, Feb. 5, 1848; Burritt to Elias Lane, May 8, [1847], Swarthmore College Peace Collection. By 1852 *The Times* had become interested in Burritt's project. Journals, Aug. 4, 1852, Jan. 22, 1853; see Burritt's article in *The Times*, August 4, 1852.

19. Journals, Nov. 5, 1847, March 6, 1848; *Second Annual Report of the Edinburgh League of Universal Brotherhood* (Edinburgh, 1849), pp. 3, 10.

20. See Fred J. Melville, *A Penny All The Way, the Story of Penny Postage* (Boston, 1908), p. 31.

gation for the Frankfort Convention, and his subsequent European travels, pushed the reform into the background. In 1849, however, he wrote a pamphlet entitled *Ocean Penny Postage: Its Necessity Shown and Its Feasibility Demonstrated.* Though restating most of the points already made in Olive Leaves, it was the fullest exposition Burritt ever attempted.

The pamphlet evinced a surer grasp of the subject than did the earlier Olive Leaves. He still used Rowland Hill's computation that it cost no more than one thirty-sixth of a penny to send a letter from Edinburgh to London as a yard-stick to determine the cost of transmitting a letter from Liverpool to Boston; and, on the basis of comparative distances, he concluded that the letter transmission would cost "only one-seventh of a penny." He made a strong point by asserting that Great Britain allowed newspapers weighing three ounces (the weight of six letters) to be sent to her colonies for only a penny, while a half-ounce letter cost at least a shilling. The total number of newspapers mailed abroad in 1846, he showed by quoting official postal statistics, though less than one-third of the number of overseas letters for that year, actually weighed slightly more than the letters. "Thus Britain has applied the penny postal system to half the contents of her mail bags, to and from her distant colonies whilst the other half is still subjected to the shilling regime."[21]

If Great Britain bestowed his postage reform upon her North American subjects, Burritt wrote, it would only be necessary for the number of letters exchanged to be quadrupled to make the three-penny rate pay as much as the shilling rate. He predicted that ocean penny postage would serve as such a stimulus to letter-writing that the number of letters would increase at least four-fold. After summa-

21. *Ocean Penny Postage; Its Necessity Shown and Its Feasibility Demonstrated* (London, 1849), *passim.*

rizing the various devices to evade sea postage, he happily concluded that his plan was practicable.[22]

The London *Nonconformist* thought Burritt's pamphlet had "fully demonstrated" the feasibility of ocean penny postage:

> Our space forbids our giving the calculations in detail; but we take it to be proved in the tract before us, that without a farthing's additional expense to Government, letters may be conveyed by the mails to every one of our colonies, and hence to all parts of the world, at the rate proposed, and that the loss incurred by the diminution of the rate charged, would be more than made up by the additional correspondence with the transmission of which the British mails would be entrusted.

There was "no impediment in the way to the adoption of this beneficent project but the *vis inertiae* of Government."[23]

In 1851, after dallying four years with the subject, Burritt determined to push hard for the reform. Several factors satisfied him that the "mind of the age is awake, and pressing forward." The Great Exhibition of 1851 filled his mind "with the most pleasing auguries and anticipations of the future"; the Crystal Palace "seemed glorious in its transfigurations, as if Heaven embosomed it with the halo of its smile, as the Temple of Universal Brotherhood." He believed ocean penny postage "should be associated with the Great Exhibition, as the complement of the grand demonstration. How graceful and magnanimous it would be in Great Britain, to open the half century, and inaugurate a new cycle of human progress, with such a gift to mankind."[24] The celebrated Thomas Carlyle talked with Burritt

22. *Ibid.*
23. Quoted in the *Christian Citizen*, Aug. 25, 1849.
24. Journals, Jan. 1, Sept. 27, Oct. 11, 1851.

about peace and made some encouraging remarks on the necessity of ocean penny postage. At the London Peace Convention of 1851 William Ewart, M.P., announced that he was a delegate to the Convention from the people of Liverpool, and that they had commissioned him "to urge O.P.P. as a method of uniting nations."[25]

Rowland Hill was now "quite favourable to the idea," wrote Burritt, "but is too much restricted by his connection with the Government to take an active part in pressing it himself." Burritt questioned Richard Cobden about the wisdom of introducing a motion in the House of Commons in favor of ocean penny postage. Cobden, who had been a vocal supporter of domestic penny postage, "thought that public opinion was not ripe enough for it yet, and that it would be necessary to draw up an accurate statistical statement to show that the measure was feasible." Burritt asked the liberal M.P. Thomas Milner Gibson to introduce a motion in the Commons for ocean penny postage. Gibson, showing "manifest interest," informed Burritt he would seek the opinion of Hill. After first discussing the subject with Cobden, Gibson was "a little more cautious." Rowland Hill's counsel left Gibson even more dubious; Hill flatly predicted that any reduction of ocean postage would contract postal revenue, and that the great increase in letters resulting from cheaper ocean postage would "occasion additional expense to the Department."[26]

To dispel doubts over ocean penny postage, Burritt wrote a tract in which he rehashed his most compelling arguments and added a few new ones. He suggested that the government take advantage of the other steamship companies that were ready to underbid the Cunard line, stating that perhaps as much as half of the £145,000 yearly subsidy

25. *Bond of Brotherhood*, Feb., 1851, p. 47; Journals, July 8, 23, 1851.

26. Journals, April 9-June 6, 1851, *passim*.

could be saved. He declared that there was "no postal charge in Christendom so anomalous and exorbitant as that imposed upon the correspondence between Great Britain and France." Paris was nearer to London than Edinburgh; yet it cost 10d to send a letter from London to Paris, and 6½d of that rate covered the Channel-passage which took only two hours. Burritt estimated that 2,000,000 letters had been conveyed between Great Britain and America in 1850. "Now, we want 8,000,000 to produce, under an Ocean Penny Postage, the amount derived from these 2,000,000, at the shilling rate." Half of the 8,000,000 letters would come from those Anglo-American correspondents of 1850, who, because of reduced postage, "would actually write two letters . . . where they write one at the existing charge." The rest would be realized through the correspondence of the thousands of Britishers who emigrated to America each year.[27]

More than a million copies of Burritt's four-page tract were circulated, and now Cobden, as well as other M. P.'s, appeared more receptive to the idea. Henry Cole was interested in Burritt's plan. Cole, a man of extraordinary ability, was an influential public servant and the chief organizer of the Great Exhibition. He had also been associated with the domestic penny postage movement during the thirties. He told Burritt that he had formed the "nucleus" of a parliamentary clique to support ocean penny postage, and that he believed the reform might be carried in two years, or "perhaps right away." Thomas Gibson had been pulled into the small group of M.P.'s who favored the project largely because of Cole's endorsement, Cobden's renewed interest, and the approval Manchester liberals, particularly George Wilson, gave to the plan. Gibson consented to introduce a motion on ocean penny postage, and Burritt

27. *Ocean Penny Postage. Will It Pay?* (London, 1851), pp. 1–4.

promised him that he would try to hold 100 public meetings and secure 1,000 petitions before the end of April, 1852.[28]

Another consideration influencing Gibson's offer to introduce a motion was the drive he was led to believe was about to take place in the United States Senate. Burritt had written Charles Sumner, elected to the Senate in 1851, to take up ocean penny postage. Sumner's favorable reply made Gibson think that Sumner could stir strong sentiment in the Senate in favor of the reform.[29] Sumner, on the other hand, was misinformed about the strength of the cause in Great Britain. Burritt had misled him by writing, "The public mind here is most favorably disposed toward it; public men are ready to act for it; there is no opposition, economical, political, or religious. *Protectionists*, Free Traders, and Radicals, Churches, Dissenters, Protestants and Catholics, are ready to lend a helping hand."[30] Burritt really was "almost astounded at the success which is attending this movement." The casual approbation of a few merchants, M.P.'s, and reformers was enough to make the politically naive Burritt think that ocean penny postage was on the verge of adoption.

From January to April, 1852, Burritt held over sixty public meetings in England and Scotland and talked to groups of prominent merchants and bankers whenever he could. His letters to newspapers in British North America were rewarded by heavily signed petitions from Halifax, Montreal, Sherbrooke, and Bytown. A petition from Kingston, Jamaica, was "signed by the mayor, rector and a large number of magistrates, curates, clergymen of different denominations, and other influential citizens." A memorial from

28. Journals, June 14, 25, Nov. 27, 1851, Jan. 3, 1852.
29. *Ibid.*, Nov. 4, 1851, Jan. 3, 1852.
30. Burritt to Sumner, London, Nov. 7, 1851, in Curti, *The Learned Blacksmith*, pp. 92–93.

the women of Great Britain to Queen Victoria was drawn up by Burritt and contained some 60,000 signatures. At many of the public meetings he assured his auditors that the "commanding eloquence and energy" of Charles Sumner was behind the measure in the United States Senate.[31] Burritt was of course not content to promote ocean penny postage during his travels in England and Scotland. He found time to establish thirteen Olive Leaf Societies; and when he returned to London after winding up his tour, he started developing "my plan for rescuing the young vagrants in London from the sewers of sin and poverty."[32] He was impatient for Gibson to introduce the motion, but yet could hardly wait until that was over so that he could get on with other reforms.

Despite numerous petitions and Burritt's successful tour, Gibson was aware of no groundswell in the Commons for ocean penny postage. He offered lame excuses and wanted to know what Cobden and others thought about the motion. Henry Cole's parliamentary "nucleus" had become mysteriously inactive. Gibson properly advised that it was "unwise to bring forward the motion in the last days of the dying Parliament." He thought it enough merely to call the attention of the Commons to the large number of petitions that had flooded Parliament. Burritt admitted to himself that the reform would not "be carried by the first attempt, for the public are not sufficiently in earnest as yet for the boon."[33] Neither, he might have added, were his parliamentary friends.

Only a few days before Parliament adjourned, however, John Bright, who had earlier shown but tepid concern for

31. Journals, Jan.-Apr., 1852; Northend, *Elihu Burritt*, pp. 440–441; *Bond of Brotherhood*, August, 1852, p. 11, Nov., 1852, p. 60; Burritt to Sumner, London, Jan. 2, 1852, in Curti, p. 95.

32. Journals, April 8, 1852.

33. *Ibid.*, April 19, 30, May 4, 1852.

ocean penny postage, spoke on the reform in the Commons. He explained the simple object of the plan and stated that cheaper communication would promote "friendly intercourse" and strengthen "the guarantees for international peace." The subject would be brought before the Commons in the next session, "either by a direct motion, or by a motion for a Committee of Inquiry," and that the Chancellor of the Exchequer "should turn his attention" to the question during the recess. Bright believed "the immediate loss in the revenue would be as speedily made up by the increase of correspondence as it had been in the case of the establishment of the present internal postage system."[34] (He obviously did not realize that domestic penny postage had not yet proved a financial success.)

Burritt was cheered by Bright's unexpected remarks. As he prepared to strike out on another campaign "to deepen and widen the measure," he received from Charles Sumner a newspaper containing the resolution on cheap ocean postage the latter had introduced in the Senate in March, 1852. The resolution asked that the President of the United States start negotiations "with the European Powers, particularly with the Governments of Great Britain and France, for the establishment of Cheap Ocean Postage." Sumner had defended the resolution by using the arguments and data Burritt had developed in his ocean penny postage pamphlets. Burritt was thankful that Sumner had kept his word but dissatisfied that the resolution did not explicitly call for ocean penny postage. He had earlier written Sumner "not to go for anything but the penny, the whole penny, and nothing but the penny, not for any installment." Now he entreated the Senator "to nail the flag of 1 penny ocean

34. Hansard's *Parliamentary Debates*, CXXII, 1852, pp. 1318–1319. Bright later spoke in behalf of the reform at some of the public meetings arranged by Burritt. (R.A.J. Walling, ed., *The Diaries of John Bright*, New York, 1931, pp. 132–133.)

postage to your masthead, and never strike or lower it. There is power in the very word *penny.*"[35]

The British government was seriously considering lowering the sea postage of letters sent to her colonies. A major reason for its concern was the pressure exerted by the Colonial and International Cheap Postage Association, formed in 1852, but operating informally since 1851. Henry Cole was "the father and founder" of the Association, Lord Granville the president. Its executive council, which included Burritt, consisted of thirty-six individuals from Great Britain, the United States, Austria, Prussia, and Spain.[36] Altogether the Association had such influence that Rowland Hill, "fearing that the Government might . . . [have] to resist a popular demand or to submit to a very serious loss of revenue," proposed to the Postmaster-General in 1851 a reduction of colonial postage from a shilling to 6d, with 4d the rate for the ocean transit of a letter and 1d the inland rate at each end of the journey. Hill never deviated from the conviction that "where very great distances are concerned, where in the nature of things answer is slow, multiplication is but moderately affected by the lowering of rate."[37] He gave Burritt the impression that he favored ocean penny postage, but in fact he was opposed to it.

Hill's plan was adopted in 1853. In March of that year a delegation from the Colonial Cheap Postage Association called on Postmaster-General Lord Canning to plead cheap penny postage for the colonies. They were told of the arrangements being made to reduce the entire cost of an overseas letter to 6d, with 4d the ocean rate. The Association

35. *Congressional Globe,* 32 Congress, 1 Session, Mar. 2, 1852, pp. 694, 1533; Journals, May 7, 1852; Burritt to Sumner, London, July 2, 1852, in Curti, p. 96.

36. Journals, Dec. 20, 1852; Frank Staff, *The Penny Post, 1680–1908* (London, 1964), p. 121.

37. Rowland Hill and George B. Hill, *The Life of Sir Rowland Hill* (2 vols. London, 1880), II, 241–242.

later agreed not to "accept as final" the new arrangement proposed by the government and endorsed Burritt's scheme for lowering the ocean rate to a penny, thereby providing a uniform three-penny rate.[38]

The Colonial Association arranged for a large deputation to confer with Lord Aberdeen, the Prime Minister, on the matter of ocean penny postage for the colonies. More than eighty M.P.'s and many merchants and bankers met with Aberdeen and presented their case in behalf of the reform. Lord Aberdeen politely professed his "great respect for the arguments and statements." But he did not feel "warranted" in reversing the proposal of Lord Canning, and he suggested rather facetiously that, since many of his callers were engaged in shipping, "the Government would be quite willing to have them undertake the mails or letters at a cheaper rate than the Post Office proposed."[39]

Burritt, a silent member of the group that called on Lord Aberdeen, misunderstood the Prime Minister's plain inferences while indulging in a little self-praise: "This was a scene of the deepest interest to me. I could hardly realize that this great company of influential men had waited upon the Premier merely to urge the very proposition which I had launched upon the tide of public opinion in 1846."[40]

Before the conference with Lord Aberdeen, Burritt had been told by Lord Granville that the government would not go beyond the proposed four-penny ocean transit rate since it was "a question of finance" with the Chancellor of the Exchequer, W. E. Gladstone. But Burritt, who had little grasp of politics and none of legislative procedures, kept pressing Gibson to introduce the motion. John Bright advised that a motion for a committee of inquiry to study the

38. *Bond of Brotherhood*, April, 1853, p. 140; London *Daily News*, March 5, 1853; Journals, March 7, 15, 1853.
39. Journals, April 16, 1853.
40. *Ibid.*

reform would be more realistic and would find Gibson less hesitant to introduce it.[41] Bright and Cobden appreciated the Treasury's concern over a pronounced postage reduction.

On August 4, 1853, Gibson finally introduced Burritt's scheme in the Commons. He referred to the large number of petitions favoring ocean penny postage that had been received by Parliament, emphasized the exorbitant cost of sea postage, and spoke of the social benefits the reform would bestow on British emigrants. On the following day in the Commons, he privately asked Gladstone if "there should be any objection to the appointment of a committee to inquire into the general question of colonial and foreign postage in the early part of [the] next session." Gladstone, alluding to the postage reform the government was initiating for the colonies, replied that it was inadvisable "at present to give a pledge on the subject, though he did think that ocean postage was a fit subject for Parliamentary inquiry . . . next session."[42]

Satisfied that ocean penny postage was "well launched" in the Commons, Burritt crossed the Channel and discussed his project with postal officials in Rotterdam, Bremen, Hamburg, and Berlin. They made it appear that Great Britain was not interested in reducing sea postage. Burritt distributed a few placards and tracts, and returned to England convinced that most of western Europe sympathized with his reform.[43]

In October, 1853, Burritt returned to the United States to begin agitation he expected would culminate in the approval by Congress of ocean penny postage. He had sent his tracts to many Congressmen and had received encour-

41. *Ibid.*, Apr. 4-June 18, 1853, *passim.*
42. Hansard's *Parliamentary Debates*, CXXIX, 1853, pp. 1294–1295; Journals, Aug. 5–6, 1853.
43. Journals, Aug. 22-Sept. 9, 1853, *passim.*

aging replies from Senators Salmon P. Chase and William H. Seward.[44] Accompanied by Henry Cole and several M.P.'s, Burritt, in May, 1852, had interviewed in London, the American minister to Great Britain, Abbott Lawrence. They had asked him to recruit important American government officials to support ocean penny postage. Lawrence agreed "to do all in his power to promote" the plan. He believed that penny postage "would pay in five years"; even if it did not, the loss in revenue was nothing compared to "the great blessings which would flow from such a system." Lawrence said that he "had written home for authority to notify the British Govt. that the present postal treaty would not be renewed at the end of the current year."[45]

Sumner's 1852 ocean penny postage resolution and Abbott Lawrence's unauthorized remarks persuaded Burritt that the "Ocean Penny Postage flag is fairly unfurled in the United States." He was encouraged by the endorsement given his plan by the New York and Boston Cheap Postage Associations, headed by Barnabas Bates and Joshua Leavitt respectively. During the forties Bates and Leavitt had been the leaders of the campaign for cheaper inland postage. Although they wanted domestic penny postage, they were pleased with the 1851 postal law which reduced the rate on inland letters not weighing over half an ounce from five cents to three. Leavitt had sanctioned Burritt's plan as early as 1848, and Bates had contributed several ocean penny postage articles to the New York *Journal of Commerce* and the New York *Evening Post*.[46] Bates, wrote Burritt, was "the American 'Rowland Hill.' "

Arriving in America, Burritt wrote Sumner of the ambi-

44. Burritt to William H. Seward, London, Feb. 14, 1851, University of Rochester Library; Burritt to [Gerrit Smith], London, July 25, 1853, Massachusetts Historical Society.

45. Journals, May 3, 1852.

46. *Bond of Brotherhood*, Jan., 1853; Journals, June 13, 1852, Feb. 15–17, 1853; *Christian Citizen*, Feb. 5, June 17, 24, 1848.

tious campaign he was preparing to undertake for ocean penny postage: "I hope to address public meetings on the subject in all the large towns, also to get a hearing at the State Legislatures . . . I intend to go to Washinton to *lobby* a little." He asked Sumner to "fix upon the middle or end of March [1854] for bringing forward the motion" and guaranteed that "before that time we shall bring an avalanche of public opinion upon congress in favor of the scheme." Burritt also apprised Gerrit Smith of how "very poor" he was.[47] Sumner sent encouragement, and Smith money.

With the aid of leading Boston citizens, Burritt organized a demonstration in Faneuil Hall on December 22. Prominent Bostonians—Josiah Quincy, Sr., H. W. Longfellow, Robert E. Winthrop, Dr. Samuel G. Howe, Mayor Benjamin Seaver—sat on the platform with Burritt before "a very respectable" audience. Burritt delivered the opening speech; a Sumner letter was read; and Dr. Howe drafted a memorial to Congress which enumerated the commercial, moral, and humanitarian advantages of ocean penny postage.[48]

Only Burritt's address, a cold statistical analysis of ocean penny postage, threw a damper on the proceedings. Many bored listeners left the hall well before he had finished speaking. "Once I paused and begged the audience to give me fifteen minutes more of patient hearing," wrote a discomfited Burritt, "but with no effect." The Boston press wrote approvingly of the meeting; and Burritt, notwithstanding his personal humiliation, told Longfellow that "a meeting in Fanueil [sic] Hall, with the Mayor of Boston in the chair, and you and Hon. Josiah Quincy on the platform is a great fact, and will make its mark."[49] From his extensive experience with public meetings in Great Britain, Bur-

47. Burritt to Sumner, New Britain, Nov. 15, 1853; Burritt to Smith, New Britain, Nov. 18, 1853, in Curti, pp. 103–107.
48. Boston *Courier*, Dec. 23, 1853; Boston *Commonwealth*, Dec. 23, 1853.
49. Journals, Dec. 22, 1853; Burritt to Longfellow, New Britain, Dec. 26, 1853, Harvard University Library.

ritt should have known better than to overestimate their value. But, in truth, he did not. With him a public demonstration was almost an end in itself.

In New York, Lewis Tappan, an officer of the New York Cheap Postage Association, arranged for Burritt to address a gathering in the Broadway Tabernacle. Chastened by the Boston reception, Burritt shortened his speech, deleted much of the statistical data, and emphasized the moral and philanthropic aspects of ocean penny postage. For three years he had been telling the British that, as the elders of the Anglo-Saxon race, it was their duty to institute his reform so that they could spread their enlightened culture around the globe. Now he informed Americans of their splendid opportunity "to Anglo-Saxonize and Christianize" the world through the adoption of ocean penny postage:

> It is for us to spread Anglo-Saxon labor, language and religion over the world . . . A hundred years ago the Anglo-Saxon race did not exceed twenty millions; it now exceeds sixty; in a century hence it may exceed 500,000,000. Would you like to see this Union the sun and center of those vast populations? What can do it better than the establishment of Ocean Penny Postage? Do you wish to see all *brought* under the religious influence of this nation? Then nothing can so well produce that effect as the system which I advocate.

A petition and memorial to Congress came out of the New York meeting, which included many merchants and bankers and at which Lewis Tappan, John P. Hale, of New Hampshire, and Mayor Jacob A. Westervelt also spoke.[50]

Burritt elucidated his project before members of the state legislatures of Massachusetts, Rhode Island, Maine, and New Jersey, and lectured in the principal cities of the

50. New York *Tribune*, Jan. 7, 1854; New York *Herald*, Jan. 7, 1854.

middle Atlantic states before arriving in Washington, D. C., in February, 1854.[51] He expected to remain in Washington only a few days before carrying his campaign into the South and West. He had talked Samuel G. Howe into forming a Boston Ocean Penny Postage Committee to raise funds for the movement. He had only fifty dollars when he reached Washington, and he wrote Howe to send another fifty so that he could begin his tour. Burritt was chary of lecturing in the South because of his "antislavery antecedents," which his over-imaginative mind had led him to believe were universally known and despised in the slave states.[52]

When Burritt arrived in Washington, Congress was furiously debating Senator Stephen A. Douglas's Kansas-Nebraska bill, which would have made possible the extension of slavery into territories that had hitherto been closed to it. Burritt called on Sumner to discuss ocean penny postage. Sumner, "lying on his sofa, hothanded and feverish from the effort and excitement of preparing for his great effort against the Nebraska Bill," was in no mood to discuss the post office. Burritt listened to Sumner declaim against "this wicked Bill," and three days later, on February 21, heard Sumner deliver in the Senate his "Landmark of Freedom" speech against Douglas' bill. Burritt was electrified by Sumner's hard-hitting eloquence: "It was the noblest oration and argument that I ever heard . . . It was an era speech. It was unanswerable."[53]

That the fiercely partisan congressional debates over slavery in the territories might serve as a major distraction

51. Burritt, *Ten-Minute Talks*, p. 43; Journals, Jan.-Feb., 1854; Burritt to Freeman H. Morse, Springfield, Mass., Jan. 16, 1854, Pierpont Morgan Library.

52. Burritt to S. G. Howe, Feb. 10, 1854, Massachusetts Historical Society; *Ten-Minute Talks*, p. 43; Journals, Jan. 31, 1854; Burritt to Anna Mary Southall, New Britain, July 11, 1854, Friends House.

53. Journals, Feb. 18, 21, 1854; David Donald, *Charles Sumner and the Coming of the Civil War*, pp. 254–255.

to ocean penny postage did not seem to occur to Burritt. He went about making inquiries among government officials as if they were eager to learn about postal anomalies. He decided to postpone his journey into the South and to remain in Washington "about a month and ply my pen, and lobby."[54] A shortage of money was as much responsible for this decision as was his realization of the importance of gaining congressional backing.

Burritt discussed his plan with officials of the Post Office Department. William King, chief secretary of the Department's foreign desk, was genuinely interested in ocean penny postage but considered it "too radical." He arranged for Burritt to meet Postmaster-General James Campbell. The Postmaster-General agreed that the current ocean postage was too high and attributed it in part to the high subsidy the government paid the Collins line. He seemed desirous of reducing the rates, but not so drastically as Burritt proposed. Money mattered to Campbell. When inland postage had been reduced to three cents in 1851, revenue showed a marked decline the following two years.[55] Hence Campbell refused to believe that ocean penny postage would not appreciably lower postal income.

Burritt rejected all arguments that suggested his plan was unfeasible. If anything, such doubts spurred him to write more articles defending it. He circulated 3,000 copies of a tract presenting the advantages of ocean penny postage to the United States. He deftly disclosed the irregularities of American sea postage, and, using his old arguments, he asserted that the plan "may be adopted without occasioning any sensible loss of revenue to the Post Office." But he chose to underline the commercial and humanitarian benefits of his reform. "Correspondence is the right hand of commerce . . . and the reduction proposed would give it an

54. Journals, Feb. 22, 1854.
55. *Ibid.*, Feb. 2–21, 1854; Roper, p. 67.

impulse and expansion which are indispensable to its legitimate development and prosperity." Through ocean penny
postage "Samples of goods, fruit and flower seeds, speci-
mens of grains, of woods, of minerals, even, as well as circulars and trade cards, would be transmitted across the
ocean." From the standpoint of national good will there
was "no measure within the constitutional competency of
the U. S. Government to bestow upon the foreign-born inhabitants of this country, which would do more to increase
their social happiness and to secure their sympathy and
gratitude, than the establishment of an ocean penny postage."[56]

Three Washington newspapers, the *Union*, the *Sentinel*,
and the *National Intelligencer*, published most of the short
articles Burritt sent them; Burritt also transmitted the same
articles to over 100 papers. To the editor of the *Union* he
explained that, while his project "advanced the greatest
interests of Commerce, and benefited, beyond description,
the mercantile community, it would be an unspeakable boon
to that great and growing mass of our population who come
from foreign lands."[57]

Senator Thomas Jefferson Rusk, of Texas, chairman of
the Senate Committee on the Post Office, had read Burritt's
articles and found them convincing. He told Burritt that
he would try to get his Committee to report in favor of
ocean penny postage, despite the fact that "the present
Post Office Administration were opposed even to the cheap
inland postage." Burritt conferred with over twenty congressmen, "all of whom were exceedingly courteous and
complimentary." Representative Edson Olds of Ohio, how-

56. *Ocean Penny Postage* (Washington, 1854), pp. 1–4.
57. Journals, Mar. 1, 1854; Washington *Union*, Mar. 1, 1854;
National Intelligencer, Mar. 1, 1854; Burritt to the Editor of the
Washington *Union*, Washington, D. C., Mar. 13, 1854, Henry E.
Huntington Library; Burritt to the Editor of the Washington *Union*,
Mar. 8, 1854, New York Historical Society Library.

ever, the chairman of the House Committee on the Post Office, doubted the practicability of the reform. Olds told Burritt that the steep subsidy to the Collins line made ocean penny postage a bad speculation. He also cited the $2,500,000 annual loss the Post Office incurred by the franking system, which allowed members of Congress and government officials to send mail free of postage, as a serious obstacle to postage reform.[58]

Congressman Olds' pessimism did not alarm Burritt, who with the assistance of William King, drafted "the form of a bill" for ocean penny postage. The bill "authorized and directed" the Postmaster-General "to enter into negotiation with the Postal Authorities of Great Britain and all other nations with . . . the view of obtaining their concurrence and cooperation in establishing, at as early a period as practicable, the uniform rate of *two cents* for the ocean transit on each letter under half an ounce in weight." Both Sumner and Rusk examined the bill, approved it, and promised to support it. Rusk praised the bill so ardently that he left Burritt "feeling that the movement had reached a new stage towards its consummation." The cooler Sumner declared that the bill could not be introduced until Congress neared adjournment because of the disputes over the Kansas-Nebraska bill.[59]

Upon Senator Rusk, not Sumner, devolved the responsibility for engineering Burritt's bill through the Senate. As chairman of the Committee on the Post Office, Rusk was in an excellent position to report the bill expeditiously. Burritt hoped to make Rusk's job a little easier by continuing to interest as many senators as he could. He was somewhat surprised to discover how well-known among many mem-

58. Journals, Mar. 9, 11, 14, 1854.
59. *Ibid.*, Mar. 16–17, 20, 1854; Burritt to Mrs. Merriam, April 27, 1854, Historical Society of Pennsylvania; Burritt to [A. Southall], Washington, D.C., April 10, 1854, Friends House.

bers of Congress were his humanitarian endeavors in Great Britain. Senators Salmon P. Chase, William H. Seward, Lewis Cass, Thomas H. Benton, Edward Everett, and Stephen A. Douglas had followed his activities in the international peace congress movement. They all seemed in accord with the importance of the project. Senator Douglas, never at a loss for words, harangued Burritt on the intrinsic correlation between cheap international postage and world peace. Burritt marvelled at Douglas's "comprehensive embrace" of the entire subject. Although Burritt realized that the Kansas-Nebraska bill had passed the Senate, he remarked that Douglas was "after all, a man of remarkable intellectual power." Senator Lewis Cass desired "the cheapest postage possible, by land or sea . . . whether it *paid* or not." Burritt dined with President Franklin Pierce, who questioned him on various League reforms and spoke understandingly of the manifold values of cheap international postage. In addition to daily conferences, Burritt posted placards throughout Washington (even putting one up himself in the rotunda of the Capitol), and wrote to his many personal friends to secure petitions to Congress from their towns.[60]

Meanwhile, William King received confirmation from a New York line of sailing packets to Australia that it would "convey letters thither and back for *two cents* each" for the ocean transit. King persuaded the Postmaster-General "to charge only the ordinary inland service on these letters in addition to the ocean transit, making in all five cents." In late March, 1854, the Postmaster-General agreed to the

60. Journals, April 7, March 21, 24, May 16, 17, 1854; (Burritt had earlier displayed similar placards in "50 of the principal Railway Stations in England." Burritt to [Gerrit Smith], London, July 25, 1853, Massachusetts Historical Society; Burritt to [?] London, July 8, 1853, Haverford College Library; *Bond of Brotherhood*, August, 1853, p. 16.); Burritt to Moses Pierce, Washington, D.C., April 14, 1854, Columbia University Library.

proposition, and ocean penny postage on letters carried by
sailing ships was established between the United States
and Australia. "This establishes the principle completely,"
wrote an ecstatic Burritt. "It is really a triumph."[61]

Encouraged by this event, which he had no direct part
in bringing about, Burritt decided to begin his speaking
tour in the South and West to reap petitions for the ocean
penny postal bill. Samuel Howe had finally given him
enough money to leave Washington. Before going, Burritt
gave Rusk a manuscript scrapbook containing several brief
articles on ocean penny postage and wrote a report that
Rusk intended to have the Committee on the Post Office
adopt in favor of Burritt's bill.[62]

From late May until the end of June Burritt did not stop
travelling or talking. In the South, he addressed large public meetings in Richmond, Petersburg, Wilmington (North
Carolina), Charleston, Augusta, Macon, Milledgeville, and
Louisville. Southerners seemed unaware of, or indifferent
to, his antislavery principles. Only Governor David S. Reid,
of North Carolina, received him with some suspicion, asking, "What wind has blown you among us?" Burritt organized numerous meetings in Ohio, Illinois, and Michigan.
In Canada, he obtained "petitions to the British Parliament
in Toronto, London, Hamilton, and other towns." He returned to New Britain on June 28, exhausted but proud of
the fact that he had travelled "about 5,000 miles on OPP"
since his arrival in America.[63] He wrote Sumner that his
journey

has been very satisfactory and successful. Although I and
many of my friends apprehended a rough reception for me

61. Journals, Mar. 27, 1854.
62. *Ibid.*, May 16, 1854; The MS Scrapbook on Ocean Penny
Postage is in the New Britain Public Institute.
63. Burritt, *Ten-Minute Talks*, pp. 43–44; Journals, May-June
29, 1854.

in the South, I was treated with great kindness and courtesy
by all I met, and the cheap ocean postage scheme was received with the liveliest sympathy. I called upon editors,
lawyers, bankers, and leading merchants, and all signed
petitions with hearty good will.[64]

Neither Barnabas Bates ("the Rowland Hill of America")
nor Joshua Leavitt had been of any assistance to Burritt.

While Burritt blazed his ocean penny postage trail in the
South and West, the trail he left behind in Washington had
disappeared. During his absence, the Senate Committee on
the Post Office made short shrift of his report and bill. Rusk
doubtless showed Burritt's handiwork to the Committee
members. Apparently they thought the proposition too
likely to involve the Post Office in further debt. Moreover,
Edson Olds had a bill before the House that proposed to
raise inland postage to five cents again because of the heavy
postal deficits incurred since the rate for letters had been
reduced in 1851 to three cents. Olds' bill, however, called
for the reduction to five cents on the ocean transit of a
letter carried not more than 3,000 miles. The Ohio Representative declared that "either . . . we should abandon the
idea of making the Post Office Department a self-sustaining
Department, and make it absolutely and unconditionally a
charge upon the General Treasury of the country, or . . .
raise the rates of postage to something near the point which
will make the Post Office . . . self-sustaining."[65] It was a
strong argument. Given Olds' concern for Post Office economy, Burritt's bill, even if it passed the Senate, would have
been stopped in the House.

Burritt was disheartened by the delay in the Senate. "If
Gen. Rusk would give notice of his bill," he wrote Sumner,
"it would be an encouraging beginning." Burritt was ready

64. Burritt to Sumner, New Britain, July 5, 1854, in Curti, p. 111.
65. *Congressional Globe*, 33 Congress, 1 Session, p. 909.

to depart for England, and he at least wanted "the Report . . . printed this session on the authority of the Senate." Then he could "take copies of it . . . to England, to distribute among the MPs and such a document would have much weight." Rusk wrote Burritt that he intended to incorporate the bill as an amendment to Olds' bill when the latter came before the Senate. Burritt was encouraged by Rusk's strategy, for he considered Olds' bill "retrogressive," even though it promised to cut substantially the ocean rate of letters.[66] The bill passed the House, but not the Senate; inland rates remained the same, but so also did sea postage.

Burritt returned to England in August, 1854, not sure what the fate in America of ocean penny postage would be. In England he found no one who would move for a committee of inquiry in the House of Commons to investigate the possibilities of his reform. The Crimean War had made ocean penny postage a highly questionable financial venture and a superfluous subject. Still, late in 1854, Great Britain and France entered into a postal agreement which established a half penny rate for the Channel-crossing of letters exchanged between the two countries. "It is now for the United States to move next," Burritt wrote in 1855, "and complete this great reform."[67] But Burritt's own interests had by then begun to shift markedly toward abolition, and he was already formulating several programs connected with that reform. He had about given up on Rusk in America and Gibson in England. "You know I wrote a *Report* for him," Burritt wrote plaintively to Sumner about Rusk in 1856. "Will you not occasionally touch him up on the question?"[68] Mostly out of courtesy to Burritt, Sumner in-

66. Burritt to Sumner, New Britain, July 5, 1854, in Curti, p. 111; *Ibid.*, pp. 112–113; *Citizen of the World*, Jan., 1855, p. 10.

67. *Citizen of the World*, Feb., 1855, p. 24; *Bond of Brotherhood*, May, 1856, p. 146.

68. Burritt to Sumner, New Britain, Feb. 13, 1856, in Curti, p. 117.

troduced in 1856 a weak resolution asking for cheap ocean postage.[69] But, like his similar resolution in 1852, nothing came of it.

Thereafter, Burritt seldom referred to ocean penny postage and never again actively campaigned for it.[70] He had done for the scheme all that a reformer working for the most part alone could possibly do. Yet notwithstanding his tenacious efforts, the ocean penny postage reform never became a movement and never came close to realization. Burritt had not succeeded in creating the powerful, sustained agitation needed to carry the measure to fulfillment. Cobden, Bright, and Gibson in Great Britain, and Rusk and Sumner in the United States, refused to assume aggressive legislative leadership over the proposal because they were not truly convinced that ocean penny postage would pay. And very likely Rowland Hill's opposition to the reform dissuaded most members of Parliament from endorsing it. What little they did to assist the reform appears to have stemmed largely from their fondness of Burritt's humanitarian fervor and good intentions. The New York and Boston Cheap Postage Associations did practically nothing to help.

Reductions on sea postage continued throughout the world in the fifties and sixties. In 1875 the ocean transit of a postcard from the United States to Great Britain cost one penny. Burritt sent a card to an old London acquaintance: "This means *Ocean Penny Postage*, for which I began to agitate in England in 1847. It has come at last and I have lived to see it and enjoy it and use it as I do now. It is a great joy to greet my friends in England with a letter however short for *one penny*."[71] In 1876 Longfellow wrote Bur-

69. *Congressional Globe*, 34 Congress, 1 Session, p. 387.

70. *Citizen of the World*, April, 1855, p. 58, July, 1855, p. 108, Nov., 1855, p. 173; *Bond of Brotherhood*, Oct. 1856, p. 47.

71. Burritt to Miss Annie E. Ridley, New Britain, July 20, 1875, Klingberg Collection.

ritt: "I was thinking of you the other day, and of how near you had come to the realization of your dream of an Ocean Penny Postage. It has nearly become a reality; near enough for all practical purposes. You may yet see it fully realized."[72] The Universal Postal Union, formed in 1875 and composed of twenty-two nations, including the United States, made rapid advancements in the direction of ocean penny postage. But not until after Burritt's death in 1879 did the nations begin to adopt his program.[73]

72. Longfellow to Burritt, Cambridge, March 29, 1876, in Curti, "Henry Wadsworth Longfellow and Elihu Burritt," *American Literature*, Vol. 7 (Nov., 1935), p. 326.
73. Staff, pp. 126–148.

10

Slavery and Civil War

In Massachusetts in 1843 Burritt had made his debut as a reformer in the antislavery movement. For nearly three years he had supported the Liberty Party, which had expected great things from him. But as an abolitionist, he had been a curious hybrid. Never wholly devoted to the Liberty Party, he had been reluctant to join in its fight against the Garrisonians. Burritt had believed that a political approach to slavery was valid; yet he had been skeptical of direct political entanglement with the Liberty Party. He had distrusted the Garrisonians because of their unceasing demand for the dissolution of the Union; yet he had respected their unambiguous moral principles. Though the Liberty Party had been delighted to have him, they had hoped he would be of more use. And though Garrison had been disturbed by his adherence to political abolitionism, he nevertheless thought that Burritt could be weaned away from that heresy. Burritt had stood between the two antislavery blocs with impunity because he had never totally committed himself to either one.

The fact is that Burritt had contributed very little to abolitionism, political or moral. Apart from his generally mediocre antislavery articles in the *Christian Citizen,* and

235

his few rather Whiggish antislavery addresses, Burritt's only constructive work had been in the organization of the New England Anti-Slavery Association. But when the Association had become inactive by the middle of 1845, after issuing only a handful of tracts, Burritt withdrew from the antislavery movement and turned his attention almost exclusively to peace. By then he had come to see slavery as a symptom of mankind's greatest sin—war. And war, he believed, was founded on ignorance, prejudice, and the lack of international fraternization. Thus, as he wended his way from antislavery to peace to universal brotherhood, he felt he was travelling on the main reform road to its obvious evangelical destination.

Burritt had not tried to escape involvement in abolitionism; he had attempted to get at the sin through what he thought was its taproot. He never entirely abandoned the cause; but when he immersed himself in programs of peace and universal brotherhood, he strayed a long way from the slave. Never having directly confronted the issue of slavery, he returned to it obliquely; never having thoroughly examined the problem, he offered indirect and unrealistic palliatives. Because he had always viewed slavery as a national concern, and because he felt a mystical attachment to the Union, he was to make a belated effort at saving the Union through a plan that required the North, South, and West to place the national interest above sectional interests. But in spite of his reverence for the Union, Burritt was a pacifist who renounced bloodletting no matter what the reason or circumstance. When after Fort Sumter the Union was in chaos, he came up with a fatuous formula that was intended not only to bring peace, but a unique kind of Union as well.

In September, 1846, not long after the formation of the League of Universal Brotherhood, Burritt wrote Garrison of the antislavery work he planned for the League. He proposed "to adopt the little plan of the Free Labor Produce

Association of Philadelphia, and expand it to a great system which should finally bring every mother's son of the non-slaveholders of the South into antagonism to their feudal barons of the lash, thus arraying against slavery the powerful interest of free labor right on its bloodstained territory." This "might be achieved by the establishment of a cotton factory in America, one in England and another in France, which should manufacture none other than free labor cotton produced in the Slave States."[1]

The idea of free labor produce was considered by some British and American abolitionists, mostly Quakers, to be an effective way of striking a mortal blow against slavery in the United States. Early in the 19th century the noted American Quaker Elias Hicks urged Friends to give up using products that involved slave labor; in Indiana, Levi Coffin, a North Carolina-born Quaker, set up depots where goods untouched by slave hands could be obtained. Joseph Sturge and other British Quakers were hoping in 1845 "to place within reach of the people of England articles manufactured out of cotton raised by free labor." They recognized, in the words of one of their manifestoes, the "undeniable facts, that the demand for the cotton of that country [the United States] in Great Britain has been a chief means of perpetuating and extending slavery in America." Sturge requested American Quaker abolitionists to promote free labor cotton goods.[2] The Philadelphia Free Labor Produce Association of Friends, organized by Samuel Rhoades and George W. Taylor, provided free labor produce for those who disliked purchasing slave labor goods.

Burritt believed strongly in free labor produce and immediately adopted the program as a principal measure of the

1. Burritt to W. L. Garrison, Frome, Sept. 8, [1846], Boston Public Library.
2. L. Filler, *The Crusade Against Slavery*, pp. 123, 163; H. Richard, *Memoirs of Joseph Sturge*, pp. 384–388.

League. With customary alacrity he laid before incredulous officers of the British and Foreign Antislavery Society "the plan of a great Free Labor Produce Association of all the abolitionists of Christendom." Burritt was not satisfied that existing organizations in Great Britain and the United States were taking full advantage of the great possibilities afforded by the project. He wrote George W. Taylor, of the Philadelphia Free Labor Produce Association, to ascertain "the means it possessed or needed to obtain Free Labor Cotton from the South" and recommended that Taylor send agents through the South to prod nonslaveholding farmers to grow more cotton. "I intend to 'agitate' total abstinence from slave grown products wherever I go," declared Burritt, supremely certain that he had engaged the League in a task of great benefit to the slave.[3]

The peace crusade impinged so drastically upon Burritt's time and efforts, however, that from 1847 to 1852 he almost completely forgot slavery. The appearance of Harriet Beecher Stowe's *Uncle Tom's Cabin* in 1852 helped redirect his attention to slavery and rekindle his interest in free labor produce. He "luxuriated" in Mrs. Stowe's "most intensely graphic thrilling book" and hoped "to take part in the great Anti-slavery struggle from which I have partially withdrawn myself, and Total Abstinence from Slave Grown Produce appears to me the most efficient measure for Abolitionists on this side of the Atlantic" to support.[4]

From 1852 until the middle of 1854 Burritt again lost sight of the slave, this time because of ocean penny postage. He did manage in 1853 to establish a Free Produce

3. Journals, Oct. 3-Dec. 17, 1846, *passim*; Aug. 20, 1847.
4. *Ibid.*, June 4, 7, 13, Nov. 22, Dec. 22, 1852. Burritt wrote an "Introduction" to one of the first British editions of *Uncle Tom's Cabin*, in which he declared that the "universal verdict anticipates and answers every question in reference to the merits of the work; insomuch that it is almost presumptuous to affirm, as to deny, its genius." H. B. Stowe, *Uncle Tom's Cabin* (London, 1852), pp. iv–v.

Depot in London with £74 worth of merchandise which he had purchased from a Manchester warehouse that handled only such commodities. Mrs. Bessie Inglis, an active Leaguer, was in charge of the depot. Burritt explained the project to Mrs. Stowe and her husband, Professor Calvin Stowe, when the couple visited Joseph Sturge in England in 1853. The Stowes promised to assist the cause upon their return to America.[5]

Burritt drafted a pledge: "Believing that the voluntary consumption of the products of the labour of the slave is a participation in the crime of the system which holds him in bondage, I do hereby pledge myself to abstain, as far as possible, from the use of any articles which have been produced by his unrequited toil."[6] He circulated tracts, one of which advanced *Twenty Reasons for Total Abstinence from Slave-Labor Produce.* Those who read this tract found out that slave labor products were the "fruits of an aggravated robbery" and were "stained with all the crime and guilt that can attach to stolen goods." Total abstinence was "a mode of antislavery action in which every man, woman and child may take a part every day, at every meal, in every article of dress they wear and enjoy." Strict British adherence to the pledge would inevitably place American slavery on the road to extinction: "If the British market were closed against American cotton, rice, sugar, and tobacco for three years, three-fourths of the land occupied with their production would be reduced virtually to a wilderness; *three-fourths* of all slaves in the United States would be without employment—a burden unless set free." The tract listed another reason for total abstinence:

5. Journals, May 1, 5, 22, June 16, July 9, 1853; H. Richard, pp. 390–392; H. B. Stowe, *Sunny Memories from Foreign Lands* (New York, 1854), pp. 247–251.

6. *Bond of Brotherhood*, August, 1853, pp. 9–10; Journals, May 23, 1853.

The present moment is a most auspicious juncture for organizing that deep, earnest, widespread sympathy which has
been excited in behalf of the slave by the delineations of
his condition in *Uncle Tom's Cabin.* This book seems to bear
the impress of a Divine mission.[7]

When Burritt arrived in the United States in 1853 to agitate ocean penny postage, he "developed to George Taylor
pretty fully my project for cultivating cotton by free Labour
in the southern states." The plan was to entice European
farmers to journey to the South and establish free labor
colonies. A dual purpose would be served: large amounts
of cotton would become available, and there would also be
an object lesson to slaveholders of the superiority of free
over slave labor. Mrs. Stowe suggested to Burritt that he
tour the South to "talk with planters" and to see for himself
where it would be best to plant free labor colonies. She
would contribute to his expenses if he supplied her with
accurate statistics on the domestic slave trade for the new
book she was planning to write. Burritt dimly perceived
the "formidable" dangers to which such a mission exposed
him. But he was "fast coming to the conviction that I am
called to this field of duty" and was thus willing to "trust
in that divine protection which has hitherto surrounded
me."[8] When shortly thereafter he travelled through the
South spreading the gospel of ocean penny postage, however, he refused to rely on Providence and uttered not a
word about his antislavery scheme.

Writing "under the roof of Harriet Beecher Stowe," Burritt sent a letter to John Ecroyd, an English Quaker from
Bradford, asking if he "would be willing to undertake to
manage a small plantation of 100 or 200 acres in South
Carolina, Georgia, or Alabama." Owing to the "want of free

7. Burritt, *Twenty Reasons for Total Abstinence from Slave-Labour
Produce*, n.d., pp. 1–4.
8. Journals, Jan. 11–12, 21–22, 1854.

coloured labour at first I have thought a few stalwart Germans fresh from the Continent might be the best hands we could find" and would excite less "suspicion as 'abolitionist agitators' in the south than any other class attainable." Astonishingly unmindful of the obvious perils of the plan, Burritt blandly assured Ecroyd that "the project has now reached a stage at which you would safely embark in it." Ecroyd, using good judgment, declined.[9]

Lewis Tappan and Benjamin Fatham, wealthy New York merchants, were interested in Burritt's plan. Fatham nonchalantly proposed that an annual cash prize be awarded the farmer who grew the most cotton by free labor. No sooner had Fatham made the suggestion than Burritt devised a prize plan. To the farmer who produced on one farm fifty bales of cotton, averaging 450 pounds per bale, a $500 prize would be given; the remaining prizes were: $300 for 50 bales, $200 for 30 bales, $100 for 20 bales, and $50 for 10 bales. Burritt planned to solicit the prize money from Northern merchants and manufacturers, and he expected a tidy contribution from Fatham. Afraid of involving himself too deeply in Burritt's "Premium System," Fatham asserted that he would not donate more than $100 annually unless Burritt could raise $2,500 in subscriptions.[10]

Burritt returned to England in August, 1854, and laid out plans for the application of the "Premium System to the production of cotton in the British Possessions." But he encountered opposition from certain reform circles. " 'The Manchester School,' " he wrote a friend, "are disinclined to the term Free Labor, as they are so extensively engaged in the manufacture of *Slave* Labour Cotton." When the Manchester Chamber of Commerce "peremptorily declined" to listen to his plan, Burritt decided that should "the 'Manchester School' . . . not take it up, I am determined to ap-

9. Burritt to Ecroyd, Andover, Jan. 21, 1854, in Curti, *The Learned Blacksmith*, pp. 123–124.
10. Journals, Feb. 11, 14–16, May 7, 1854.

peal to the Philanthropic, of the Earl of Shaftesbury order."[11]

Rebuffed by Manchester liberals, Burritt concentrated on the establishment of a free labor colony in the United States. He urged Gerrit Smith to "exchange some of your wild land for about 500 acres of the same quality in Georgia," on which Burritt "would . . . plant 20 vigorous freemen . . . from England, Scotland, and Germany in the course of a year." He coaxed a young Englishman named Charles Dowman to go to America to cultivate cotton. Dowman, who had planned to migrate to Australia, agreed. Burritt advised him to purchase a 500 acre farm near Griffith, Georgia, keeping 200 acres for himself and setting aside the remaining 300 for the colonists to be sent to America. Though it was Dowman who might have to face the fury of Southerners, it was Burritt who wrote, "This is the most precarious and delicate enterprise. that I ever endeavored to set on foot. It may get me in difficulty; but I feel inclined to go forward."[12]

Positive that Dowman would be but the first of many British farmers to go to America to grow cotton, Burritt wrote the wealthy Bostonian Amos A. Lawrence of the "little farm colony [that] may be established in Georgia." He asked Lawrence to purchase 500 acres of Georgia land and permit the settlers he would send over to work the land free of rent for five years, "on condition that they employ no slave labour." At the end of five years, he estimated that the value of the land would have increased by 250%, making Lawrence's purchase "a profitable investment."[13]

11. Burritt to [A. Southall], London, August 26, 1854, Friends House; Journals, Sept. 21, Oct. 31, Nov. 2, Dec. 5, 1854.

12. Burritt to Smith, London, Oct. 6, 1856, in Curti, pp. 129–130; Journals, Oct. 6, 14-Nov. 3, 1854, *passim*; Burritt to [A. Southall], London, Nov. 18, 1854, Friends House.

13. Burritt to Amos A. Lawrence, London, Nov. 3, 1854, Massachusetts Historical Society; Journals, Nov. 3, 1854.

In January, 1855, while still in England, Burritt began
editing a new monthly reform periodical published in Philadelphia by George Taylor, who, Burritt noted happily, had
"agreed to bear *all* the loss, and share with me all the
profits."[14] Entitled the *Citizen of the World*, the journal
espoused the free-produce and premium plans and also
dealt with major European political questions. Late in 1854
Burritt had taken over editorial duties of *The Slave*, a
small British monthly that served as an organ for the British
free-produce movement. With Edmund Fry's considerable
assistance, he was still publishing the monthly *Bond of
Brotherhood*.[15]

The *Citizen of the World* forthrightly condemned slavery
but professed "the most brotherly feeling towards the people of the slave states." The antislavery articles aspired
"to show, that the slave labor of the South costs the farmers
and planters of those States more by the day or year than
is paid for the most skilful and faithful agricultural labor
employed in England, or in any country in Europe." On
"this simple fact" Burritt based his "economical argument
in favor of free and fully requited industry." Slaveholders
"not only pay more for their labor than European farmers,"
he affirmed, "but also get the worst in Christendom for
their money." For anyone could "see by intuition that the
slave must be naturally the most stolid, spiritless, eye-serv-
ing, uninventive piece of human machinery ever set at work
in field or factory, mine or mountain"; such "leaden lethargy . . . would be the same . . . in the best race . . . if reduced to the condition of slavery." Burritt decried the
"plantation system as undemocratic, monopolistic, and lead-

14. Burritt to [A. Southall], New Britain, July 11, 1854, Friends
House; Journals, Aug. 28, 30, Oct. 16, 1854. Taylor was the publisher
of *The Non-Slaveholder*, an organ of the Philadelphia Free-Produce
Association, which was superseded by the *Citizen of the World*.

15. Journals, Nov. 24, Dec. 26, 1854; Burritt to Elizabeth Stanley,
London, July 27, 1855, New Britain Public Institute.

ing to sullen, emasculated yeomanry and faded social institutions." Free labor was the panacea: "Free Labor would change all this, and cover all the South with those homesteads which make the glory and greatness of New England."[16]

Burritt had expected the League to be the mainstay of the free labor premium system. But by 1854 the League was crumbling in Great Britain and was stone dead in America. Important Leaguers refused to commit themselves to the plan and were sorry that Burritt had established a free produce depot in London. Benjamin Fatham, the New York merchant, had condemned the colonization project and scolded Burritt for attempting to launch a premium system in Great Britain. Fatham's subsequent defection forced Burritt to write to Mrs. Stowe, Amos Lawrence, and other Americans for $100.00 donations to the premium plan. Only $100.00 had been subscribed, and Burritt worried lest "much of the expense . . . fall on me." Charles Dowman, after disclosing the free labor plan to Southern planters, finally settled down on a farm outside of Atlanta, Georgia, and wrote Burritt that he would "try" to grow one bale of cotton during the year. George Taylor was having financial problems with the cotton factory he had rented near Philadelphia to convert free labor cotton into finished cloth. The Philadelphia Free Labor Produce Association was stagnating, and Burritt's free labor depot in London was losing money.[17] Since the slaves were in the United States, and since most British reformers were either indifferent or hostile to his premium plan, Burritt decided to go to America in 1855 "to give myself actively to setting the plan in operation there." He hoped that those few Britishers who sub-

16. *Citizen of the World*, March, 1855, p. 40; April, 1855, p. 56; May, 1855, p. 72; July, 1855, pp. 104–105; Aug., 1855, p. 123.

17. Journals, July 25, Dec. 9, 1853, Mar. 12, 25, July 19, 25, Nov. 20, Dec. 11, 1854, Jan. 11-Aug. 6, 1855, *passim.*

scribed and "paid" to the premium plan "will not feel that the plan has been a *feint* because it is suspended for a few months."[18] Grudgingly he admitted that the plan was in a peculiar "state of betweenity—partly something and partly nothing."[19] In truth, it was mostly nothing.

Before leaving England in September, 1855, Burritt wrote an article on "National Emancipation." He declared that "slavery, on a single acre of the remotest State of the Union, is not a *sectional*, not a *peculiar*, but an *American* institution." Emancipation, therefore, required a *"National Act."* And there was "but one way by which the entire nation may bear the burden of Emancipation: that is—*Compensation for the Manumission of the Slaves."* Three months after his arrival in the United States, he wrote Charles Sumner of his "new 'iron in the fire'—Immediate and National Emancipation by Compensation, devoting all the Public lands west of the Mississippi to the object. Intend soon to take the field and send in petitions to the end."[20] Burritt's mercurial mind had uncovered another antislavery plan. Unlike the others, this one proposed a frontal assault on slavery. And because his other antislavery programs had amounted to so very little, he now wisely dropped them.[21]

Burritt delineated his compensated emancipation project in a pamphlet entitled *A Plan of Brotherly Co-Partnership of the North and South for the Peaceful Extinction of Slav-*

18. Burritt to [A. Southall], London, Aug. 11, 1855, Friends House.
19. Burritt to Elizabeth Stanley, London, July 27, 1855, New Britain Public Institute.
20. *Citizen of the World*, Oct., 1855, pp. 153–154; Burritt to Sumner, New Britain, Jan. 11, 1836, in Curti, p. 116.
21. Burritt and George Taylor helped organize the North American Free Labor Produce Association in Philadelphia in February, 1856. Fewer than twenty persons, most of them Quakers, lent their support to the ambitious Association which was supposed to inspire the free produce movement in America with "a new attitude and vigor." *Bond of Brotherhood*, Mar. 1856, p. 143, Aug., 1856, p. 13; Journals, Feb. 15, Mar. 17, Apr. 13, 1856.

ery. The slavery issue, he wrote, had turned the "harmonies" of the nation "into grating discords" and had engulfed "its fraternities in a sea of fierce and endless agitation [pitting] the two great divisions of the country against each other in a struggle embittered with every element of strife." He was shocked because "bloodshed and civil war are threatened and expected in some quarters, with but a slight show of affliction at the catastrophe." Slavery must be abolished "in a way and in a spirit that should attach all the members of the confederacy to each other by stronger bonds than had ever existed between them." Only "by compensating the slaveholders, out of the public treasury or the public domain, for the act of manumission" can the whole nation honorably eradicate slavery. Slavery was a national sin and the guilt must be shared by everyone:

> By popular sentiment, commercial partnership, and legislative action, the free States have lived in guilty complicity with the system of slavery from the foundation of the Republic. It is far too late for them to cleanse their garments of the stains and the guilt by the flames and fumigation of indignant emotion.[22]

Burritt had figures to prove that his plan for national compensated emancipation was well within the fiscal reach of the nation. At the rate of "$250 per head, taking young and old, sick and disabled," it would cost $875,000,000 to free 3,500,000 slaves. If western public lands, which by official estimate comprised 1,600,000,000 acres and which did not include the Gadsden Purchase of 1853, were sold at the average of 75 cents per acre, the revenue would be $1,200,000,000. "Thus, the public lands would not only defray the expense of emancipating all these slaves, but would

22. Burritt, *A Plan of Brotherly Co-Partnership of the North and South for the Peaceful Extinction of Slavery* (New York, 1856), pp. 12–20.

also yield a large surplus for their education and moral improvement." And since the public domain was "a free gift from Providence," what better way could the nation "more appropriately recognize this gift, than by consecrating it to freedom, than by making it the ransom price from slavery of all the chattelized human beings in the Union?"

Using the Census of 1850, Burritt listed the number of slaves in each Southern state, and in the District of Columbia, and the remuneration each state would receive at the rate of $250 per slave. Apart from outright compensation there were important hidden pecuniary considerations the South would find palatable. With slavery at an end, the value of Southern real estate would at least double, as multitudes "of intelligent and vigorous men from the North and Europe would pour into" the cleansed South. New towns and cities would sprout up, old ones would flourish, and the entire South would undergo a remarkable economic renascence.

The plan allowed each slave state the "prerogative . . . to retain or abolish slavery." There would be no "Federal compulsion." The national government "only makes a generous offer to each and every Southern State," leaving it to the state "in the freest exercise of its sovereign will to accept or reject that offer." Burritt did not expect all the Southern states to accept "simultaneously" the proposition. "One State after some hesitation, would lead the way, and be followed one after the other by the rest."[23]

Such were the highlights of Burritt's program. Like the man himself, it was conciliatory and compassionate, for Burritt believed "that the anti-slavery sentiment of the Free States would have ten times its present influence upon the South if repentance, rather than indignation, were its chief element."[24] He was attempting to duplicate in Amer-

23. *Ibid.*, pp. 33–38.
24. *Citizen of the World*, Nov., 1855, p. 170.

ica the example set by Great Britain in 1833 in emancipating the slaves in the West Indies and compensating the owners. He thought his plan "quite distinct from any other mode ever proposed for the extinction of slavery in America."[25] But it was not original. A resident in New Britain showed him a passage from Daniel Webster's writings which advocated the sale of public lands for the emancipation of slaves and their subsequent colonization abroad. Rufus King, a conservative statesman of an earlier year, had spoken out in the Senate in favor of using part of the revenue from public lands for emancipation. As late as February, 1855, Ralph Waldo Emerson had lectured in the Broadway Tabernacle on the necessity of compensated emancipation: "We will give up our coaches, and wines and watches. The churches will melt their plate . . . The mechanics will give; the children will have cent societies . . . I don't think that any price, founded on a sum that figures could tell, would be quite unmanageable." Burritt also learned that the Reverend John Rankin, of Ohio, had for years entertained a similar plan.[26] Though the scheme was not new, Burritt was prepared to give it an audience that it never had before. No reform that he either originated or supported suffered from underexposure.

Burritt's proposal encountered opposition from abolitionists and critics of slavery. The New York abolitionist William Goodell wrote Burritt a strong letter "declaiming against the principle of compensation." Amasa Walker thought the plan was "impracticable." Lewis Tappan disapproved because "the South would not part with the political power or the sensual gratification which slavery gave them for any pecuniary consideration."[27] Horace Greeley did not object

25. Burritt to [A. Southall], New Britain, April 22, 1856, Friends House.

26. Journals, April 11, 1856; *Dictionary of American Biography*, X, p. 399; New York *Herald*, Feb. 7, 1855; Journals, Dec. 30, 1856.

27. *Ibid.*, Nov. 23, 1855, Jan. 1, Aug. 4, Dec. 2, 1856; New York *Tribune*, Dec. 3, 1856.

to the proposition, although he felt "there was not enough antislavery sentiment North or South sufficient to carry the plan."[28] The Quincy (Massachusetts) *Patriot* disagreed with Burritt's plan because "the most peaceable way to get rid of the evil is to let it alone; if agitation ceases, it will naturally die out of itself."[29]

The intransigent Garrison also attacked compensated emancipation, but for very different reasons. First, slave-masters "not only have no disposition to sell out, but declare their purpose never to part with it on any consideration"; second, Burritt had to convince the South, not the North, of the fairness of the plan; third, the South, "were it willing to abandon her slave system for a pecuniary consideration," would "justly estimate" the number of slaves at 4,000,000 and the average value of each slave at $500; fourth, "the South owns her lawful proportion" of the public lands, and therefore "will not be so demented as to vote to pay herself *with her own* money!"; fifth, "the Slave Power has all these lands within its grasp, and means to use them for its own aggrandizement"; sixth, "congress has no power to make such a contract for the abolition of slavery"; and seventh, "The whole thing is preposterous."[30]

Compensated emancipation was unquestionably much more complicated than Burritt had made it out to be. Yet, despite some of Garrison's cogent objections, the plan was reasonable and fair. It was reasonable because it offered the one solution short of war for the abolition of slavery; it was fair because it recognized the great capital investment of Southern planters in slaves. Above all, the plan was

28. Journals, Dec. 3, 1856. Henry Raymond, editor. of the *New York Times*, told Burritt that he fully assented to the principle of compensated emancipation. But Amos Lawrence, according to Burritt, "seems to believe that Emancipation was neither practicable or desirable, the negroes were so degraded."

29. Quoted in the *Liberator*, April 17, 1857.

30. *Ibid.*, April 10, 1857. Garrison's article was entitled, "How to Draw Out Leviathan With a Hook."

geared to the extirpation of slavery and not simply to its nonextension. Doctrinaire abolitionists, who favored the immediate abolition of slavery with no strings attached, and lukewarm antislaverymen, who apparently did not wish their share of the public domain squandered, failed to see that an equitable solution to slavery involved some sort of financial compensation.

Obviously the major impediment to the plan was the South itself. Even if morally and financially fair, it still left the South with 3,500,000 slaves to integrate into a white society which clung tenaciously to the doctrine of white supremacy. Burritt did not provide for the colonization of slaves once freed, but instead advocated the employment of funds in excess of emancipation costs for the "education and moral improvement" of the freedman. The plan did not propose what Southerners would have considered basic to any notion regarding the abolition of slavery—race-adjustment to subordinate the Negro. Burritt had no solution to this problem. A Mississippian, after listening to Burritt lecture on emancipation in Indiana, asked him if "the Emancipated negroes should be placed on a social and political equality with the whites." Burritt evasively replied: "public sentiment and policy would regulate all that, and that question might be safely left to adjust itself."[31] It was understandable that Burritt should not have faced this issue, for his brand of brotherhood was color blind.

Burritt conducted an extensive campaign for compensated emancipation in practically all of the free states and in the slave states of Delaware and Missouri. Audiences averaged from two to three hundred people, the majority of whom appeared in favor of the plan. Usually Burritt passed around petitions for signatures. By November, 1856, he was "greatly encouraged by the reception of the Emancipation scheme." Many antislaverymen in Illinois and Ohio

31. Journals, Jan. 2, 13, 1857.

were interested, and he had the opportunity to discuss the plan with William Herndon, of Springfield, Illinois, Abraham Lincoln's law partner.[32]

After discussing compensated emancipation with Longfellow, Dr. Eliphalet Nott, Gerrit Smith, and Ralph Waldo Emerson, Burritt decided in February, 1857, to organize a national society to sponsor the program. He had written Gerrit Smith that he was "anxious . . . for a national convention, such as we spoke of," and suggested that "we had better let the West take the *apparent* lead in the matter. They constitute a kind of middle ground between the North and the South."[33] Burritt made plans for a convention in Cleveland in August.

Burritt advertised the forthcoming Cleveland convention in numerous newspapers. To many prominent people he sent the "Call", a slip of paper explaining the purpose of the convention and requesting the signature of the receiver.[34] Gerrit Smith was the first to sign, though such individuals as Longfellow, Whittier, and Emerson, who had earlier approved the plan, did not. By July the "Call" had received the signatures of "hundreds of influential men of all parties & professions, from Maine to Nebraska—including 100 from *Delaware* alone."[35] Nearly the entire faculty of Wesleyan University, including the president, signed the "Call"; Dr. Mark Hopkins, president of Williams College, and Dr. Eliphalet Nott, president of Union College, also signed. President Theodore D. Woolsey of Yale sent his

32. *Ibid.*, June-Nov., 1856; Burritt to the editor of the Elmira (Pa.) *Advertiser*, New Britain, Sept. 4, 1856, Klingberg Collection.

33. Burritt to [Gerrit Smith], Pittsfield, Feb. 13, 1857, in Curti, pp. 131–132.

34. Burritt to Emerson, New Britain, May 21, 1857, Harvard University Library; Burritt to Smith, New Britain, Aug. 12, 1857, Syracuse University Library; Journals, Mar. 23-July 1, 1857, *passim.*

35. Burritt to the Rev. Dr. Theodore D. Woolsey, New Britain, July 13, 1857, Yale University Library; see Burritt's letter to Gerrit Smith in Curti, pp. 134–135.

approbation but not his signature, while Dr. Leonard Bacon and Professor Benjamin Silliman signed. Burritt distributed thousands of copies of a brief extract of his *Plan of Brotherly Co-Partnership* entitled the *Equity and Expediency of Compensated Emancipation*. *Littell's Living Age* printed the abstract, and endorsed its "great and magnanimous" proposal.[36]

Burritt believed that at the Cleveland convention "a beginning will be made from which a great movement may grow."[37] He hoped that the "nucleus of a new National Political Party" founded on his plan might result from the convention, or at least a national compensated emancipation society. There were personal reasons for desiring such a party or society. Edmund Fry had recently written him that the League of Universal Brotherhood had merged with the London Peace Society and no longer existed as a separate organization. With no funds, heavy debts, and no Burritt to direct it, the League had withered away. To Burritt it seemed that with compensated emancipation he had reached the end of his career as a reformer. Sadly he reflected on his humanitarian endeavors:

> The League of Brotherhood is dead. I gave it ten of the best years of my life; but it could not live while I was absent from England. The Christian Citizen died because of my absence from America. The Ocean Penny Postage Movement is suspended. The Free Labor Undertaking has miscarried.[38]

Only the slave remained.

36. For a list of "Call" signatures, see *Bond of Brotherhood*, Sept., 1857, pp. 25–29; Burritt, *Equity and Expediency of Compensated Emancipation*, n.d.; *Littell's Living Age*, XVII (June 20, 1857), p. 754.

37. Burritt to [A. Southall], New Britain, July 28, 1856, Friends House.

38. *Journals*, May 16, July 23, 1857.

The Cleveland Compensated Emancipation Convention met from August 25–27, 1857. Mark Hopkins was the chairman, and Gerrit Smith and Burritt delivered the principal addresses. Spectators who were not members of the convention and who were opposed to the principle of compensated emancipation were allowed to express their opinions. Two opponents, one of them a Negro, reproved the plan because it recognized "the right of the slaveholder to property in man" and because the government had no right to dispossess "the people" of their God-given inheritance of public lands. The Reverend Henry C. Wright, an implacable Garrisonian, equated compensated emancipation with moral recreancy.[39]

Smith, who delivered the best speech, startled Burritt when he proposed an amendment to Burritt's resolution that the government pay $250 for each slave set free. The amendment stipulated that the government pay $150 to the slaveholder, give $25 to each slave, and have the slave states contribute $75 per slave to the owner; slaveholders would thus receive $225 and the slaves enough money "to aid them in starting here, or in removing to another continent if they should so prefer." Burritt "deeply regretted" the amendment, arguing that the South was being asked to pay too much since the public domain was not the monopoly of the North. In effect, he maintained, the South would be paying $150 per slave while the North would pay only half that amount: "Such a proposition exposes us to the scorn and ridicule of the South." After much debate, Burritt's figures prevailed.[40]

A constitution establishing the National Compensated Emancipation Society was adopted on the last day of the Convention. Professor Benjamin Silliman, who did not attend the Convention, was elected president and Burritt

39. *Bond of Brotherhood*, Oct., 1857, pp. 41–46.
40. *Ibid.*; Ralph Harlow, *Gerrit Smith*, pp. 371–372.

corresponding secretary. Gerrit Smith contributed $100.00
on the spot "as a beginning." Headquarters for the Society
were to be located in New York City. "This was a gladden-
ing moment for me," wrote Burritt, "and I felt my best
hopes had been realized." But in a rare moment of detach-
ment he evaluated with some perturbation his newest reform venture: "I am now about to enter upon what I regard
my last public enterprize. If it should follow the fate of my
other undertakings, I intend to retire to the plough, and
give myself entirely to farming."[41] (He was assuming that
he could keep up the payments on the New Britain farm
he bought in 1856.[42])

In October, 1857, Burritt entered upon his duties as "Sec-
retariat" by renting a small office in the Bible Society Building in New York. The year 1857 was inauspicious for the
start of a new reform association because of the severe economic depression. Several New York members of the Society urged Burritt "to go home, and not undertake any
enterprize involving contributions for philanthropic objects
in such a fearful financial crisis." The treasurer of the Society, Robert L. Murray, a New York merchant, was near
bankruptcy due to the panic, and Burritt was relieved to
find out that "all funds"—$75.00—were safe. Undaunted
by the depression and having but a few dollars of his own,
he foolishly assumed responsibility for paying the office
rent.[43]

Burritt practiced self-mortification in order to manage on
the Society's exiguous funds. "You know I am one of the
sawdust-pudding kind," he told Gerrit Smith, "and can stand
a severe economy." He bought a desk and three chairs for
the office and "a husk bed for $2" and "a few yards of
coarse unbleached cotton for sheets," and put himself "on

41. Journals, Aug. 27, 31, Oct. 7, 1857.
42. *Ibid.*, Mar. 22-Apr. 24, 1856, *passim.*
43. *Ibid.*, Oct. 9, 1857.

[a] short allowance of 25 cents a day for food," later cut down to eighteen cents. He was willing to live "on bread and cold water." After having slept a few nights on his "seaweed" bed he was told by the janitor of the building, who found him dressing one morning, that regulations forbade the use of office rooms as a hotel. "It may work for [the] good," mused Burritt, "for I have caught a fearful cold by sleeping on the floor."[44]

Money was not the only problem that perplexed Burritt in his effort to get the Emancipation Society functioning. He could find nobody to assist him.[45] Dr. Nott had accepted the presidency of the Society after Professor Silliman had refused the office; Mark Hopkins, Erastus Fairbanks, former governor of Vermont, the Reverend F. M. Post, of Missouri, and John W. Tatum, of Delaware, were vice-presidents. But with the possible exception of Hopkins, none of the officers, save Burritt, took an active interest in the Society. Gerrit Smith, once "full of hope and zeal for the cause," contributed only his name and a few dollars. Garrison had been hard on Smith for his part in the movement; and Smith, though assured by Burritt that Garrison's animadversions "will strengthen our cause," was not sure he was on the right antislavery course.[46]

To secure Southern support for the Society, Burritt sent a barrage of letters into all parts of the South. John R. Underwood of Kentucky, a former United States Senator, and 160 residents of Delaware joined the organization. But this was almost the extent of Southern interest. Burritt also transmitted many articles describing his emancipation plan

44. Burritt to Gerrit Smith, New York, Oct. 13, 1857, Syracuse University Library; Journals, Oct. 15, 21, 23, 28, 1857.

45. Burritt to Gerrit Smith, New York, Oct. 13, 1857, Syracuse University Library.

46. *Liberator*, Sept. 4, Oct. 9, 1857; Gerrit Smith to Samuel J. May, Sept. 5, 1857; Garrison to S. J. May, Sept. 14, 1857, Boston Public Library; Harlow, pp. 372–373.

to Southern newspaper editors. When these articles were summarily returned, he rightly inferred that "editors in the Slave States are determined to admit no discussion on the subject of Emancipation."[47]

Burritt could not even obtain significant support in the North. David Sears, one of Boston's wealthiest citizens, joined the Society, but his was, said Burritt, "the first name that has come in from all those I have written to."[48] Burritt magnified the progress of the movement in order to win partisans. He wrote Nathan Appleton, a wealthy Boston manufacturer, that the subject of compensated emancipation was about to be brought before Congress, "and, probably, will come to discussion and vote this present session." Appreciating Appleton's cautious political mind, he played up the "conservative spirit" which "animates and inspires the undertaking."[49] Burritt's notice to Appleton of impending legislative action was based solely on the few letters he had written to Congressmen to act as "champions of the measure." Connecticut's Senator Lafayette S. Foster was one such legislator beseeched to "act as its pioneer in the Senate."[50]

By January, 1858, Burritt estimated that he had "travelled 15,000 miles this past year in connection with the Compensation Movement." Only $25.00 had been contributed to the Society since he opened the New York office. "Emancipation audiences barely pay expenses," he complained. He himself had "all the pecuniary responsibilities," he told Gerrit Smith, but he hoped that after the depression had

47. Burritt to Gerrit Smith, New Britain, Sept. 18, 1857, Syracuse University Library; Bond of Brotherhood, Jan., 1858, p. 90; Journals, Nov. 13, 1857.

48. Journals, Nov. 5, 1857.

49. Burritt to Nathan Appleton, New York, Jan. 19, 1858, Massachusetts Historical Society.

50. Burritt to L. S. Foster, Zanesville, Wisconsin, Dec. 15, 1857, New York Public Library.

run its course "contributions will begin to flow in." Not more than "a *solitary dollar*" had he received after despatching "600 circulars . . . to persons most likely to sympathize." Sometimes, as in Lancaster, Pennsylvania, where Burritt lectured before a large audience after an introduction by Thaddeus Stevens, he managed to make a few dollars and fill up several petitions; at other times, he met with a "cold reception," as in Harrisburg, Pennsylvania, where one person "stamped out of the house demanding his 15 cents."[51]

The first annual meeting of the National Compensated Emancipation Society was held in New York in May, 1858. Burritt had sent out scores of invitations. "We must have *you*," he wrote Gerrit Smith, "for you know how much we lean upon your advocacy & championship." He asked President Woolsey of Yale to accept one of the offices of vice-president.[52] Three days before the meeting, Burritt anticipated failure, as he had received no answers to his invitations.

Fewer than a hundred people attended the meeting, which was held in spacious Cooper Institute, and of these only a small proportion were members, the rest being spectators. Until the late arrival of Dr. Mark Hopkins, Burritt was the only officer who bothered to show up. The Reverend Theodore Bourne had to recruit a few gentlemen from the audience to sit on the platform and make Burritt less conspicuous. Bourne read letters from Dr. Nott and David Sears endorsing compensated emancipation. Burritt descanted on the Society's activities (or rather his own) and tried hard to sound optimistic. Because of a lack of speakers, the Reverends George W. Bethune and T. C.

51. Journals, Jan. 1, Feb. 9, 10, 1858; Burritt to Gerrit Smith, Harrisburg, Pa., Feb. 11, April 6, 1858, Syracuse University Library.

52. Burritt to Gerrit Smith, New Britain, April 6, 1858, Syracuse University Library; Burritt to the Rev. Dr. Theodore D. Woolsey, New Britain, May 3, 1858, Yale University Library.

Cuyler were beckoned from the listless audience to deliver impromptu addresses.[53] The drab proceedings confirmed what Burritt had suspected: the Society was not only his brainchild, he was its sole caretaker.

Burritt had hired Cooper Institute without having inquired about the cost. He was flabbergasted to discover that the charge was $150.00. Borrowing $40.00 to make a down payment, he proceeded to sell the spare office furniture and bed for $2.50. He returned to New Britain, "grateful that I had seen the end of my responsibilities connected with the Society." His "zeal" for the cause "has bled me to the amount of $200, besides all my labors."[54] The National Compensated Emancipation Society did not collapse after his departure because it had never really existed. It simply shifted its location to wherever Burritt happened to be at the moment.

Three days before the New York meeting, Burritt had issued the first number of a new weekly journal he had begun in New Britain. The *Citizen of the World* had come to an end in 1856, and he felt he needed an organ to disseminate the principle of compensated emancipation "not only for generating sympathy but for *collecting* expressions of it." Called the *North and South*, the journal bore "the general character of the old *Christian Citizen*." The Society was not to "have any moral or pecuniary responsibility in connection with it,"[55] probably because he knew the Society did not concern itself with financial responsibility.

The progress of the *North and South* was no better than that of the stillborn compensated emancipation movement. Longfellow subscribed to the journal, but not many persons emulated the poet's courtesy. After the first few numbers

53. *North and South*, May 15, 1858; Journals, May 8, 11, 1858.
54. Journals, May 12, 1858.
55. Burritt to Gerrit Smith, Feb. 20, 1858, Syracuse University Library.

Burritt realized that the "enterprise threatens to involve me
in another *Citizen* shipwreck . . . I feel incompetent to
direct my own steps."[56] He wrote most of the articles after
a gruelling ten or twelve hours of work on his hardscrabble
farm. At first, he enjoyed "the mingling of pen-work, and
plow-work," and he "never felt so robust, hearty and active." But soon he admitted to Gerrit Smith that he had
never "passed through such a process of labor, physical &
mental." His crops "were rotting"; his pigs "nearly all died
and everything seemed to go the wrong way."[57] The *North
and South* showed the effects of bouts between pen and
plow. It was skimpy and lacked his old spontaneity and
enthusiasm. The editorials on compensated emancipation,
while generally good, were repetitious, since he had little
news to relate about recent practical developments. At
times the paper said nothing about compensated emancipation and rather resembled a quaint agrarian journal extolling the blessings of the farmer's life.

Burritt made clumsy efforts in the *North and South* to
win the endorsement of the Democratic and Republican
parties to compensated emancipation. He lightly reprimanded the Democratic party for truckling to the dictates
of the South, even though "the anti-slavery element is per-
meating its rank and file" in the North. His appeal to the
Democratic party to adopt the principle of compensated
emancipation lacked conviction because he knew how much
that party depended on the Southern vote. He was far less
charitable to the Republican party, which he believed had
done great harm to the abolitionist cause. Reluctantly he
voted for the Republican presidential candidate in 1856,
John C. Frémont. The Republican principle of the nonex-

56. Journals, May 14, June 13, 1858.
57. Burritt to Mrs. [Merriam], New Britain, July 27, 1858, Historical Society of Pennsylvania; Burritt to Gerrit Smith, Utica, Aug.
16, 1858, Syracuse University Library.

tension of slavery in the territories was to Burritt a perver-
sion of the antislavery tenets of the old Liberty Party, a
party that had been "composed mostly of earnest antislavery
men, who had labored, prayed, and hoped for the utter
extinction of slavery." The Free Soil Party had diluted "the
radicalism of antislavery sentiment" so as to make it "smooth
and easy for the adhesion not only of conservative, but of
moderately pro-slavery men." Finally, the Republican party
was formed with an antislavery platform "lowered and
bevelled off . . . so as to render it accessible to slaveholders
themselves." Even the "accommodating platform" of nonextension, Burritt declared, might "be reconstructed for the
campaign of 1860."[58]

By 1859 Burritt spent most of his time toiling on his farm
and lecturing on topics unrelated to compensated emancipation. He still attempted to bring his plan "more fully and
forcibly before the country." He organized two state compensated emancipation conventions in the capital cities of
New York and Connecticut.[59] The aged Dr. Nott delivered
the main address at the Albany Convention before a small
gathering of ministers, college professors, and businessmen.
He remarked that compensated emancipation "has at least
the merit of furnishing an opportunity and a motive for
the North and South, to meet on common ground, and in a
fraternal spirit, for the consideration of a plan for effecting
at the national expense . . . the abolition of slavery." A Garrisonian got up denouncing the movement for "compro-
mising the inalienable rights of man, and making easy conditions with sinners, letting them off without repentance."
Burritt cut him down by asserting that the Garrisonians
themselves "had proved beyond a shadow of doubt that the
North had as great work of repentance to perform as the

58. *North and South*, July 10, 17, 1858.
59. Burritt to Luther Bradish, New Britain, Dec. 27, 1858, Connecticut State Library.

South." The Hartford Convention, attended by a "small, but quite influential group of Connecticut clergymen and professional people," was as dull as the Albany conference.[60]

The brooding, self-righteous John Brown had a plan for emancipation without compensation. His abortive raid on the federal arsenal at Harpers Ferry in 1859 not only failed miserably, but, according to Burritt, "suddenly closed the door against all overtures or efforts for the peaceful extinction of slavery"; by his rash act Brown had "put his foot on 'Compensated Emancipation' and stopped its march forever." At the time of Brown's raid the compensated emancipation movement, Burritt went on, "had reached that stage at which congressional action was about to recognize it as a legitimate proposition."[61]

So wrote Burritt in his autobiography several years after the Civil War. It was a highly erroneous declaration. No one knew better than he how badly the movement had foundered, how it had failed to arouse the North or to obtain a hearing in the South. He knew, too, that even the supposed friends of compensated emancipation were actually men of little faith.

When the Civil War came, American peace reformers had their principles put to the acid test. At the annual meeting of the American Peace Society, in May, 1861, shortly after the firing on Fort Sumter, the use of armed force against the South was justified on the grounds that the Society, in the words of Amasa Walker, "has ever protested against the confounding of war with preservation of civil government."[62] George C. Beckwith, Lewis Tappan, Gerrit Smith (now president of the Peace Society) and an overwhelming majority of peace men pronounced the right of the North to

60. *Bond of Brotherhood*, April, 1859, pp. 139–140; *North and South*, March 5, 1859.
61. Burritt, *Ten-Minute Talks*, pp. 49, 51.
62. *Advocate of Peace*, July and August, 1861, p. 271.

crush the Southern rebellion.[63] Writing in the *Advocate of Peace*, Beckwith declared that the right of governments to quell insurrections by force "underlies every form of civil government, and is essential to its very existence."[64]

Since Burritt was to address the annual meeting of the Peace Society, Amasa Walker inquired about his views on the war. Walker was worried that Burritt might advocate a policy that digressed from the militant policy Walker knew the Society would endorse. Burritt's reply was unclear: "I can hardly say what direction my thoughts will take when I sit down to elaborate something."[65] Walker sent Burritt's letter to Beckwith, who was also concerned about what Burritt might say, with the comment, "from this we will learn about our friend Burritt's intention."

Burritt's oration was one of the best he ever delivered on any subject and also one of the most artful. He did not clearly reveal his beliefs regarding the right of the North to fight the South. But it was easy for his hearers to infer that he thought the South ought to have been allowed to depart in peace. He declared that the individual who entered

> his protest against the awful carnage and desolation of a civil war, becomes instantly subject to the charge, if not the punishment of treason . . . His own familiar friend, with whom he took sweet counsel and walked to the house of God in company, rises against him as a member of the great Government of the people, and taunts him with treason to its authority.

The strength and integrity of the peace cause lay

63. Curti, *Peace or War, The American Struggle*, pp. 54–55.
64. *Advocate of Peace*, Sept. and Oct., 1861, p. 296.
65. Burritt to Amasa Walker, New Britain, April 15, 1861, University of Indiana Library.

in the spirit and the teachings of the Christian religion. If these teachings do not condemn war, and make it a sin against God and man, where shall we go for arguments against the bloody and delusive arbitrament of the sword?

How strange it was, said Burritt, that the Churches in the North and South supported the cause of their section, "cheering them on, blessing their banners, and praying for their triumph." It only showed "how much remains to be done, and how long it will take to do it, to bring the conscience of the Christian Church to one common, fixed and unchanging standard of sentiment and duty on the subject of war."[66]

Appalled by the war, and convinced that the North had grievously erred in not recognizing the independence of the Southern Confederacy, Burritt retired to his farm. The Union was still an emotion-stirring symbol to him, but one not worth the price being paid to keep it intact. He wrote Henry Richard, secretary of the London Peace Society, that he had been "saddened to silence" by the "quicksand footing" of the American Peace Society. He maintained that its "sophistry and position have shorn the locks of the Society of all the strength of principle" and regretted "that 49 in a hundred of all the *Quakers* in America have drifted from their moorings in this storm of passion or indignation." His own "inability to put forth a feather's weight of influence against the war spirit," distressed him greatly.[67]

Having developed a compensated emancipation plan for the purpose of preventing war, Burritt now formulated a scheme to stop the war. His "Plan of Adjustment and Reunion" was presented in a series of lectures in numerous Northern cities. Its underlying supposition was that after

66. Burritt, *Lectures and Speeches*, pp. 230–243.
67. Burritt to Richard, New Britain, May 26, 1861, in Curti, *The Learned Blacksmith*, pp. 138–141.

the rebellion was suppressed an anomalous Union would still exist. Slavery would remain, since the war was being fought to preserve the Union, not to free the slaves. The only solution for the maintenance of a peaceable Union was to enlarge it so as to include the entire North American Continent. In the beginning there would be three great Republics: the Northern Republic (including the West), the Southern Confederate States, and Mexico. In bringing Mexico into this arrangement it would not

> be necessary to concede to them that absolute and unrestricted independence which would be dangerous to us, or incompatible with such a Union of American nations. We might concede to them their Congress, and a few other prerogatives of a limited Nationality, strickly [sic] and clearly defined.

This "Nations-Union" would have a "General Congress . . . composed of two delegates from each of the States, forming the nation represented, with 'reserved seats' for the Canadas, and the other British Provinces in America, whenever they and the mother country might think the connection would favor their interests." All matters which affected the safety and welfare of the three Republics would have to "be submitted to the General Congress for consideration, sanction, and execution." Slavery would "be rigidly local to the Confederate States." The Nations-Union could easily "establish a North American Zollverein or Customs-Union, . . . by which all importations from foreign countries should be placed on the same footing, and pay the same duties"; a uniform penny postage system would operate on the Continent.[68]

Burritt sent a digest of his plan to Senators Sumner and Salmon P. Chase, explaining to the latter that it "might . . .

68. Burritt, MS Lecture on A Plan of Adjustment & Reunion, Central Connecticut State College Library.

not only restore to us practically, the Old Union, in all its entirety and power but also realize those larger and legitimate ambitions which we have long indulged as a nation." Chase replied that there were aspects of the plan, "especially the feature of a North American Zollverein, which seem to me to deserve attentive consideration." But Chase was against the recognition of "a Southern Confederacy formed out of the United States."[69] Burritt received in general a "respectful hearing" for his plan, but he found that "the whole people go for a *vigorous prosecution of the war*, to the bitter end. I have gone as far as I could, without exposing myself to arrest in opposing the war."[70]

In 1855 Burritt had devised a similar plan for the political reorganization of North America.[71] Though the idea went unnoticed then, he thought that the awesome realities of the Civil War made it both feasible and exigent. In 1855 he had said that the "social tendencies" of the age pointed to such a future political order; in 1861 he believed the War necessitated it. The plan was manifestly based on high evangelical hopes and an incredibly low level of political astuteness. It was predicated on a vision of a new world by a man who had difficulty understanding the one in which he lived.

Painfully and imperfectly realizing that the only plan for adjustment and reunion that could end the war was war itself, Burritt again removed himself to his farm in utter disgust. Since civil war was a bloody fact, he hoped that at least it would lead to the overthrow of slavery. Hence he

69. Quoted in J. W. Shuckers, *The Life and Public Services of Salmon Portland Chase* (New York, 1874), pp. 380–381; see Burritt's letters to Sumner and Chase in Curti, *The Learned Blacksmith*, pp. 141–144.

70. Burritt to E. W. Coggeshall, New Britain, Dec. 13, 1861, New Britain Public Institute.

71. See his article on "The Extension of the American Union", *Citizen of the World*, May, 1855, pp. 76–77.

was first gratified by General Frémont's unauthorized proclamation freeing those slaves in Missouri whose owners supported the Confederacy and then disquieted that President Lincoln had quashed both Frémont and the proclamation. "Well at the very moment when we were most hopeful and jubilant over Frémont's edict, and were most confident that it was to be the rule of the conflict, and the beginning of the great consummation so devoutly to be wished, the Government comes out and virtually repudiates the principle of the proclamation," Burritt indignantly wrote. If the North felt impelled to fight, then let it fight "a war for freedom."[72]

Burritt expected the slaves to be liberated as a consequence of the war, but he opposed the indiscriminate seizure of other forms of Southern property. For this reason he thought the second confiscation bill considered by Congress in 1862 too drastic in the long categories of Southern property it empowered the President to order seized. In a letter to Lincoln, Burritt asked the President not to sign the bill, "which, if put in force, must be a burning caustic upon the life strings of the Union, producing imitations as annoying and repulsive to the North as they would be maddening to the South." Burritt cautioned Lincoln to "let the despotisms of the Old World see, that, in putting down and punishing this great Rebellion, our Government is not constrained to copy or countenance . . . vindictive policies, or to reproduce, under our banner, a Poland, a Hungary, or even an Ireland."[73]

Lincoln took issue with the confiscation bill for reasons quite different from Burritt's. Whereas Burritt thought it right that slave property be confiscated, Lincoln feared that

72. Burritt to the Editor of the New York *Daily World,* [1862], Columbia University Library.
73. Burritt to Lincoln, New Britain, June 2, 1862, Library of Congress.

part of the bill mainly because it encroached upon his authority over the slavery question. Had Congress not passed an explanatory resolution that diluted the stringency of the bill, Lincoln would probably have vetoed it. Burritt hailed Lincoln for the congressional act which abolished slavery in the District of Columbia and which included Lincoln's proposals for compensation to the slaveowners and colonization for the freedmen if they so desired. "The whole civilized world is honoring you with its sincere homage, as the first of all the list of American Presidents that ever had the moral courage to propose a plan for the extinction of slavery, so just, generous and noble as to be hailed with admiration in both hemispheres."[74]

In the fall of 1862 Burritt decided to go to England. He wrote Henry Richard to ask for a loan to pay his passage, since he was still beset by "floating debts." He told of how he was regarded in certain quarters in the North "as almost a *secessionist*" and how he tried "to modify that impression by calling myself a *separationist*." Burritt believed the South had "developed an energy, a willingness and capacity of endurance that have had few parallels in history." For the North he envisioned a "winter of discontent," in spite of Lincoln's Emancipation Proclamation that would go into effect on the first day of the new year. He saw "no light in the working of that proclamation" since "either the whites or the negroes of the South will have to evacuate that section, especially if the slaves should be armed and assist in the subjugation of the former masters." But Lincoln, "very cautious and conservative," would not "incite the slaves to insurrection, and I doubt if he even consents to arm them against the South even as a *military necessity*. Of course, his proclamation will lie inoperative until the Southern

74. Allan Nevins, *The War for the Union: War Becomes Revolution, 1862–1863* (2 vols. New York, 1960), II, 145–146; Burritt to Lincoln, June 2, 1862.

States are pretty much all subjugated, for as fast as the federal armies march southward, the negroes will be withdrawn into the Gulf States." Burritt declared that the desire for Union was still strong in the North, where the "people cling to it as the sheet anchor of their political being." He had "not a doubt that millions of the North would rather accept Jeff. Davis and his constitution, than consent to separation."[75]

With nothing to do in America but read and hear about sanguinary battles and brilliant or not-so-brilliant generals, Burritt returned to England early in 1863, happy to have 3,000 miles of water between himself and the holocaust. He had labored unsparingly for compensated emancipation, but to no avail. In a decade of intensifying strife and vituperation he had offered his countrymen a plan for the eradication of slavery that was fair and practicable. He had failed, but so also had his country. He had proposed a compromise based on brotherhood; the nation had chosen war.

75. Burritt to [Richard], New Britain, Oct. 27, 1862, in Curti, pp. 144–148.

11

The Faith Remains Firm

The twilight of Burritt's humanitarianism coincided with the Civil War. From its outbreak to his death in 1879 his reform labors decreased substantially, and he had nearly reached the end of his distinguished career of benevolence. Yet these years were far from anti-climactic. Burritt travelled extensively, spent four rewarding years as American consular agent at Birmingham, wrote several interesting books, resumed his language study, and managed to play a vital if indirect role in the latest phase of the peace movement. Though he had retired from active philanthropy, his evangelical earnestness remained. His obsession to perform good works never abated; his belief that he was his brother's keeper never faltered. During his last few years he re-affirmed those moral principles which had been his guide-posts throughout his life.

When Burritt arrived in England in 1863, he was not altogether sure what he was going to do now that the League of Universal Brotherhood was dead and he himself was all out of reforms. Seven years had elapsed since his last trip to Great Britain, and, as he wrote in his autobiography, he did not return "with the expectation of reviving the movements he had originated there, but rather to see friends of former years."[1] He had spent his happiest years in England, where he had won a measure of acceptance and acclaim far greater than in America. He had to borrow money to get to England. Once there he took to lecturing to support himself. With the aid of former Leaguers, he arranged a lecture tour in England and Scotland. "I hope in most cases," he carefully wrote a friend, "a small charge at the door for admission would be made."[2] He had three first-rate lectures to deliver upon invitation: "The Higher Law and Mission of Commerce", "The Physiology of Free Nations", and "The Benevolent Associations of the Day—Their Philosophy and Power".[3] These lectures incorporated his fundamental beliefs in free trade, peace and brotherhood, and benevolence. Burritt's prolonged absence from England had not diminished his popularity, and he had no problem in arranging speaking engagements.

In the summer of 1863 he began a foot tour from London to John O'Groat's in Scotland for the purpose of visiting farms along the way and taking notes on the latest agricultural techniques. Before he had purchased his farm in New Britain, Burritt's interest in agriculture had been largely sentimental. He had since, however, become a serious student of husbandry. In 1858 he had helped organize the New Britain Agricultural Club, of which he was secretary, and he took an active part in the meetings.[4] Before leaving for England in 1863, several members of the Agricultural Club requested that he "write them letters about farming in the Mother Country, and on other matters of interest that I might meet with on my travels there." The possibility of publishing a book on pastoral life from London to John

1. Burritt, *Ten-Minute Talks*, p. 52.
2. Burritt to Elias Lane, Islington, Jan. 5, 1863, Swarthmore College Peace Collection.
3. Burritt, *Lectures and Speeches*, pp. 1–69.
4. *North and South*, March 5, 1859.

O'Groats was uppermost in his mind as he set off on his journey.

His walk took him over three months. "I feel that I have done what no other American ever did," he wrote a friend on the day he reached his destination, "and [I] have acquired a knowledge of the country and people which, I hope, may be of some advantage to me hereafter."[5] From a rather sketchy journal of his travels he composed *A Walk From London to John O'Groats*. Published in London in 1864, the book went through two editions within a few months.

On June 1, 1864, he began a second tour on foot, this time to Land's End. "Here I am at last!", he wrote upon completing the walk. He had traversed the length of Great Britain, and he believed that "no other living man had done this before."[6] *A Walk From London to Land's End and Back* was published in 1865, and quickly also went through two editions.

John O'Groats and *Land's End* were admirable travel works, describing simply and entertainingly British agriculture, animals, landscapes and historical sites. The style of both books was supple and lucid, and there is scarcely a trace of the heavily ornamented prose of his early lectures and essays. With maturity had come a more graceful style. As a writer, Burritt could, as he admitted, "expand facts and embellish them a little," but he could "do nothing in absolute fiction."[7] In each book there was a freshness that derived in part from the great pleasure and recreation his walks had given him and from the fact that he knew what he was writing about. He had crossed the English country-

5. Burritt to Annie Ridley, John O'Groats, Sept. 28, 1863, Klingberg Collection.

6. *Ibid.*, June 28, 1864.

7. Burritt to John Lovell, July 13, 1868, American Antiquarian Society.

side on many previous occasions, but always with a cause
to plead or reform to explain. Now he came to observe the
people at work and at play. Knowing a great deal about
farming and having a sharp eye for detail, he described
British agricultural methods in a masterly and sparkling
manner. In *John O'Groats* he wrote delightfully of the uses
and abuses of the donkey ("a kind of Ishmaelite in the
great family of domestic animals") and informatively of the
differences between English and American birds.[8] Longfellow enjoyed the book because it took him "across the
breezy fields," and gave "glimpses of landscape which are
so lovely, and which one never gets from a carriage window
on the dirty highway." It was, wrote Longfellow, "full not
only of pleasantries, but also of information, not found in
other books of travel."[9]

Land's End was a larger and more interesting volume.
Burritt thought it better because it was "more descriptive
and less speculative, and also embraces more of the pic-
turesque sceneries of England." Filled with what Van Wyck
Brooks called "unassuming information,"[10] *Land's End* emphasized the economic aspects of British agriculture and
rural industries, especially the wages and working conditions of farm laborers. On Burritt's return from Land's End
to London he stopped off at Windsor to visit the Queen's
Dairy and to inspect the procedures by which the royal
family was supplied with dairy products. He was impressed
by the whole operation, but thought that the milk pails

8. Burritt, *A Walk From London to John O'Groats* (London,
1864), pp. 29–49, 63–76; for an excellent review of *John O'Groats*,
see *Christian Examiner*, (1864), p. 385.

9. Longfellow to Burritt, Cambridge, Oct. 2, 1865, Klingberg Collection.

10. Burritt to Longfellow, Birmingham, April 25, 1866, Historical
Society of Pennsylvania; Van Wyck Brooks, *The Flowering of New
England* (New York, 1936), p. 422.

were too heavy—he recommended that "seamless, white-cedar pails" be used instead."[11]

Shortly after Burritt finished writing *John O'Groats*, he received official notification of his appointment as American consular agent at Birmingham. In his autobiography he stated that he had not solicited the office and that he "accepted the post with some hesitation, and even reluctance, fearing it would be a bar to all literary labor."[12] Though he had not sought the position, he had made an earlier effort to become the consul at Newcastle. In 1861, the Bristol consul, Zebina Eastman, an old friend of Burritt, had suggested to Secretary of State Seward that Burritt would make an excellent choice for the vacant consulate at Newcastle. Upon learning of Eastman's recommendation, Burritt wrote Seward that he would "esteem it a great honor and pleasure to serve the Government in the capacity suggested." Burritt promised Seward that, if appointed consul, he would "by speech and pen . . . give a rightful direction to those sources of public opinion which I might reach, and bear in favor of our country's cause" in the Civil War. Further, he had "made as many different circles of acquaintance with the movers of public opinion, as any other American living," and he was "confident that through these sources of influence I might be of some service to the Government and nation."[13]

The Birmingham district was not an independent consulate, but an agency under the jurisdiction of the consul at Bristol, Eastman; thus Burritt was a consular agent and not a consul. He began his official duties in the summer of

11. Burritt, *A Walk From London to Land's End and Back* (London, 1865), pp. 455–462.

12. Burritt, *Ten-Minute Talks*, p. 53.

13. Burritt to William H. Seward, New Britain, Sept. 2, 1861, University of Rochester Library.

1865, taking up residence in the village of Harborne, three
and a half miles from Birmingham. His two nieces crossed
the Atlantic to keep house for him. With a clerk to assist
him in his duties, Burritt had ample time to write and to
lecture. His office did not encroach upon the new literary
career he was diligently pursuing. Longfellow wrote him
that, as Nathaniel Hawthorne had "found the hidden romance" of his life at the Salem customs house, so would he
"find some good, and some unexpected poetry" at the Birmingham consulate. Burritt was making a concerted effort
to discover new "poetry" in his life while he lived well and
quietly. "I am pleasantly situated here—," he wrote Gerrit
Smith, "the business is simple, merely commercial, and I
am able to put forth some thoughts beyond the duties it
invokes, while the income makes me easy and comfortable."[14] Such financial security was a new experience for
him.

The greater part of the consular duties concerned "the
industrial pursuits and productions" of his agency. Not satisfied that his annual reports described sufficiently the industrial and agricultural economy of the "Black Country",
as the Birmingham district was popularly called, Burritt
wrote *Walks in the Black Country and Its Green Borderland*. The book was a charming study of the resources and
industries of the Birmingham district. Like *John O'Groats*
and *Land's End*, it was filled with historical information
and effective characterizations of the landscape and the
people. Seward, to whom Burritt sent a copy, commended
"the character and value of the book."[15]

14. Longfellow to Burritt, Cambridge, Oct. 2, 1865, Klingberg
Collection; Burritt to Smith, Birmingham, Mar. 28, 1867, in Curti,
The Learned Blacksmith, p. 161.

15. Burritt, *Walks in the Black Country and Its Green Borderland*
(London, 1868); Burritt, *Ten-Minute Talks*, p. 54; Burritt to William
H. Seward, Birmingham, May 9, 1868, University of Rochester Li-
brary.

Burritt was pleased that he had the opportunity "to write whole books on continuous subjects." The only books he had written previously had been compilations of articles from the *Christian Citizen* and a few abstracts containing the vital statistics of nations which he called *The Year-Book of the Nations*. Published irregularly in Great Britain and the United States from 1855 to 1863, *The Year-Book of the Nations* was a carefully compiled and useful abstract, but Burritt had trouble even giving them away. He wanted, as he wrote a London publisher, "to get the writings which I think may do some good in a book form" because he felt "exposed to a very sudden call from this scene of labor."[16] This inference of imminent death was meant to rouse the publisher to action and it succeeded. Some of Burritt's best lectures and speeches were now printed in book form, as were selections from his periodical and newspaper writings from 1850 to 1855.[17] After the death of Edmund Fry in 1866, Burritt converted the *Bond of Brotherhood* into a literary journal; and in 1868 he changed the title of the former peace periodical to *Fire-Side Words*, a title more suitable to the didactic nature of its articles, most of which were written for juvenile readers. Two pages were usually devoted to "Fireside Lessons in Forty Languages".[18]

The most thoughtful book Burritt wrote while consular agent was *The Mission of Great Sufferings*, which he con-

16. Burritt to William H. Seward, New Britain, Feb. 13, 1856, Unversity of Rochester Library; Burritt to Clement M. Clay, New Britain, April 11, 1856, Duke University Library; Burritt to Henry Barnard, Jan. 2, 1855, Jan. 19, 1856, Connecticut Historical Society; Burritt, *The Year-Book of the Nations* (London, 1855), (New York, 1856), (New York, 1863); Burritt to Edward Marston, Birmingham, May 21, 1868, Klingberg Collection.

17. Burritt, *Lectures and Speeches* (London, 1869); *Thoughts and Notes at Home and Abroad* (London, 1868).

18. Burritt, *Fire-Side Words* (London, 1868); this periodical lasted only one year.

sidered "the best thing I ever did."[19] Inspiration apparently came in part from the Quaker Meetings for Sufferings he had attended. The book's purpose was "to show what the ministry of suffering and self-sacrifice has done in the development of Christianity, Patriotism and Philanthropy." The Quakers emerged as the heroes of this study because "they were the true reformers, gifted with the clearest and fullest comprehension of civil and religious freedom." Through endless "trial and obloquy, they held up those principles with the quiet and even valour of a faith which no persecution could weary or weaken."[20] With only a Journal entry in 1842 to remind him how he had mocked the Quakers, he warmly praised the sect which had been a steady source of comfort and assistance to him. Though a diffuse and at times tediously moralistic book, it affords a revealing insight into the nature of evangelicalism.

Burritt assumed his consular duties about the time the Civil War had drawn to a close. The assassination of Lincoln had filled him with grief. In an article in the *Bond* on "The Mission of Great Deaths" he paid an eloquent tribute to the trials of the late President.[21] Soon after he had written the article, Thomas H. Dudley, United States Consul at Liverpool, asked Burritt to distribute copies of the *Narrative of the Sufferings of Our Prisoners in the Hands of the Rebel Authorities*. Burritt refused to comply:

> As the war is over now, and the great work of reconstruction inaugurated, all good and patriotic men both North and South must feel it desirable and necessary to the restoration of the Union, to bridge chasms, heal wounds, and bleach the earth from blood, in a word, to let by-gones be by-gones as soon as possible. No human nor divine power can civilise

19. Burritt to Miss Vansittart, Nov. 27, 1867, Klingberg Collection.
20. Burritt, *The Mission of Great Sufferings* (London, 1867), p. 55.
21. *Bond of Brotherhood*, June, 1865, pp. 482–487.

war—especially civil war—and I am inclined to think the sooner the records of atrocities on both sides of this long and terrible conflict are buried in oblivion, the sooner will a better future dawn upon our country.[22]

Burritt was for a speedy restoration of the Confederate States into the Union. He was disturbed by the violent quarrel in America between President Andrew Johnson and the radical Republicans over the process and terms of Reconstruction. He sympathized with Johnson's liberal policy toward the South, though some British observers disagreed with the President's program. John Bright wrote Burritt that he was "glad to see" that the Johnson Republicans had been defeated in the crucial congressional elections of 1866: "I hope the President will see the error of his ways—and that the process of an honest reconstruction may now come rapidly."[23] Burritt kept abreast of political developments at home, but he discreetly avoided choosing sides.

Early in 1869 he learned that the Birmingham consular agency was soon to be made an independent consulate. He asked his old friend Charles Sumner to use his influence to obtain the position for him. "During my present sojourn in England I have performed a good deal of literary work and acquired some additional literary reputation, a quality which, perhaps, it would not be undesirable to associate with American officials abroad." Though Congress had in 1868 reduced the salaries of consuls and consular agents, causing Burritt to send a letter of remonstrance to Seward, he very much wanted to retain his post. But he suspected that the incoming Grant administration would make wholesale consular changes. Nervously awaiting news of any

22. Burritt to [Dudley], Birmingham, June 8, 1865, in Curti, pp. 148–149.

23. John Bright to Burritt, Nov. 28, 1866, New Britain Public Institute.

"sudden change," he was saddened to hear that the "new
broom at Washington" had "swept me out of the place."
He was indignant that capable men of unimpeachable
character like himself and Zebina Eastman (who had also
been removed) should be ousted for purely political reasons. "I hope he will be a decent man, and not a low politician of immoral habits," he wrote of his replacement.[24] Burritt had fulfilled his consular assignment very capably, but
he did not realize that in politics patronage frequently out-
weighed performance.

Since his return to England in 1863, Burritt made no
effort to revive any of his old reform projects. He attended
most of the annual meetings of the London Peace Society
from 1863 to 1869, addressing three of them. In 1867 he
began inserting a monthly Olive Leaf in two or three German journals but only "as a pleasant souvenir of the enterprise."[25] He felt that his day as a reformer was "pretty
much done." Now that he had been turned out of the Birmingham consulate, however, he turned to benevolence
again. In the fall of 1869 he established the International
Land and Labour Agency of Birmingham to assist prospective emigrants to America.[26]

Throughout the 19th century the British government had
become increasingly involved in protection of emigrants.
Passenger acts had attempted to regulate the process of
emigration so as to provide the greatest safety and security
for British emigrants. These acts never sufficiently elim-
inated the unscrupulous practices of speculating brokers

24. Burritt to Sumner, Birmingham, Feb. 26, 1869, in Curti, pp.
163–170; Burritt to Zebina Eastman, Birmingham, March 31, April
1, May 3, 1869, Chicago Historical Society; Burritt to David A.
Wells, Birmingham, May 14, 1869, Library of Congress.

25. *Lectures and Speeches*, pp. 244–274, 311; see pp. 312–333 for
a sample of some of these Olive Leaves.

26. Burritt to [the American consul at London], Birmingham, May
12, 1869, Pierpont Morgan Library.

who contracted for space aboard ships and then sent agents to round up prospective passengers by false promises of low passage rates and large, well-provisioned ships; nor did they effectively cope with the misery and possible death that faced emigrants packed aboard small, filthy ships. Yet the acts, despite limitations, made emigration cheaper, safer, and healthier.[27] Burritt's Agency, however, was not concerned with getting emigrants to America; it wanted "to render it more safe, comfortable, and profitable to those who go to that country for land or labour." For those emigrants with money enough to buy farms in America the Agency endeavored "to secure the purchase of a farm of any size or price, in any of the States, at the charge of only 1 per cent to the buyer." For a fee of £5 the Agency supplied emigrants "with a list of farms in any State and other information"; farm leases "for those who lack capital" were also available. Finally, Burritt offered to "obtain situations and employment in the United States for labourers of all occupations . . . at the charge of £1 for a man, and 10s. for a female servant."[28]

Twenty years earlier he had tried to make emigrant-aid a key reform of the League, but he was then too enmeshed in other projects to concentrate on the idea, and, as Edmund Fry dryly remarked at the time, "not very willing to let a favorite idea pass out of his own hands."[29] Burritt worked hard to make the Agency a success. "Although our Agency has been opened only about two months," he wrote the editor of the Albany *Cultivator and Country Gentle-*

27. Oliver MacDonagh, *A Pattern of Government Growth, 1800–1860, The Passenger Acts and their Enforcement* (London, 1961), chapters 1–3.

28. *Washington's Words to Intending English Emigrants to America, With Introduction and Appendix by Elihu Burritt* (London, 1870), p. 128.

29. *Christian Citizen*, April 28, June 16, 1849; Edmund Fry to Zebina Eastman, Mar. 14, 1852, Chicago Historical Society.

man, "more than a thousand farms has [*sic*] been committed
to it for sale to English purchasers, from Maine to California
and from $500 to $5000 in price."[30] He composed a pamphlet in which he described the soil, climate, and resources
of every American state and territory; "and soon young
English farmers, and men of other occupations, acted upon
it, and went out, under the auspices of the Agency, to New
England, the Middle States, Virginia, North Carolina, Ten-
nessee, and other parts of the country." To an interested
American he wrote, "We can supply any number of good
servant girls out of Shropshire and other agricultural countries at the shortest notice."[31] Because most of the servant
girls were without means to get to America, Burritt arranged for prospective American employers to send passage
fare to him, money they later deducted from wages paid the
servants.

Burritt's International Land and Labour Agency lasted
less than a year. A well-intended but pretentious operation,
it lacked capital and effective organization and moreover
had to compete with numerous similar agencies. After its
collapse Burritt travelled throughout England, spending six
weeks at Oxford University, before late in 1870 he decided
to return to America.

Once home in New Britain Burritt "entered upon the en-
joyment of a quiet literary life, while taking part in all the
pleasant duties of a citizen of his native town."[32] Having
written during his short stay at Oxford a slim book on
*Prayers and Devotional Meditations, Collated from the
Psalms of David*, he followed it up with a tiny volume of

30. Burritt to the Editor of the Albany *Cultivator and Country
Gentleman*, Nov. 12, 1869, Historical Society of Pennsylvania.
31. Burritt, *Ten-Minute Talks*, p. 60; Burritt to [the Rev. J. Wil-
liams], Birmingham, Oct. 11, 1869, in Curti, pp. 172–173.
32. Burritt, *Ten-Minute Talks*, p. 63.

appropriate Biblical sayings for children, called *The Children of the Bible*.[33]

In 1872 he had published in London a serious religious study entitled *A Voice From the Back Pews*. (It was published anonymously because he wanted to send "it out into the religious world to stand or fall on its own intrinsic merits, without the influence of a name for or against it."[34]) Explaining at the outset that he had been a Congregationalist for over forty years and had heard sermons by ministers of all Protestant denominations, Burritt declared that there was "little Bible foundation . . . to many beliefs, theories, or doctrines which are preached and held as necessary to salvation!" He analyzed what he understood to be the basic tenets of Christianity as it evolved from Judaism. His major argument was that "God never revealed to mankind the immortality of the soul before the coming of Jesus Christ": Christ was the ultimate Messiah. Burritt criticized the "thousands of [C]hristian ministers and millions of professed [C]hristians" who

seem to admit, and even to insist, that Jesus Christ had not yet realized what the Jews have reason to expect in the Messiah promised them; but that if they will believe in the common Saviour of the world, and wait a few hundred years longer, [H]e will fulfill their expectations; [H]e will come again in human form on the earth and gather them all back to Jerusalem, and reign over them in great glory, and be to them all they ever hoped and expected in their Messiah.[35]

33. Burritt, *Prayers and Devotional Meditations, Collated From the Psalms of David* (London, 1870); Burritt, *The Children of the Bible* (New Britain, 1871).

34. Burritt, *Ten-Minute Talks*, p. 64.

35. Burritt. *A Voice From the Back Pews* (London, 1872), pp. 6–8, 230, 247.

The reason so many Christians believed "in two Messiahs, one the Saviour of the world and giver of spiritual life, and the other the Restorer of the Jews . . . as [H]is peculiar people," was that they were unable "to spiritualize fully the predictions of the prophets."

More than half of *A Voice From the Back Pews* rebuts those Christians who, claimed Burritt, confused Christ's nature and mission. Christ had come as a Universal Deliverer "to impart to sinful men a new and eternal life, an immortality that death shall not interrupt; to breathe into their natures [H]is own . . . that their spiritual life may be hidden in [H]is." The revelation of God "as the universal and equal Father of mankind" appeared only through Christ. Burritt distinguished between "Christ's Theology" found in the New Testament and the "Creed Theology" propounded by many Protestant ministers. The former was what Christ plainly said and meant about His being and purpose, while the latter was the misunderstanding of theologians. To Burritt "the alpha and omega of Christ's own teaching" was "to give [H]is life, not [H]is *death*" to the world. Christ's theology made Him one and inseparable with God the Father"; the creed theology made Christ "a separate being, a distinct person, another God, who must be recognized, worshipped, sung, and prayed to as such"; Christ's theology emphasized "Life! Life!"; the "creed theology says Death! Death!" Burritt could not "find a single word uttered by Christ in the four Gospels that puts forth, sanctions, or suggests the creed-doctrine that [H]is death was the penalty for the sins of mankind, or a substitute for their eternal death, or that [H]is human blood atoned for sin, or cleansed the human soul from sin."[36]

All in all, it was a remarkable book which disclosed the evangelical bent of Burritt's religious beliefs. He was a competent student of the Bible. But because he lacked

36. *Ibid.*, pp. 285, 289, 419.

theological training, he was incapable of making a careful exegetical study of the Scriptures. He had practically nothing to say regarding such fundamental and much-debated Christian tenets as original sin, grace, freedom of the will, and the atonement. His theology was essentially the theology of evangelical common sense, and his basic arguments, however compelling, were not original. Neither were they when he wrote as controversial as he had thought. Indeed, Horace Bushnell, in a less forthright manner, had advanced most of Burritt's propositions on the nature of Christ some thirty years earlier. The Reverend Dr. George L. Walker, a Yale theologian, wrote Burritt at length praising the work and commenting that most of its views were in accord with his own. Burritt replied that he was "highly gratified that these views coincide with yours on so many points, for I cannot expect that many theologians or ministers could or would go so far with me as you seem to do."[37] But had Burritt inquired, he would have discovered that most of his religious ideas were rather commonplace.

Burritt's literary pursuits were interrupted by news of the Treaty of Washington of 1871. This reactivated his interest in the cause of peace and plunged him into a final reform fling. The Treaty of Washington provided for the arbitration by the Geneva Tribunal of several complicated Anglo-American disputes that had arisen out of the Civil War. The most incendiary problem concerned the *Alabama* claims. Charles Sumner's bombastic Senate speech in 1869, in which he strongly suggested that England owed America a huge indemnity for the "indirect" or "consequential" damages caused by the Alabamas, had strained relations between the two countries. In view of the taut diplomatic background the Treaty of Washington was a major accomplishment.

37. Burritt to the Rev. Dr. George Walker, Mar. 27, 1875, Yale University Library.

The Joint High Commission which drafted the Treaty and the Geneva Tribunal established to settle the *Alabama* dispute represented to Burritt "the nearest approximation to that Congress and High Court of Nations which the friends of peace had been pressing upon the governments of Christendom for forty years." The American Peace Society held a series of public meetings in celebration of the Treaty. The Reverend James B. Miles, the new secretary of the Society, invited Burritt to participate in the demonstrations. Burritt spoke at over thirty meetings, most of which he helped to organize.[38] When the Geneva Tribunal came close to settling nothing, as the United States' representatives pressed for indirect damages, Burritt accused the Republican party of trying to win the Irish vote by "twisting the lion's tail" a little. He wrote Sumner that he felt "exceedingly anxious about your relation to this great difficulty" and that "nine in ten in England regard you as the author of these consequential claims, which bar the way to a fair & satisfactory settlement."[39] The American representatives finally dropped the indirect claims, and a settlement of the controversy was reached in September, 1872.

In February, 1872, Burritt and James B. Miles had decided to capitalize on the favorable peace propaganda generated by the Treaty of Washington by holding an international peace congress in America. They issued a "Call" to the friends of peace in Europe and America to attend a congress in New York, in September, 1872, "for the purpose of elaborating and commending to the governments and

38. Burritt, *Ten-Minute Talks*, p. 66; see Burritt's correspondence in Curti, pp. 175–195.

39. *Ibid.*, pp. 196–203; Cyrus W. Field to Burritt, New York, April 24, 26, 1872; Charles Sumner to Burritt, Washington, D.C., June 1, 1872, New Britain Public Institute.

peoples of Christendom, an INTERNATIONAL CODE, and other measures" to promote peace.[40] But the peace congress never met. Money problems and few replies to the "Call" convinced Burritt and Miles that it was foolhardy to continue plans for a meeting in the United States and they decided to hold the congress in Europe instead. Burritt was unable to accompany Miles to Europe in 1873 because he had been involved in a railway accident.

After much persistent effort, Miles, a persuasive and indefatigable peace reformer, laid the groundwork for a conference at Brussels which was to prepare "an international code, as a permanent provision and basis for the adjustment of difficulties at the bar of reason." Miles returned to America and began to make preparations for the convention. He received little support from the Peace Society, which thought it was too formidable an undertaking. Burritt begged Miles to go ahead: "I earnestly hope you will have *back-bone* enough to hold you up stiff and strong through this contest with senseless crotchets."[41]

About thirty-five delegates attended the Brussels conference on October 10, 1873, including such jurists as David Dudley Field, Montague Bernard, Pasquale Mancini, Johann Bluntschli, Sheldon Ames, and Sir Travers Twiss. No international code of laws was drawn up at the conference, but an Association for the Reform and Codification of the Laws of Nations was established.[42] Burritt congratulated Miles: "Truly you have won a great triumph and a great crown of glory in your wonderful success, and I am almost

40. The University of Rochester Library has a copy of the "Call" sent to Seward.

41. *The New York Times*, July 16, 1873; Curti, pp. 212–213; Burritt to Theodore D. Woolsey, New Britain, Sept. 4, Oct. 3, 1873, Yale University Library.

42. For an account of this entire movement, see Curti, *Peace or War*, pp. 90–101.

glad I was not with you to share it with you; for you richly deserve it all, and I have had my share of whatever reputation attaches to a pioneer in former Congresses."[43]

Burritt urged Miles "to go to New York and settle down there in his office of Secretary of the *International Code Association*, which will be the great peace work hereafter." He was disgruntled by the failure of "the old fogies" of the Peace Society to offer Miles any assistance.[44] But Miles died in 1875, and leadership of the Association lapsed into British hands.

He spent the last few years of his life writing and spreading odd bits of benevolence in New Britain. He established "three little wayside chapels" in his native town and invited local clergymen of various denominations to hold afternoon church services on Sunday and prayer meetings during the week.[45] In New Britain and surrounding towns he organized "Union" church meetings, or gatherings of "lay members and ministers of different churches and denominations within an hour's ride." He had children attend the prayer meetings and read "verses of scripture between the prayers, talks and songs." For the moral benefit of the poorer townspeople he rented a large hall in which religious readings and group singing under the direction of teachers and students from the local schools were conducted.[46]

43. For the correspondence between Burritt and Miles, see Curti, *The Learned Blacksmith*, pp. 174–233.

44. Burritt to Amasa Walker, New Britain, Jan. 16, 1875, New York Historical Society.

45. Burritt to Zebina Eastman, New Britain, July 28, 1874, Chicago Historical Society; Burritt to Jeremiah Beach, New Britain, Aug. 28, 1875; Burritt to A. A. Lyman, Nov. 28, 1877, Central Connecticut State College Library; Burritt to Mr. Parker, May 2, 1876, New York Public Library.

46. Burritt to the Rev. Mr. Knight, New Britain, Aug. 4, 1875, Klingberg Collection; Burritt to Horatio C. King, New Britain, June 28, 1875, Newark, New Jersey, Public Library; C. Northend, *Elihu Burritt*, p. 182.

In 1875 Burritt suffered a sudden stroke which left him a semi-invalid and forced him to "shut myself up in the house almost hermetically." One of his "most enjoyable recreations" was to teach Sanskrit to a small class of young ladies. "There are six in the class," he informed a prospective student. "You need no books, and would be at no other expense than an hour's time one evening a week."[47] The class met for over a year; and, as a "last graduating exercise," the young ladies had to translate into Sanskrit Longfellow's "The Psalm of Life," Burritt's favorite poem. He sent Longfellow each of the translations bound in an album. The poet assured Burritt that he prized "most highly this mark of your remembrance and regard. I often think of you, Dear Mr. Burritt, and of all the sweet influences of your life."[48] Burritt himself wrote *A Sanskrit Handbook for the Fireside*, published in 1875, as well as primers in Persian, Hindustani, Arabic, and Turkish, which were never published.[49]

Though his health was failing, Burritt managed to keep up with the major political issues in the United States. A confirmed Manchester liberal, he viewed with contempt the high tariff policy of Grant Republicans. "I think political economy is the great field now," he wrote Zebina Eastman, advising him to join the Liberal Republicans in their fight against the protectionism of the Grant administration. "I hope . . . you will wheel into line with David A. Wells, Amasa Walker, [and] Horace White." Earlier he had urged the American free trader David Wells to "become the *Cobden* of America, and . . . win for our country the same vic-

47. Burritt to Frederick T. Stanley, New Britain, Feb. 13, 1875, Connecticut Historical Society; Burritt to Hattie Butler, New Britain, Jan. 25, 1875, New Britain Public Institute.

48. Longfellow to Burritt, Cambridge, Sept. 16, 1876, in Curti, "Henry Wadsworth Longfellow and Elihu Burritt", *American Literature*, p. 327.

49. The manuscripts are in the New Britain Public Institute.

tory and honor he won for his." Burritt was disappointed by the Liberal Republican presidential fiasco of 1872, and distressed by Grant's government by crony. The President, he wrote Amasa Walker, seemed "determined" to have no one in his Cabinet "to overtop his small stature."[50] Burritt also contributed many articles on national and international questions to the New York *World*, several of which he later had published in *Chips From Many Blocks*,[51] his last book.

Burritt was a celebrity in his native town, receiving much attention and adulation. He modestly accepted the homage, though he may have recalled how during his youth "they used to cast upon me all manner of jeering epithets for my apparent stupidity and bashfulness."[52] In 1837 he had left New Britain as a poor young blacksmith seeking a more suitable station in life. When in 1870 he returned to stay, he had labored nearly three decades for the moral betterment of mankind. The process through which he had turned his talents to philanthropy need not be repeated here. If he was not a born moralist, he was born in an aggressively moralistic generation and grew up in an intensely religious household. His transition from learned blacksmith to crusader for universal brotherhood had not been inspired by any single social reform or dictated by unique personal experiences. Burritt had been drawn into the vortex of benevolent reform because he was truly convinced that all men were their brothers' keepers and that he had been divinely appointed to help redeem a sinful world. He belonged to

50. Burritt to Zebina Eastman, New Britain, July 28, 1874, Chicago Historical Society; Burritt to David Wells, Birmingham, May 14, 1869, Library of Congress; Burritt to David A. Wells, New Britain, Nov. 21, 1874, Illinois Historical Society; Burritt to Amasa Walker, New Britain, Jan. 16, 1875, New York Public Library.

51. Burritt, *Chips From Many Blocks* (Toronto, Canada, 1878).

52. In 1872 Yale University conferred an honorary Master of Arts degree on him; Franklin B. Dexter to Burritt, July 24, 1872, Yale University Library; Journals, Aug. 5, 1842.

that singular breed of 19th century social reformers who devoted themselves to Christianity, morality, and humanity. He always operated under an exalted sense of mission. Thus he was at times authentically abashed by the lionizing he was subjected to. Since God had selected him for a noble task, it was both irrelevant and irreverent for him to take himself too seriously. He meant what he had written a British admirer in 1850:

> If man could see what God sees in my heart and life, how it would modify these expressions of regard! My constant prayer is, that He would keep me in a meek and humble spirit; that I may walk softly before Him and my fellow-men. You must not *lionize* me; you must sink persons; and raise aloft principles to the admiration of the world. Persons, the best in the world, may fail and fall, but principles never change.[53]

Burritt had truly believed that the League of Universal Brotherhood would succeed in effecting the moral reformation of mankind and in ushering in the millennium. Much that he wrote and did was disconcertingly sentimental and moralistic, but this was because he was an uninhibited sentimentalist and moralist who had learned nothing and had forgotten nothing. He always allowed his evangelical heart to shout down whatever doubt might have existed in his mind. He was an extraordinary idealist who thought good intentions would automatically produce good results. He had no conception of the processes of social or moral change, and he invariably confused agitation with accomplishment. Not until late in his career did he carefully consider the line in Longfellow's "The Psalm of Life" which admonished, "Learn to labor and to wait." He finally ad-

53. Quoted in *Friends' Quarterly Examiner*, XIV (London, 1880), pp. 571–577.

mitted that "This is the right doctrine . . . Many can do the
first, but the last lesson in the line comes rather hard to impatient expectation."[54]

Most British and American philanthropists and reformers
had accepted Burritt and his grandiose League because
both exuded the ebullient Christian optimism which had
attracted them to reformism. On either side of the Atlantic
he was welcomed into the highest circles of reform and
treated with respect. As Longfellow wrote, "Nothing ever
came from his pen that was not wholesome and good."[55]
Burritt had more than fulfilled his own definition of the reformer's role: "The true reformer is calm and mild, mighty
against sin, hurling burning truths at every wrong, but still
preserving amid it all a loving heart."[56] He was no Albert
Brisbane or Orestes Brownson. He had the moral intensity
of a Savonarola, but he also possessed the compensating
quality of Christian compassion. He neither ridiculed nor
reviled; he spoke meekly and acted humbly. People had
listened to him because in their hearts they had wistfully
hoped that his words were prophetic of a new and better
dispensation. He had stood for peace, freedom, charity, and
love. It would have been awkward, to say the least, for anyone to disavow these principles, particularly when they
were so earnestly embodied by Burritt himself. If he had
received little direct assistance in his moral crusades, he
had met with even less opposition.

Burritt had faced the uncertain buffetings of the reformer's life with the equanimity of a stoic. Until his later
writings and position as a consular agent had brought him

54. From an undated note in the Central Connecticut State College Library. In 1853 and 1854, on at least three occasions, Burritt
wrote a stanza from "The Psalm of Life" on scraps of paper, Klingberg Collection and New York Public Library.
55. Quoted in *Messenger of Peace*, new series, April, 1910.
56. *Christian Citizen*, April 27, 1844.

a modicum of financial security, he had been plagued by paralyzing money problems. His creditors had hounded him relentlessly. In 1850, for example, the timely financial assistance of a friend had prevented the sheriff of Worcester County, upon the complaint of a creditor, from carrying Burritt off to jail; in 1853 he had been hesitant to return to America to campaign for ocean penny postage because he did not wish "to be thrown into jail as a welcome."[57] Burritt's Journals are riddled with tales of financial woes.[58] Sometimes he had to rely on the gratuitous needlework of ladies to keep his clothes presentable.[59] Though one of the greatest of 19th century philanthropists, he was surely one of the poorest.

In 1878 Burritt wrote his will. He ordered that most of his property be sold and the sum realized divided into twenty-five shares, most of which were to be distributed among his relatives. He directed a nephew "to . . . act as a trustee for the Burritt Mission Chapel, or my barn prepared and occupied for religious services." His more substantial Cherry Street Chapel was to be kept up through a special fund set aside for that purpose. Though he never had much use for the American Peace Society, he bequeathed that organization one share "as a small token of my earnest sym-

57. Journals, May 13, 1850; Burritt to [Almira] Burritt, London, April, 1853, Central Connecticut State College Library.

58. In 1856 a Worcester creditor humiliated Burritt by sending an open letter to the Worcester *Aegis* in which he labeled Burritt "a humbug and insolvent" and "a *philanthropic* loafer." The creditor, the postmaster of Worcester, claimed that Burritt owed him a postage bill of $25.12. The bill had been incurred by Thomas Drew while he had been assistant editor of the *Christian Citizen*. Burritt, the champion of ocean penny postage, was not aware of this debt. He sent a letter to the *Aegis* stating how little "philanthropy had repaid me during the last ten years" and how costly benevolence had been for him. Worcester *Aegis*, May 7, 1856; Journals, April 29–May 26, 1856, *passim*.

59. Burritt to Mrs. Frederick T. North, New York, Feb. 13, 1854, Central Connecticut State College Library.

pathy and deep interest in its long and faithful work of good will to men, which I labored to promote during many years of my active life." He asked "that no needless expense . . . be incurred either for my funeral or monument, but that both shall conform to the simplicity of life that I have maintained from my youth up." To the town of New Britain he left "the undying affection of a son who held its esteem and special token of consideration above all the honors which he received elsewhere."[60] Burritt was ready, almost eager, to begin that immortal life for which he had prepared so religiously. On March 6, 1879, he died.

It is true that Burritt had not been able to carry to completion a single reform he had sponsored, and that frustration, if not disillusionment, had been his lot as a reformer. But the measure of his career was not in what he had done, but in what he had been and in what he had tried to do, not in his projects, but in his unspotted commitment to peace and brotherhood. Repeated failures had never led him to question the ultimate triumph of his evangelical errand of mercy. As Lord Dufferin, the governor-general of Canada had written him in 1876, "If the world at large were animated by the same unselfish and liberal feelings which have characterized everything you have ever said or written, the prospects of the human race would indeed be promising."[61] Indeed they would.

60. A copy of Burritt's will is in the Central Connecticut State College Library.

61. Lord Dufferin to Burritt, Ottawa, Mar. 13, 1876, New Britain Public Institute.

Bibliography

MANUSCRIPT MATERIAL

A. Correspondence

Appleton, Nathan, MSS., Massachusetts Historical Society.

Burritt, Elijah H., MSS., American Antiquarian Society, Boston Public Library, Columbia University Library, Klingberg Collection (letters belonging to the Reverend Haddon E. Klingberg, New Britain, Conn.), Wesleyan University Library, Yale University Library.

Burritt, Elihu, MSS., American Antiquarian Society, Boston Public Library, Central Connecticut State College Library, Chicago Historical Society, Columbia University Library, Connecticut State Library, Dartmouth College Library, Duke University Library, Friends House Library (London), Haverford College Library, Historical Society of Pennsylvania, Henry E. Huntington Library, Klingberg Collection, Massachusetts Historical Society, Newark Public Library, New Britain Public Institute, New York Historical Society, New York Public Library, Pierpont Morgan Library, Rochester University Library, Swarthmore College Library.

Burritt, Elizabeth, MSS., Central Connecticut State College Library.

Eastman, Zebina, MSS., Chicago Historical Society.

Emerson, Ralph W., MSS., Harvard University Library.

Garrison, William L., MSS., Boston Public Library.

Herrick, Edward C., MSS., Yale University Library.

Lawrence, Amos, MSS., Massachusetts Historical Society.

Lincoln, Abraham, MSS., Library of Congress.

Longfellow, Henry W., MSS., Harvard University Library, Historical Society of Pennsylvania, Klingberg Collection, New Britain Public Institute.

May, Samuel J., MSS., Boston Public Library.

Polk, James K., MSS., Library of Congress.

Quincy, Edmund, MSS., Boston Public Library.

Seward, William H., MSS., Rochester University Library.

Smith, Gerrit, MSS., Harvard University Library, Klingberg Collection, Massachusetts Historical Society, New Britain Public Institute, Syracuse University Library.

Southall, Anna Mary, MSS., Friends House Library.

Sturge, Joseph, MSS., Central Connecticut State College Library, Swarthmore Friends Historical Library.

Sumner, Charles, MSS., Harvard University Library, Klingberg Collection, New Britain Public Institute.
Tappan, Lewis, MSS., Library of Congress.
Walker, Amasa, MSS., Boston Public Library, Harvard University Library, Indiana University Library, Klingberg Collection, New York Historical Society, New York Public Library.
Wells, David A., MSS., Illinois Historical Society, Library of Congress.
Weston, Maria Chapman, MSS., Boston Public Library.
Woolsey, Theodore D., MSS., Yale University Library.

B. Burritt Manuscripts

"Album and Letter Book, 1822–1838", American Antiquarian Society.
"A Plan of Adjustment and Reunion", Central Connecticut State College Library.
"Arabic, Hindustani and Persian Languages", New Britain Public Institute.
"Cashbook, 1839", American Antiquarian Society.
"Elements of Genius", Central Connecticut State College Library.
"International Law", Chicago Historical Society.
"Journal of Elihu Burritt, A Connecticut Blacksmith", Central Connecticut State College Library.
"Journals, 1841–1859", 21 vols., New Britain Public Institute.
"Natural Philosophy Prior to the Newtonian System", Central Connecticut State College Library.
"Scrapbook on Ocean Penny Postage", Central Connecticut State College Library.
"The Constitutional Unity of Christians and the Natural Bonds of Brotherhood", Connecticut Historical Society.
"The League of Universal Brotherhood", American Antiquarian Society.
"The Social Principle", Connecticut Historical Society.

C. Miscellaneous Manuscripts

Coues, Samuel E., "Peace Album", Harvard University Library.
Holland, Frederick W., "History of the American Peace Cause" (3 vols., compiled about 1865), Boston Public Library.

BURRITT WRITINGS

A. Books

A Sanskrit Handbook for the Fireside (Hartford, Brown & Gross, 1875).

A Voice From the Back Pews to the Pulpit and Front Seats (London, Longmann, Green & Co., 1872).
A Walk From London to John O'Groats (London, Sampson, Low & Marston, 1864).
A Walk From London to Land's End and Back (London, Sampson, Low, Son & Marston, 1865).
Chips From Many Blocks (Toronto, Rose-Medford Co., 1878).
Lectures and Speeches (London, Sampson, Low, Son and Marston, 1869).
Miscellaneous Writings (Worcester, Published by Henry J. Howland, 1850).
Prayers and Devotional Meditations, Collated from the Psalms of David (London, Samuel Bagster and Sons, 1870).
Sparks From the Anvil (Worcester, Published by Henry J. Howland, 1846).
Ten-Minute Talks on All Sorts of Topics (Boston, Lee and Shepard, 1873).
The Children of the Bible (New Britain, George L. Allen, 1871).
The Mission of Great Sufferings (London, Sampson, Low, Son, and Marston, 1867).
The Year-Book of the Nations (London, Unwin & Co., 1855; New York, D. Appleton & Co., 1856 & 1863).
Thoughts and Notes at Home and Abroad (London, Charles Gilpin, 1868).
Thoughts and Things at Home and Abroad (Boston, Phillips, Sampson, and Co., 1854).

B. Pamphlets

A Journal of a Visit of Three Days to Skibbereen, and its Neighborhood (London, Charles Gilpin, 1847).
A Plan of Brotherly Co-Partnership of the North and South for the Peaceful Extinction of Slavery (New York, Dayton & Burdick, 1856).
Equity and Expediency of Compensated Emancipation (n.d., n.p.).
Jemmy Stubbins, or the Nailer Boy (Worcester, Published by Elihu Burritt, 1850).
Ocean Penny Postage (Washington, n.d.).
Ocean Penny Postage, Its Necessity Shown and Its Feasibility Demonstrated (London, 1849).
An Ocean Penny Postage. Will It Pay? (London, 1851).
Olive Leaves for the People (Worcester, Published by Elihu Burritt, 1850).
Proposition of A Universal Ocean Penny Postage (n.p., n.d.).

The Neighbors, or the Samaritan Mirror (Philadelphia, Merrihew & Thompson, 1844).

Twenty Reasons for Total Abstinence from Slave-Labour Produce (n.p., n.d.).

C. Miscellaneous Pamphlets

Address of the Southern and Western Liberty Convention, Held at Cincinnati, June 11, 1845, To the People of the United States; Also The Letter of Elihu Burritt to the Convention (Cincinnati, Printed at the *Gazette* Office, 1845).

Melville, Frederick J., *A Penny All The Way, The Story of Penny Postage* (Boston, Warren H. Colson, Publisher, 1908).

Postage Rates, 1789–1930, Abstract of Laws Passed Between 1789 and 1930, Fixing Rates of Postage and According Free Mail Privileges (Washington, Government Printing Office, 1930).

Second Annual Report of the Edinburgh League of Brotherhood (Edinburgh, H. Armour, 1849).

Washington's Words to Intending English Emigrants to America, With an Introduction and Appendix by Elihu Burritt (London, Sampson, Low, Son, and Marston, 1870).

Worcester Almanac, Directory, and .Business Advertiser for 1846 (Worcester, Printed by Henry J. Howland, 1846).

Zollikofer, G. J., *The Moral Education, or the Culture of the Heart of the Young*, Trans., E. Burritt (Providence, B. Cranston & Co., 1840).

D. Newspapers and Periodicals Edited or Published by Burritt

Advocate of Peace and Universal Brotherhood, 1846.
Bond of Brotherhood, 1846–1867.
Christian Citizen, 1844–1851.
Citizen of the World, 1855–1856.
Fire-Side Words, 1868.
Literary Geminae, 1839–1840.
North and South, 1858–1859.

NEWSPAPERS

Albany *Evening Journal*, 1841–1842.
Baltimore *Patriot*, 1842.
Baltimore *Sun*, 1841.
Boston *Commonwealth*, 1853.
Boston *Courier*, 1853.
Christian Freeman, 1844–1845.
Emancipator, 1843–1846.
Kennebec (Maine) *Journal*, 1843.

Liberator, 1844–1848, 1857.
London *Daily News*, 1853.
Manchester Guardian, 1846.
Massachusetts Spy, 1843–1844.
National Intelligencer, 1842, 1854.
Newburyport *Herald*, 1841.
New Haven *Herald*, 1842.
New York *Evangelist*, 1840–1843.
New York *Herald*, 1854–1855.
New York *Journal of Commerce*, 1841.
New York *Observer*, 1840–1843.
New York *Tribune*, 1841–1842, 1848, 1854, 1856.
Pennsylvania Inquirer and National Gazette, 1842.
Providence *Journal*, 1842.
Richmond *Inquirer*, 1842.
Taunton *Whig* (Massachusetts), 1838.
The Times (London), 1846, 1849–1851.
The New York Times, 1873.
Washington *Union*, 1854.
Worcester *Aegis*, 1841–1843, 1856.
Worcester *County Gazette*, 1845.
Worcester *Palladium*, 1843–1844.

PERIODICALS

Advocate of Peace, 1844–1845, 1847–1848.
American Eclectic, 1841–1842.
American Journal of Science, 1834.
American Literature, 1935.
American Phrenological Review, 1840, 1846.
Annual Report of the American Historical Association for the Year 1903.
Blackwood's Magazine, 1849, 1853.
Chambers's Edinburgh Journal, 1851.
Christian Examiner, 1848, 1864.
Dictionary of American Biography.
Friends' Quarterly Examiner (London), 1880.
Journal of Southern History, 1938.
Littell's Living Age, 1846–1847, 1857.
Messenger of Peace (Indianapolis), 1910.
New York Review, 1838.
Patriarch, 1841–1842.
People's Journal (London), 1846.
Proceedings of the American Antiquarian Society, XVI (1905).
Proceedings of the New York Genealogical Society, XXXVI (1881).
Southern Literary Messenger, 1840–1843.

GOVERNMENT DOCUMENTS

Congressional Globe, 30 Congress, 2 Session; 32 Congress, 1 Session; 33 Congress, 1 Session; 34 Congress, 1 Session.
Hansard's *Parliamentary Debates*, VI (1849), CXII (1852), CXXIX (1853).

SECONDARY SOURCES

Aptheker, Herbert, *To Be Free: Studies in American Negro History* (New York, International Publishers, 1948).

Ausubel, Herman, *John Bright, Victorian Reformer* (New York, John Wiley and Sons, 1966).

Bartlett, David W., *Modern Agitators: or Pen Portraits of Living American Reformers* (New York, Miller, Orton, and Mulligan, 1855).

Beales, A. C. F., *The History of Peace* (New York, Dial Press, 1931).

Beckwith, George, ed., *The Book of Peace: A Collection of Essays on War and Peace* (Boston, Published by the author, 1845).

Benson, Adolph B., ed., *America of the Fifties: Letters of Fredrika Bremer* (New York, American Scandinavian Foundation, 1924).

Billington, Ray A., *The Protestant Crusade, 1800–1860* (New York, Rinehart Co., 1938).

Bode, Carl, *The Anatomy of American Popular Culture, 1840–1861* (Berkeley, University of California Press, 1959).

———, *The American Lyceum: Town Meeting of the Mind* (New York, Oxford University Press, 1956).

Branch, E. Douglas, *The Sentimental Years, 1836–1860* (New York, D. Appleton-Century Co., 1934).

Brooks, Van Wyck, *The Flowering of New England* (New York, E. P. Dutton & Co., 1936).

Camp, David N., *History of New Britain* (New Britain, William B. Thomson & Co., 1889).

Channing, William E., *Works*, II (Boston, American Unitarian Association, 1871).

Cole, G. D. H., *Chartist Portraits* (London, Macmillan & Co., 1941).

Cremin, Lawrence A., *The American Common School* (New York, Bureau of Publications, Columbia Teachers College, 1951).

Cross, Whitney R., *The Burned-Over District* (Ithaca, Cornell University Press, 1950).

Curti, Merle E., *The American Peace Crusade, 1815–1860* (Durham, Duke University Press, 1929).

———, *Peace or War, The American Struggle* (New York, W. W. Norton & Co., 1936).

———, *American Philanthropy Abroad* (New Brunswick, Rutgers University Press, 1964).

——, *The Growth of American Thought* (New York, Harper & Brothers, 1943).

——, *The Learned Blacksmith, The Letters and Journals of Elihu Burritt* (New York, Wilson-Erickson, Inc., 1937).

Donald, David, *Charles Sumner and the Coming of the Civil War* (New York, Alfred A. Knopf, Inc., 1960).

Dumond, Dwight, *Antislavery, The Crusade For Freedom in America* (Ann Arbor, University of Michigan Press, 1961).

——, *Letters of James Gillespie Birney*, II (New York, D. Appleton-Century Co., 1938).

Einarsson, Stefan, *A History of Icelandic Literature* (New York, Johns Hopkins Press, 1957).

Filler, Louis, *The Crusade Against Slavery, 1830–1860* (New York, Harper & Brothers, 1960).

Fletcher, Robert S., *A History of Oberlin College From Its Foundation Through the Civil War*, I–II (Oberlin, Oberlin College, 1943).

Foster, Charles I., *An Errand of Mercy, The Evangelical United Front* (Chapel Hill, University of North Carolina Press, 1960).

Foster, Frank H., *A Genetic History of the New England Theology* (Chicago, University of Chicago Press, 1907).

Galpin, W. Freeman, *Pioneering for Peace, A Study of American Peace Efforts to 1846* (Syracuse, Bardeen Press, 1933).

Garrison, F. J. and W. P., *William Lloyd Garrison, the Story of His Life Told by His Children*, II (New York, Century Co., 1885).

Goodell, William, *Slavery and Antislavery* (New York, William Harned, 1852).

Griffin, Clifford S., *Their Brothers' Keepers, Moral Stewardship in the United States, 1800–1865* (New Brunswick, Rutger University Press, 1960).

Harlow, Ralph V., *Gerrit Smith, Philanthropist and Reformer* (New York, Henry Holt & Co., 1939).

Haroutunian, Joseph, *Piety Versus Moralism: The Passing of New England Theology* (New York, Henry Holt & Co., 1932).

Helmstadter, Richard J., "Voluntaryism, 1828–1860" (unpublished Ph.D. dissertation, Columbia University, 1961).

Hill, Rowland and George B., *The Life of Sir Rowland Hill*, II (London, T. De LaRue & Co., 1880).

Hobson, J. A., *Richard Cobden, The International Man* (T. Fisher Unwin Co., 1918).

Hofstadter, Richard, *Anti-intellectualism in American Life* (New York, Alfred A. Knopf, Inc., 1964).

Hughes, Sarah Forbes, *Letter and Recollections of John Murray Forbes*, I (Boston, Houghton Mifflin & Co., 1899).

Kitson, Clark, G. R., *The Making of Victorian England* (Cambridge, Harvard University Press, 1962).

Krout, John A., *The Origins of Prohibition* (New York, Alfred Knopf, Inc., 1925).

Ladd, William, *Essay on a Congress of Nations*, ed., James B. Scott (New York, Oxford University Press, 1916).

MacDonagh, Oliver, *A Pattern of Government Growth, 1800–1860, the Passenger Acts and Their Enforcement* (London, MacGibbon & Kee, 1961).

McLoughlin, William G., *Modern Revivalism: Charles Grandison Finney to Billy Graham* (New York, Ronald Press, 1959).

Martineau, Harriet, *Retrospect of Western Travels*, II (New York, Harper & Brothers, 1838).

Merrill, Walter M., *Against Wind and Tide, A Biography of Wm. Lloyd Garrison* (Cambridge, Harvard University Press, 1963).

Meyers, Marvin, *The Jacksonian Persuasion* (Stanford, Stanford University Press, 1957).

Miller, Perry, *The Life of the Mind in America, from the Revolution to the Civil War* (New York, Harcourt, Brace, and World, 1965).

Minnigerode, Meade, *The Fabulous Forties* (New York, G. P. Putnam, 1924).

Mott, Frank Luther, *A History of American Magazines*, I (New York, D. Appleton & Co., 1930).

Nagel, Paul, *One Nation Indivisible, the Union in American Thought* (New York, Oxford University Press, 1964).

Nevins, Allan, *The War for the Union: War Becomes Revolution, 1862–1863*, II (New York, Scribner Co., 1960).

Niebuhr, H. Richard, *The Kingdom of God in America* (New York, Harper Torchbooks, 1959).

Northend, Charles, *Elihu Burritt: A Memorial Volume* (New York, D. Appleton & Co., 1879).

Nye, Russell B., *The Cultural Life of the New Nation* (New York, Harper & Brothers, 1960).

Owen, David, *English Philanthropy, 1660–1960* (Cambridge, Harvard University Press, 1964).

Phelps, Christina, *The Anglo-American Peace Movement in the Mid-Nineteenth Century* (New York, Columbia University Press, 1930).

Pierce, E. L., *Memoirs and Letters of Charles Sumner*, III (Boston, Roberts Brothers, 1887).

Pym, Horace N., ed., *Memories of Old Friends, Being Extracts From the Journals and Letters of Caroline Fox, of Penjerrich, Cornwall* (Philadelphia, J. B. Lippincott & Co., 1882).

Richard, Henry, *Memoirs of Joseph Sturge* (London, S. W. Partridge, 1865).

Robinson, Howard, *The British Post Office, A History* (Princeton, Princeton University Press, 1940).

Roper, Daniel C., *The United States Post Office* (New York, Funk & Wagnall, 1917).

Shuckers, J. W., *The Life and Public Services of Salmon Portland Chase* (New York, D. Appleton & Co., 1874).

Smalley, Edward, *The Worcester Pulpit: With Notices Historical and Biographical* (Boston, Phillips, Sampson & Co., 1851).

Staff, Frank, *The Penny Post, 1680–1918* (London, Lutterworth Press, 1964).

Stowe, Harriet Beecher, *Uncle Tom's Cabin*, with an "Introduction" by Elihu Burritt (London, Partridge and Oakey, 1852).

———, *Sunny Memories From Foreign Lands, I* (Boston, Phillips, Sampson, and Co., 1854).

Sumner, Charles, *The Works of Charles Sumner, II* (Boston, Lee & Shephard, 1870).

Thistlethwaite, Frank, *American and the Atlantic Community, Anglo-American Aspects, 1790–1850* (New York, Harper Torchbooks, 1959).

Thomas, Benjamin, *Theodore Weld, Crusader for Freedom* (New Brunswick, Rutgers University Press, 1950).

Walling, R. A. J., ed., *The Diaries of John Bright* (New York, William Morrow & Co., 1931).

Woodham-Smith, Cecil, *The Great Hunger* (New York, Harper & Row, 1962).

Index

Aberdeen, Lord, 220
Advocate of Peace, 116, 121ff., 134, 140, 262
Albany Convention, 260
Albany *Evening Journal*, 56
Alden, J. W., 90, 94, 99
Allen, George, 103
American Antiquarian Society, 15–16
American Committee for a Congress of Nations, 187–88
American Eclectic, 29ff., 37–39
American Journal of Education, 44
American Journal of Science, 8
American Peace Congress Committee, 187ff.
American Peace Society, 116ff., 122ff., 141ff., 158, 174, 187, 197, 261ff., 284ff.
American Phrenological Journal, 24
Amherst College, 35
Andover Theological Seminary, 25
Anti-Corn Law League, 137, 148ff., 154
Antiquitates Americanae, 30, 34
"Anti-Slavery League of the World", 143
Antislavery, Ch. 5, *passim.*, Ch. 10, *passim.*
Appleton, James, 94, 99–100
Appleton, Nathan, 256
Arbitration treaties, 185ff.

Bacon, Leonard, 47, 97, 101, 252

Bailey, Rufus W., 31–37, *passim.*
Baltimore *Sun*, 56
Bancroft, George, 29, 56
Bastiat, Frederic, 188ff.
Bates, Barnabas, 222, 231
Beckwith, George C., 116ff., 124ff., 141, 158, 261–62
Beecher, Henry Ward, 196
Beecher, Lyman, 54, 111
Bellamy, Joseph, 66
Benton, Thomas H., 229
Bernard, Montague, 285
Blackwood's Magazine, 159
Blanchard, Joshua P., 120ff., 125, 132ff., 158, 171, 187
Bluntschli, Johann, 285
Bodenstedt, Arthur, 195ff.
Bond of Brotherhood, 140ff., 152ff., 157, 275–76
Boston Relief Committee, 164ff.
Bourne, Theodore, 257
Bowdoin College, 189
Bowring, John, 180
Bradshaw, George, 137, 175, 211
Bright, John, 137, 192–93, 217ff., 277
Broadway Tabernacle, 49, 59, 77, 193, 224
Brooklyn Lyceum, 60
Brown, John, 261
Brussels Peace Convention, 179ff., 191
Bryant, William C., 188
Burleigh, William H., 103
"Burned-Over District," 73
Burritt, Almira, 198
Burritt, Ann (Mrs.), 17

Burritt, Clarissa (Mrs.), 17
Burritt, Elihu, Sr., 3, 7
Burritt, Elihu, family of: 3–8, 17–18, 74, 106; youth and education: 5–11; characteristics: 21, 24–26, 53, 64; language study of: 10–16; lectures of: 44–64 *passim*; early writings: 12–13, 21–22, 28–32, 36–40; religious views: 67–69 *passim*; and temperance: 80–83; and antislavery: 85–113 *passim*; and pacifism: 119–44 *passim*; and League of Universal Brotherhood: 146–52; and Irish famine: 162–65; and Friendly Addresses: 165–66; and Olive Leaf Societies: 166–69; and international peace conventions: 179–95 *passim*; and arbitration treaties: 185–86; and ocean penny postage: 203–32 *passim*; and free labor produce: 236–39; and free labor colonies: 240–45; and compensated emancipation: 245–57 *passim*; views of Civil War: 263–65; consular agent at Birmingham: 273–75; land agency of: 278–80; later writings: 270–76, 280–83; peace activities: 284–86; death: 291–92
Burritt, Elijah, 7–10, 14–15, 18, 84ff.
Burritt, Elizabeth Hinsdale (Mrs.), 3–5, 74, 106
Burritt, Emily, 17–18
Burritt, George, 18
Burritt, Isaac, 18, 60
Burritt, William, 17–18
Bushnell, Horace, 70, 283

Calvinism, 4–5, 65ff.
Campbell, James, 226, 229–30

Campbell, John, 149
Canning, Lord, 219ff.
Capital punishment, 122, 124
Carlyle, Thomas, 213–214
Carpenter, Mary, 156, 160ff.
Cass, Lewis, 229
Chalmers, Thomas, 97, 101
Chambers, William, 160
Chambers's Edinburgh Journal, 160, 211
Channing, William E., 10, 26, 115
Chapin, Calvin, 97, 101
Chapman, Maria Weston, 161
Chartism, 134, 149, 177
Chase, Salmon P., 108, 110, 122, 265
Cherokee Indians, 86–87
Chevalier, Michel, 188ff.
Christ, 54, 67–88, 281
Christian Citizen, 101ff., 120ff., 130ff., 151, 161ff., 171ff., 183, 207
Christian Freeman, 103
Christian Observer, 142
Christian Reflector, 158
Citizen of the World, 243, 258
Clarke, Julius, 90, 93
Clarkson, Thomas, 99
Clay, Cassius M., 99, 110
Cobden, Richard, 137, 143, 180ff., 185ff., 195, 199ff., 214ff., 287
Coffin, Levi, 237
Cole, Henry, 215, 217, 219, 222
Colonial and International Cheap Postage Association, 219ff.
Compensated emancipation, 247ff.
Congress and Court of Nations, 131ff., Ch. 8, *passim*.
Conn, William, 147
Cornwall, Jabez, 17–18
Coues, Samuel, 120ff., 132ff., 169, 171
Crimean War, 199ff.

Crosfield, Joseph, 136ff., 155
Cross, George, 147
Cunningham, William, 137, 155
Cutter, W. H., 31
Cuyler, T. C., 257–58

Dick, Thomas, 9, 97, 101, 107, 130, 134
Dodge, David Low, 115ff.
Dodge, William E., 137
Dorr Rebellion, 93, 177
Dowman, Charles, 242
Douglas, Stephen A., 255ff.
Dresser, Amos, 170
Drew, Thomas, 103, 162, 171
Dudley, Thomas H., 276
Dufferin, Lord, 292
Durkee, Charles, 189
Dwight, Theodore, 128

Eastman, Zebina, 273ff., 278, 287
Eaton, Elizabeth, 74–75
Ecroyd, John, 240–41
Edinburgh Peace Convention, 197
Edwards, Jonathan, 65–66
Egils saga, 30
"Elements of Genius," 62
Ellsworth, William, 103
Emancipation Act (1833), 148
Emancipator, 90, 94, 101–03
Emerson, Ralph W., 51, 58–59, 248, 251
Essay on a Congress of Nations, 131ff., 176
Estlin, J. B., 154ff.
Evangelicalism, 70, 73–74ff., 143ff.
Evangelist (New York), 29ff., 34, 36, 39
Everett, Edward, 19ff., 64
Ewart, William, 180, 214

Fatham, Benjamin, 240
Felton, Cornelius, 142–43

Field, David Dudley, 285
Finney, Charles G., 73
Fire-Side Words, 275
First International, 130
Fitch, Eleazar, 67
Forbes, Robert F., 164
Foster, Charles, 96
Foster, Lafayette S., 256
Foster, Theodore, 40
Frankfort Assembly, 194, 198
Frankfort Peace Convention, 193ff.
Free Labor Produce, 237ff.
Free Soil Party, 261
Free trade, 137, 155
Fremont, John C., 259, 266
Friendly Addresses, 136ff., 164ff.
Fry, Edmund, 157, 252

Gale, George W., 26
Garrison, William L., 86, 104, 112, 118, 148, 150, 236, 249, 255
Geneva Peace Society, 173
Gibbs, Josiah, 57
Gibson, Thomas M., 214ff., 221ff.
Giddings, Joshua, 188, 193
Giles, Henry, 56–57
Gilpin, Charles, 157
Girardin, Emile, 188ff.
Gladstone, William E., 220ff.
Gloucester Journal, 159
Goodell, William, 99, 112, 248
Gough, John B., 81–82
Grant, Ulysses S., 277, 287–88
Great Exhibition (1851), 213
Greeley, Horace, 57, 110, 248–49
Griscom, John, 49

Harper and Brothers, 34–35, 39
Hartford Convention, 261
Haughton, James, 149
Harvard College, 21, 33
Harvey, Thomas, 149
Hawes, Joel, 70–71

Hedge, Frederic, 95
Herndon, William, 251
Heyworth, Lawrence, 149
Hicks, Elias, 237
Hildreth, Richard, 99, 111
Hill, Rowland, 207ff., 214, 219, 233
Hillard, George, 138
History of the Conquest of Florida, 40
History of the Hartford Convention, 128
Hoar, Samuel, 90–91
Holbrook, Josiah, 43
Holmes, Oliver W., 51
Hopkins, Mark, 251, 253, 255, 257
Hopkins, Samuel, 66, 78
Howe, Samuel G., 188, 223ff.
Hubbard, R. B., 102
Hugo, Victor, 188ff.

"Influence of Mythological Figures and Metaphors on Education," 43
Ingersoll, J. R., 200
International Land and Labour Agency, 278ff.
International peace movement, Ch. 8, *passim.*
International Sunday School Association, 169
Irish Famine, 162ff.

Jackson, James C., 99–100
James, John A., 96, 101, 134, 136
Jaup, Heinrich, 195ff.
Jay, William, 185
Jefferson, John, 135, 149
"Jemmy Stubbins," 161ff.
Jerrold, Douglas, 141ff.
Jocelyn, Simeon S., 86
Johnson, Andrew, 277
Journal des Economistes, 188

Journal of Commerce (New York), 51, 222

Kennebec Journal (Maine), 100, 125
King, Rufus, 248
King, William, 226ff.
Knickerbocker, 32

Ladd, William, 116ff., 130, 188
Lamartine, 166, 187–88
La Presse, 188
Lawrence, Amos, 242
Leaflets of the Law of Kindness, 169ff.
League of Universal Brotherhood, 144, Ch. 7, *passim.*
Leavitt, Joshua, 87–88, 94, 104, 222, 231
Lewis, Samuel, 109
Liberal revolutions of 1848, 176ff.
Liberator, 86, 160ff.
Lincoln, Abraham, 266ff.
Lincoln, William, 19
Liberty League, 112ff.
Liberty Party, 88, 90, 93, 97–99ff., 104ff., 110ff., 142
Literary Geminae, 21ff., 31–32, 36
Locofocoism, 92
London *Nonconformist*, 211, 213
London Peace Convention, 197, 214
London Peace Society, 155ff., 165ff., 174, 182ff., 192, 196ff., 278
Longfellow, Henry W., 22–23, 25, 98, 134, 169, 187, 223, 233–34, 251, 274, 290
Lovett, William, 138
Lyceum movement, 42–43

Manchester Peace Convention, 197

Mancini, Pasquale, 285
Mann, Horace, 193
Manual labor schools, 26
Marsh, George, 29–30
Massachusetts Peace Society, 115
May, Samuel, J., 110, 118, 140
Metternich, 176ff.
Mexican War, 124ff., 135–36
Milledgeville (Georgia), 8, 85
Millennialism, 78–79
Miller, Rodney, 70, 73, 77
Miller, William, 78–79
Mission of Great Sufferings, 275–76
Morning Chronicle (Boston), 109
Morse, Samuel F. B., 29
Morse, Sidney, 40, 50, 61
"Motives and Tendencies of International Peace," 119
Mott, Lucretia, 139
Murray, Robert L., 254
Music Fund Hall, 54
My Brother's Grave, 12

Napoleon III, 197, 199
National Association for Promoting the Political and Social Improvement of the People, 138
National Intelligencer, 56, 227
Natural Bridge, 46, 49
"Natural Philosophy Prior to the Construction of the Newtonian System," 43
Nelson, Thomas, 24, 61
New Britain, Conn., p. 3, 14–15, 27, 166, 286ff.
Newburyport *Herald*, 45
New England Antislavery Tract Association, 95, 97, 101
New England Conference of Wesleyan Ministers, 170
New England Non-Resistance Society, 118

New England Puritan, 122
New Haven *Herald*, 54, 61
New Haven *Patriot*, 54
New Haven Theology, 67
Newton, Isaac, 43
New York Lyceum, 49, 51–52
New York Mercantile Library Association, 47–48, 51–52
New York Peace Society, 115, 117
New York *Tribune*, 43, 48, 50, 57, 60, 182–83
Niebuhr, H. Richard, 78
Njals saga, 30
Non-Resistance, 119ff., 177ff.
North American Review, 19, 32, 37
North and South, 258ff.
Nott, Eliphalet, 80, 134, 251, 257, 260

Oberlin College, 26, 109, 170, 189
Observer (New York), 29ff., 34, 36, 40, 61
Ocean penny postage, Ch. 9, *passim.*
Old South Church (Worcester), 68, 73, 75–78
Olds, Edson, 227–28, 231ff.
Olive Leaf Societies, 166ff.
Olive Leaves, 132ff.
Oneida Institute, 26
Oregon boundary dispute, 135–36, 144

Paris Peace Convention, 183ff.
Park, Edwards, 25
Parker, Theodore, 170
Parley, Peter, 37
Patriarch, 31–32, 37–39
Peace movement in Great Britain, 204ff.
People's Journal, 154

Peters, Absalom, 29, 34, 36, 39
Pierce, Franklin, 199ff., 229
Pierpont, John, 97
Philadelphia Methodist Conference, 170
Phrenology, 24, 55, 63
Poems on Slavery, 98
Polhill, Mr., 86–87
Political abolitionism, 89ff.
Princeton College, 52
Providence *Journal*, 56

Quakers, 72, 136ff., 146, 152ff., 166, 237, 263
Quincy, Edmund, 112, 118, 143, 156, 160
Quincy, Josiah, 138, 223
Quincy *Patriot*, 249

Rathbone, Richard, 154, 158ff.
Rathbone, William, 154
Reedtz, Baron von, 196ff., 231
Reid, David S., 230
Religious Tract Society, 142
Rhoades, George, 237
Richard, Henry, 183ff., 188ff., 263, 267
Richmond *Inquirer*, 61
Ritchie, Thomas, 61–62
Rogers, Nathaniel P., 104
Roman Catholicism, 70–71
"Roman Patriotism," 44, 47
"Rubicon of St. Peter," 62
Rusk, Thomas J., 227, 231–32
Russell, John, 163ff., 185ff.

Salem Lyceum, 54
Samaritans, 30
Say, Horace, 179ff.
Sears, David, 256–57
"Self-Cultivation," 49, 54, 62
Self-Culture, 10
Seward, William H., 110, 222, 277
Shilling Magazine, 141–142

Sigourney, Lydia H., 13, 22, 138–39, 152, 169
Silliman, Benjamin, 8, 57, 252ff.
Smalley, John, 4
Smith, Gerrit, 113, 171, 187, 223, 242, 251, 253ff., 258, 261
Smith, Isaac, 49
Society of Christian Morals, 173, 180, 189
Southern Literary Messenger, 23–24, 30
Southern and Western Liberty Convention, 105
Spring, Gardiner, 70
Stanton, Henry, B., 90
Stewart, Alvan, 99–100
Stevens, Thaddeus, 257
Stowe, Calvin, 238
Stowe, Harriet B., 238, 240–41
Sturge, Joseph, 137, 139, 143ff., 148ff., 166, 174ff., 185, 195, 239
Sumner, Charles, 134–135, 138, 140ff., 158ff., 179, 183, 187, 199ff., 216ff., 222ff., 225, 232–33, 245, 265, 277, 283–84

Tappan, John, 187
Tappan, Lewis, 139, 144, 169, 185, 224, 240, 248, 261
Tariff of 1828, 85
Taunton (Mass.) Educational Convention, 19ff.
Taylor, George W., 237–38, 240, 242
Taylor, Nathaniel, 67
Temperance, 80ff., 146
The Slave, 243
The Times, 159, 200
Tocqueville, Alexis de, 189
Treaty of Washington (1871), 283–84
Troup, George M., 85–86
True Grandeur of Nations, 134–35

Tuck, Amos, 188
Twiss, Travis, 285

Uncle Tom's Cabin, 238
Underwood, John R., 255
Unitarianism, 72, 154ff., 170
Universal Postal Union, 234

Vam Andel, Adrian, 167ff.
Van Buren, Martin, 91
Vincent, Henry, 160, 180
Vinet, Alexandre, 29
Visschers, Auguste, 179ff., 194

Walker, Amasa, 120ff., 132ff.,
    143, 170ff., 187ff., 248, 262,
    287
Walker, George L., 283
Walker's Appeal, 85–86
"Want of Individuality of Char-
    acter," 62
War and Peace, 185
War of 1812, 115, 128
Washington Temperance Society,
    81
Webb, Richard D., 156
Webster, Daniel, 248
Weed, Thurlow, 56

Weld, Theodore, 90
Wells, David A., 287
Wheeler, Frederic, 196
Whig Party, 91–92, 95
Whipple, E. P., 51
White, Horace, 287
Whittier, John Greenleaf, 89–90,
    183, 251
Wigham, John, 155
Wilder, Sampson, 79
Williams College, 7–8
Wilson, George, 155, 192, 215
Woolsey, Theodore, 29, 251
Worcester *Aegis*, 54
Worcester County Jail, 78–79
Worcester County Peace Society,
    121ff.
Worcester Lyceum, 52, 56, 60
Worcester, Noah, 115ff.
Worcester Union Congregational
    Church, 79
World's Temperance Convention,
    140
Wright, Henry C., 118, 253

Yale College, 10, 33
Year-Book of the Nations, 275

Zollikofer, G. J., 28ff.